W9-DEL-696

IRENAEUS OF LYONS

During the second century the Christian world was shaken by the Gnostics. Irenaeus came from Asia Minor via Rome to become Bishop of Lyons, clarify Christian doctrines and fight the Gnostics with a major, five-volume work. He was a living part of his contemporary culture and his approach filled early Christian thought with new life.

The writings of Irenaeus exist as a whole only in Latin and Armenian. This study offers new translations of significant parts of his work, critically based on a complete reconstruction of the original Greek in the French series Sources Chrétiennes. It will be invaluable to students of the Early Church, both as an introduction to Irenaeus' thought, and as a collection of sources.

Robert M. Grant has taught for nearly fifty years at the Divinity School of the University of Chicago, working and writing intensively on second-century Gnosticism. His most recent book is *Heresy and Criticism* (1993).

THE EARLY CHURCH FATHERS
Edited by Carol Harrison
University of Durham

The Greek and Latin Fathers of the Church are central to the creation of Christian doctrine, yet often unapproachable because of the sheer volume of their writings and the relative paucity of accessible translations. This series makes available translations of key selected texts by the major Fathers to all students of the early church.

Already published:
Maximus the Confessor
Andrew Louth

Further books in this series will be on Ambrose, Gregory of Nyssa and Origen.

IRENAEUS OF LYONS

Robert M. Grant

London and New York

First published 1997
by Routledge
2 Park Square, Milton Park, Abingdon, Oxon, OX14 4RN

Simultaneously published in the USA and Canada
by Routledge
270 Madison Ave, New York NY 10016

Transferred to Digital Printing 2005

© 1997 Robert M. Grant

Typeset in Garamond by
Harper Phototypesetters Limited, Northampton

All rights reserved. No part of this book may be reprinted or
reproduced, or utilized in any form or by any electronic,
mechanical, or other means, now known or hereafter
invented, including photocopying and recording, or in any
information storage or retrieval system, without permission in
writing from the publishers.

British Library Cataloguing in Publication Data
A catalogue record for this book is available from
the British Library

Library of Congress Cataloguing in Publication Data
Grant, Robert McQueen, 1917–
Irenaeus of Lyons/Robert M. Grant.
p. cm. – (The early church fathers)
Includes bibliographical references and index.
1. Irenaeus, Saint, Bishop of Lyons. 2. Christian saints – France –
Biography. i. I. Title. II. Series.
BR1720.I7G73 1996
270.1'092–dc20
[B] 96–7705

ISBN 0–415–11837–9
ISBN 0–415–11838–7 (pbk)

CONTENTS

ABBREVIATIONS

HTR	*Harvard Theological Review*
JBL	*Journal of Biblical Literature*
JTS	*Journal of Theological Studies*
LCL	Loeb Classical Library
NHS	Nag Hammadi Studies (Leiden: Brill)
PG	Migne, Patrologia Graeca
PL	Migne, Patrologia Latina
RE	*Realencyclopädie der classischen Altertumswissenschaft*
Robinson	J. M. Robinson (ed.), *The Nag Hammadi Library in English*, rev. edn (San Francisco: Harper & Row, 1988)
SC	Sources Chrétiennes
TU	*Texte and Untersuchungen*
VC	*Vigiliae Christianae*

1

THE LIFE OF IRENAEUS

Irenaeus of Lyons was the most important Christian controversialist and theologian between the apostles and the third-century genius Origen. He gathered up and combined the traditions of predecessors from Asia Minor, Syria, and Rome and used them to refute the Gnostics who were subverting the Gospel. He built up a body of Christian theology that resembled a French Gothic cathedral, strongly supported by columns of biblical faith and tradition, illuminated by vast expanses of exegetical and logical argument, and upheld by flying buttresses of rhetorical and philosophical considerations from the outside. In his own person he united the major traditions of Christendom from Asia Minor, Syria, Rome, and Gaul, although his acquaintance with Palestine, Greece, and Egypt was minimal. We cannot say that he represents the whole of second-century Christianity, but he does represent the majority views outside Alexandria, where Christian speculative thought was closer to the Gnosticism he fought. He represents the literary categories of his predecessors as well as the areas through which he had passed.

He knew most of the New Testament rather well, though it did not include Hebrews or any books of the "apocryphal New Testament," and he was acquainted with the writings of most of the so-called Apostolic Fathers: 1 Clement (not 2 Clement), Ignatius, Polycarp, and Hermas (not the Didache or Barnabas), as well as two of the apologists: Justin and Theophilus, plus Justin's renegade disciple Tatian. In addition he was rather well informed about Gnostics and their writings, and used several treatises recently found in Coptic versions at Nag Hammmadi, Egypt.

Irenaeus tells something about his early life in his major treatise *On the Detection and Refutation of the Knowledge Falsely So Called* (cited hereafter as *Heresies*) and in two letters partly saved in

Eusebius' *Church History*. First, writing to Florinus to dissuade him from heresy, he sets forth early memories of what must be Smyrna, on the Aegean coast, where long ago he and Florinus encountered his life-long hero the bishop and martyr Polycarp. He insists that early memories are best, for presumably critics were questioning his claims about traditions.

> When I was still a boy I saw you in lower Asia with Polycarp, when you were shining brilliantly in the royal palace and trying to win favor from him. I remember the events of those days better than recent ones, for childhood learning grows up with the soul and is united with it, so that I can speak of the place where the blessed Polycarp sat and discussed, his entrances and exits and the character of his life, the appearance of his body, the discourses he made to the multitude, how he related his life together with John and with the others who had seen the Lord, and how he remembered their words, and what he heard about the Lord from them, about his miracles and teaching – how Polycarp received this from the eyewitnesses of the life of the Word and proclaimed it all in accordance with the scriptures. Because of God's mercy given me I heard these things eagerly even then, and I recorded them not on paper but in my heart, and I meditate on them accurately by God's favor.
>
> And I can testify before God that if that blessed apostolic presbyter had heard anything of this kind he would have shouted and stopped his ears and said, as was his custom, "O good God, for what sort of times have you preserved me, that I should put up with this?" He would have fled from the place where he was sitting or standing when he heard such words. This can be made plain from his letters which he sent to the churches nearby, strengthening them, or to some of the brothers, exhorting and warning them.[1]

The whole passage suggests that Irenaeus' insistence on memory and tradition was under fire, chiefly from Gnostics but no doubt from more orthodox and probably younger colleagues. *Heresies* shows that for him a "boy" could be nearly 15 years old; if so, he was born about AD 140.

Some years later, probably around 155, Polycarp visited Rome. Irenaeus knows something about the visit, whether he himself was at Rome or not, and in *Heresies* repeats his statement about early memories.

And there is Polycarp, who not only was taught by the apostles and conversed with many who had seen the Lord, but also was established by apostles in Asia in the church at Smyrna. We ourselves saw him in our early youth, for he lived long and was in extreme old age when he left this life in a most glorious and most noble martyrdom. He always taught the doctrine he had learned from the apostles, which he delivered to the church, and it alone is true. All the churches in Asia bear witness to this, as well as the successors of Polycarp to this day, and he was a witness to the truth of much greater authority and more reliable than Valentinus and Marcion and the others with false opinions. For when under Anicetus he stayed in Rome he turned many away from the heretics we have mentioned and brought them back to the church of God by proclaiming that from the apostles he had received this one and only truth transmitted by the church. Some heard him say that John the Lord's disciple was going to the bath in Ephesus when he saw Cerinthus inside and jumped out of the bath without bathing, saying that he feared the bath would fall down since Cerinthus, the enemy of the truth, was inside.[2] And when Polycarp himself once met Marcion, who ran to him and said, "Recognize us," he answered, "I do recognize you, firstborn of Satan."[3] . . . There is also a very powerful letter of Polycarp, written to the Philippians, from which those who desire and care for their salvation can learn the nature of his faith and the preaching of the truth. In addition, the church of Ephesus, founded by Paul, with John continuing with them until the times of Trajan, is a true witness to the tradition of the apostles.[4]

At Rome Polycarp argued not only with heretics but also with the bishop Anicetus, and they finally agreed to disagree. Irenaeus discusses this topic when he writes to the later bishop Victor.

When the blessed Polycarp was staying in Rome under Anicetus and they had modest disagreements about some other matters they made peace at once, since they had no desire for strife on this topic. For neither could Anicetus persuade Polycarp not to observe what he had always observed with John our Lord's disciple and the other apostles with whom he had associated, nor did Polycarp persuade Anicetus to observe this, for he said that he ought to hold fast the custom of the presbyters before him. In spite of this, they had fellowship with each other and in the church Anicetus yielded the Eucharist to Polycarp, obviously out of respect, and they parted from each other in peace, for those who observed and those who did not observe kept the peace of the whole church.[5]

Irenaeus insists on peace because he is criticizing Victor's militancy.

Later on, Irenaeus was eager to take part in the worldwide mission of the church and became a missionary among the Celts of Gaul. Why Lyons? The social and economic history of the city gives some explanation. Migration from Asia to Gaul was common in the second century, as inscriptions and temple ruins prove. Asian culture and pagan cults were accompanying Asian traders.[6] Frend refers to the Greek names of L. Taius Onesimus, Onesiphorus, and Epagathus, and to one woman described as *Asiana*, another as *natione Graeca*.[7] Especially notable is T. Flavius Hermes, named with T. Romanius Epictetus and Flavia Melitine.[8]

Greek culture seems to have flourished at Lyons, but sometimes Irenaeus regretted his absence from the deeper culture of Christian Asia. He addressed his readers with an apology of sorts.

You will not expect from us, who live with the Celts and most of the time use the language of barbarians,[9] either the art of rhetoric which we did not learn, or the skill of a writer which we have not exercised, or elegance of language or persuasion which we do not know. You may, however, accept with love what we have written for you with love, simplicity, and truth, and without technique, and yourself develop it, being more capable than we are.[10]

Some have thought he viewed Latin as barbaric but this is hard to believe in view of his admiration for the church of Rome and, indeed, the Roman empire.[11]

For him the church's mission is both universal and unified.

If the languages in the world are dissimilar, the power of the tradition is one and the same. The churches founded in Germany believe and hand down no differently, nor do those among the Iberians, among the Celts, in the Orient, in Egypt, or in Libya, or those established in the middle of the world. As the sun, God's creature, is one and the same in the whole world, so the light, the preaching of truth, shines everywhere and illuminates all men who wish to come to the knowledge of truth. And none of the rulers of the churches, however gifted he may be in eloquence, will say anything different – for no one is above the Master (Matt.10:24) – nor will one weak in speech damage the tradition. Since the faith is one and the same, he who can say much about it does not add to it nor does he who says little diminish it.[12]

Many barbarian peoples who believe in Christ and ... possess salvation, written without paper or ink by the Spirit in their hearts, and they diligently protect the ancient tradition ... Those who have believed this faith without letters are "barbarians in relation to our language" (1 Cor.14:11) but most wise, because of the faith, as to thinking, customs, and way of life, and they please God as they live in complete justice, chastity, and wisdom. And if someone told them, speaking in their own language, what has been invented by heretics, they would immediately shut their ears and flee far away, not even enduring to hear this blasphemous discourse.[13] Because of that ancient tradition of the apostles they do not admit even to thought any of the lying inventions of these people.[14]

In the sixth century Gregory of Tours imagined that Polycarp sent Irenaeus on his mission to Lyons and that he converted practically the whole city to Christianity before becoming a martyr. There is no evidence for this, though it reflects the later enthusiasm for Irenaeus found in the churches of Gaul. If one asks what became of Irenaeus' converts, Gregory explains that they were killed in great numbers, along with Irenaeus himself.[15]

When persecution began about 177, the martyrs Gregory knew have names mostly Greek, a few Latin, but none Celtic, and their Acts criticize non-Christians as barbarians. "Incited by a wild beast [the Devil] wild and barbarous tribes could hardly stop," while "the governor and the people (*démos*) showed the like unjust hatred."[16] The Celtic population remained resolutely non-Christian.

Around this time a letter from the Gallican confessors commended Irenaeus to Eleutherus of Rome.

Again and always we greet you in God, Father Eleutherus. We have urged our brother and colleague Irenaeus to bring this letter to you and we ask you to hold him in esteem, for he is zealous for the covenant of Christ. For if we had known that rank confers righteousness on anyone, we should especially have commended him as a presbyter of the church, which in fact he is.[17]

Perhaps Irenaeus as a presbyter was the local equivalent of the bishops found elsewhere. He seems to regard "bishop" and "presbyter" as substantially identical.

Around the same time the confessors were sending "the brothers in Asia and Phrygia" their "pious and most orthodox judgment" about Montanism. These were the brothers to whom they also sent the book of *Gallican Martyrs*.[18] The Montanist schism, based on widespread prophetic ecstasy, had recently originated in Phrygia,[19] but we do not know exactly what Irenaeus thought of it. In Irenaeus' *Heresies* he insists on the existence and importance of spiritual gifts among Christians. Eusebius quotes passages from him about raising the dead, exorcism, prediction, visions, prophetic speech, and cures, concluding with words about gifts of prophecy and speaking "through the Spirit with various tongues."[20] If he really opposed Montanism he must have agreed with the other critics cited by Eusebius. They objected to its disorderly character, not its emphasis on spiritual gifts.[21]

At some point during the Roman episcopate of Eleutherus (c.175–189) Irenaeus produced his five books against the Valentinians. In his view they were the most dangerous heretics of the time, obviously because they impelled Christians to leave the tradition transmitted in the apostolic succession. His treatise, entitled *On the Detection and Refutation of Knowledge Falsely So Called*, was not written for Christians either in Gaul itself or at Rome, where there was no need of a list of bishops, but more probably those in Asia and Phrygia. We have just seen that Christian letters were being sent from Lyons specifically to Asia and Phrygia.

The first book concerns the Valentinian Gnostics and their eccentric predecessors as far back as Simon Magus. The second provides rational proofs that their doctrines are false. The prefaces to the fourth and fifth books show what he thought he was doing. The third supplies proofs from the apostles, that is, the gospels taken as a whole. The fourth book emphasizes the sayings of Jesus, especially his mysterious parables, and shows the unity of the Old Testament and the Gospel, while the fifth, relying especially on other words of Jesus and the letters of Paul, culminates in Irenaeus' old-fashioned Asian picture of the future reign of God on earth. He first sent Books I–II to his unnamed correspondent, then III, IV, and V in succession.[22] The whole treatise, commonly called *Against Heresies*, was quite popular, especially among anti-Gnostic Christians in churches related to Rome. The oldest fragment of the work, a papyrus scrap from Oxyrhynchus in Egypt, can be dated before the end of the second century and suggests that foes of Egyptian Gnosticism early found it helpful.[23] Clement soon used it in Alexandria, Tertullian in Carthage, Hippolytus in Rome.

As a whole the work survives only in a Latin translation of the third or early fourth century (hardly later, since Valentinianism was fading away), though there are many Greek fragments, the most important being provided by Eusebius and Epiphanius, especially from Books I and III, as well as a valuable old Armenian version of Books IV and V. Most of Book II is found only in Latin, perhaps because the rational arguments were not remarkably convincing.

The treatise shows that Irenaeus was trying to maintain those traditions of the Roman church reported by Clement, Hermas, and Justin which he believed were consistent with his own Asian traditions from John, Polycarp, and Papias. He also believed in the apostolic succession of presbyter-bishops – but did not report that the Valentinians believed that their own tradition and succession were superior to his.[24]

He describes the Roman succession in some detail.

> After founding and building up the church, the blessed apostles delivered the ministry of the episcopate to Linus; Paul mentions this Linus in the letters to Timothy (2 Tim.4:21). Anacletus succeeded him, and after him, in the third place from the apostles, Clement received the lot of the episcopate; he had seen the apostles and met with them and still had the apostolic preaching in his ears and the tradition before his eyes. He was not alone, for many were then still alive who had been taught by the apostles. Under this Clement, when there was no slight dissension among the brethren at Corinth, the church at Rome wrote a most powerful letter to the Corinthians to reconcile them in peace and renew their faith and the tradition which their church had recently received from the apostles: one God almighty, Creator of heaven and earth, the fashioner of man, who brought about the deluge and called Abraham and brought the people out of the land of Egypt, who spoke with Moses, who gave the law and sent the prophets, who prepared fire for the devil and his angels.

This does not accurately reflect the content of 1 Clement, although B. Botte argued that Irenaeus is combining 1 Clement with 2 Clement, where fire is mentioned.[25]

Those who wish can learn that the God proclaimed by the churches is the Father of our Lord Jesus Christ, and can understand the apostolic tradition by this letter, older than those who now teach falsely that there is another god above the Demiurge and Creator of all that exists. Evaristus succeeded this Clement; Alexander, Evaristus; then Xystus was appointed, sixth from the apostles; from him, Telesphorus, who achieved martyrdom most gloriously; then Hyginus; then Pius, whose successor was Anicetus. After Soter had succeeded Anicetus, now in the twelfth place from the apostles Eleutherus holds the episcopate. With the same sequence and doctrine the tradition from the apostles in the church, and the preaching of truth, has come down to us. This is a complete proof that the life-giving faith is one and the same, preserved and transmitted in truth in the church from the apostles up till now.[26]

Irenaeus' relations with Eleutherus' successor Victor were less cordial. In *Heresies* he had insisted that the church of Ephesus had been founded by Paul and that John stayed there until the reign of Trajan; it is an authentic witness to the tradition of the apostles.[27] Evidently he could not imagine disagreement with the church of Rome. Later, however, he wrote to Victor to complain about his treatment of the bishop of Ephesus over the Paschal problem. Victor had requested metropolitans to convoke synods, and Eusebius still had access to a dossier including protocols from Palestine (presidents, Theophilus of Caesarea and Narcissus of Jerusalem), Rome (Victor), Pontus (Palmas by seniority), Gaul (Irenaeus), Osrhoene and cities, Bacchyllus of Corinth individually (*idiôs*), and others unidentified. He says all agreed with Victor.[28]

Other bishops in Palestine, however, included Cassius of Tyre and Clarus of Ptolemais. Their letter discussed apostolic tradition and ended thus:

> Try to send copies of our letter to every diocese [?] (*paroikia*) so that we may not be liable for those who easily deceive themselves. We are showing you that at Alexandria they observe the same day as ourselves, for letters have been exchanged between them and us so that we may observe the holy day harmoniously and in agreement.

Eusebius seems to suppose that the letter supported Victor's position,[29] but the title of a lost letter does not agree with his opinion: "To an Alexandrian, that it is right that we should celebrate the Feast of the Resurrection upon the first day of the week."[30] It thus appears that Palestine and Alexandria followed another tradition, as in later times. Presumably this means that Irenaeus was defending Roman usage against that of Alexandria and Palestine.

Irenaeus' own letter to Victor on the Paschal feast is conciliatory but firm.

The controversy is not only about the day but also about the actual form of the fast. Some think they must fast for a day, others two days, others even more. Some count their day as forty hours, day and night. Such variety among the participants did not begin recently in our time but much earlier under our predecessors who, it seems, disregarded rigidity and maintained a custom both simple and individual, transmitting it to those after them. None the less all these were at peace and we also are at peace with one another, and the divergence in the fast confirms our unity in the faith. Among them were the presbyters who before Soter presided over the church you now govern, I mean Anicetus, Pius, Hyginus, Telesphorus, and Xystus. They did not keep it themselves and did not commit it to their successors; none the less they were at peace with those who came to them from the churches in which it was observed, even though the observance was opposed to those who did not keep it. No one was ever expelled because of this form, but the presbyters before you who did not observe it sent Eucharist to those from the churches that did observe it, and when the blessed Polycarp was staying in Rome under Anicetus and they had modest disagreements about some other matters they made peace at once, since they had no desire for strife on this topic. For neither could Anicetus persuade Polycarp not to observe what he had always observed with John our Lord's disciple and the other apostles with whom he had associated, nor did Polycarp persuade Anicetus to observe this, for he said that he ought to hold fast the custom of the presbyters before him. Under the circumstances, they had fellowship with each other and in the church Anicetus yielded the Eucharist to Polycarp, obviously out of respect, and they parted from each other in peace, for those who observed and those who did not observe kept the peace of the whole church before Soter.[31]

Irenaeus took his writing against heresy with great seriousness. Indeed, he placed a solemn oath at the end of a work addressed to Florinus, tempted by the Valentinian heresy. "I swear by our Lord

Jesus Christ, and by his glorious coming when he comes to judge the living and the dead, that when you copy this book you must compare what you copy and carefully correct it by the original, and also copy this oath and put it in the copy."[32] Dionysius of Corinth had already warned Soter of Rome about heretics who were editing his own letters as well as the "dominical scriptures."[33]

Later Irenaeus wrote the *Epideixis* or *Proof of the Apostolic Preaching*, mentioned by Eusebius[34] but now extant only in an Armenian version. It is a relatively simple summary of the main points of the rule of faith as supported by biblical texts. Irenaeus refers back to his earlier work and repeats many of the major topics. He omits the references to authorities other than the Bible – save for "the presbyters (disciples of the apostles)."[35] It is not included here because it is more exegetical than theological and lacks the actuality and polemical quality of the basic anti-heretical work.

2

GNOSTIC ORIGINS

No one knows how the Gnostics originated, though they obviously came out of "fringe" Judaism and Christianity. They knew something of Greek philosophy, more about theosophy, and their fondness for dualistic thought, speculative cosmology, mythology, and spiritualizing ideas about Christ, all expressed in mysterious language, won them some converts. Gnostics "knew" the real meaning of Christianity (not what others supposed it was) and kept it fairly secret. No one knows how many there were. If the mediaeval Albigensians present any parallel, there were relatively few. There were few Christians, fewer Gnostics.

Though Irenaeus wrote primarily against the Valentinians, he used earlier Gnostic heresies to indicate their "source and root" and their unapostolic succession, claiming that thus the system would be overthrown (1.23–31) and relying primarily on Justin's lost treatise *Against all Heresies*, which Justin himself said discussed Simon Magus, his disciple Menander, and Marcion (and others not listed).[1] Since in his *Dialogue* Justin also mentions the followers of Saturninus, Basilides, and Valentinus, he may have discussed them in the lost work too.[2] Irenaeus has done his own research for Valentinus, and presumably also for Carpocrates, whose successful missionary Marcellina was at Rome under Anicetus, and Cerinthus, active in Asia. Supposedly the Ebionites and the Nicolaitans shared the Christology of Carpocrates and Cerinthus. Irenaeus promises a separate refutation of Marcion with use of his writings. His own (later?) research involved the *Oration* and other writings of his contemporary Tatian, Justin's disciple but a heretic after his master's death. He investigated what we know as the *Apocryphon of John* for the doctrines of the "Barbelo-Gnostics" and did further research for his account of what must be the Ophites, without troubling to see how repetitious the description was. He could not stop writing until he had dealt with the "Cainites," whose literature, including the *Gospel of Judas*, he says he has read.[3]

Irenaeus' basic approach was genetic. He believed that he could undermine contemporary Valentinians by showing that they had forerunners and that these forerunners were wrong and perverted. Justin had pointed out that the demons inspired the Gnostic teacher Simon Magus only in the reign of Claudius (41–54), after the ascension of Christ, and that he had a disciple named Menander; then he skipped to Marcion in his own time.[4] The argument that wrong interpretations of school teaching are late comes from the philosophical schools, notably in the debates over correctness as to what Plato taught.[5]

The first of Valentinus' supposed ancestors was Simon Magus. Irenaeus begins his account of him by weaving together several sources, prefacing quotations from Acts 8:9–11 and 20–23, adding anti-heretical materials derived from Justin on Simon's expertise in magic and his statue erected by Claudius Caesar, and ending with the heretical theological statement that Simon appeared among the Jews as Son, descended in Samaria as Father, and came to the other nations as Holy Spirit.

Then he turns to sketch the Simonian myth. In the beginning Simon conceived his First Thought, the Mother of all, so that she would give birth to the angels and archangels by whom this world was made. Farther on, in the account of Simon's fallen Thought, Helen, the duplication is fairly obvious. We hear twice about the attitude and activities of the rebellious angels, in accounts we may call A and B, presumably reflecting two sources again.

A	B
	Simon was unknown to them
After she generated them	
she was held captive by them	but his Thought was held captive
out of envy	by the powers and angels
since they did not want to be	
considered the offspring of	she had emitted.
anyone.	And she suffered complete
	disgrace from them,
	unable to return upward
	to her father.

She was enclosed in a human body, and through the ages passed into other female bodies as from one case into another.	She passed from body to body and always suffered disgrace. Finally she was in a brothel; She was the "lost sheep."

Since she was in Helen of Troy, when the poet Stesichorus cursed her in his poems he went blind, but later when he repented and praised her in his "palinodes," he saw again. Stesichorus did write a *Helen* and two *Palinodes* on Homer and Hesiod,⁶ but the story about recovering sight is in Plato, where Simonian theologians may have found it.⁷ Finally she stood in a brothel in Tyre, the "lost sheep" (Luke 15:4–6), where Simon found her and took her with him (1.23.2).

There also seem to be two accounts of Simon's descent to earth.

He himself came in order to recover her and set her free and provide salvation by the Gnosis of himself.	When the angels misgoverned the world, since each desired the primacy, he came down in order to correct the situation.
When Simon came down to earth he appeared as a man, though not a man, and was thought to suffer in Judaea, though he did not suffer.	He appeared among the Jews as Son, He came down in Samaria as Father, and arrived among the other nations as Holy Spirit. He was really the Supreme Power.

He was the Father above all, though he was willing to be called Zeus or other names.

In his ethical teaching he rejected the Old Testament prophets, claiming that they were inspired by the angels who made the world, no doubt because of the diverse divine names in the Old Testament. "Those who have hoped on him and Helen" can ignore the prophets and do whatever they will. Like Pauline Christians, they are saved by his grace, not by just works (Eph.2:8–9).

Both Justin and Irenaeus regard Menander as Simon's successor, though Irenaeus reports that Menander was sent by the first unknown Power as another Savior of mankind. Menander therefore must have been not Simon's successor but an independent religious teacher who demanded baptism into himself, not Simon or Helen. Unfortunately he promised immortality on earth and lost credibility when his followers died (1.23.5).

Saturninus, in turn, knows Menander's Father unknown to all, who made various spiritual powers, seven of whom then made "the world and everything in it." When a luminous image appeared from the Supreme Power, the angels could not prevent its upward escape, but then encouraged one another to "make man after *the* image and *the* likeness" (1.24.1–2). They were too weak to make a product that could stand erect. Instead, it wriggled like a worm until the Power from above took pity on it (for it was made in its likeness) and emitted a spark of life that raised the man, set him on his feet, and made him live. After death this spark of life runs back above, but the rest returns to the original material elements.

Saturninus' story of redemption is based on the Christian one. He himself is not the Savior. Once more, we perceive a double narrative, with Christian sources more transparent in the first one.

The god of the Jews is one of the angels.	Two races of men were fashioned by the angels. one bad, the other good.
Because the Father wanted to destroy all the Archons, the Christ came for the destruction of the god of the Jews and for the salvation of those who believe in him.	As the demons helped the evil, the Savior came for the destruction of evil men and demons and for the salvation of the good.
Marriage and generation are from Satan. Many disciples also abstain from meat and by feigned "abstinence" lead many astray.	The Savior was ungenerated, incorporeal, and shapeless, and he was seen only in appearance.
As for the prophecies, some have been spoken by the angels who made the world, others by Satan. He is an angel opposed to those who made the world, especially the god of the Jews.	

Perhaps the term "the god of the Jews" is a Christian Gnostic alternative to "the God of the Hebrews" in Exodus 7:16 and other passages. After this point the double narrative disappears. Presumably Justin or some other source described no one later than Saturninus.

Irenaeus' picture of Basilides' doctrine (1.24.3–7) is often neglected in favor of a different one by Hippolytus,[8] more philosophical and poetic, which scholars tend to suppose came first though perhaps kept secret in Basilidian circles. It seems just as likely that a later theologian developed Basilides' theology in a new direction, and that Irenaeus' account is relatively reliable.

Basilides postulated five primal psychological powers: Mind, first born from the ungenerated Father, from Mind Logos, from Logos Forethought, from Forethought Wisdom and Power, and from Wisdom and Power the powers, archons, and angels whom he calls first, who made the first heaven. Later they made further copies of those above them to a total of 365, equivalent to the days of the solar year and summed up in the magical name Abrasax.[9]

Like Saturninus, Basilides explains salvation out of biblical passages though he calls "the god of the Jews" the chief of the hostile angels. The most important passage is Psalm 2:2: "The kings of the earth rose up and the archons gathered together against the Lord and against his Christ." When the god of the Jews wanted to subject the other nations to his own people, the other archons rose up against him and fought him, and the other peoples rose against his people. The Father, however, sent his First-Begotten Mind, called Christ, to liberate believers. After Christ appeared on earth as a man and worked miracles, a certain Simon of Cyrene was pressed into service to carry his cross and was crucified by ignorance and error,[10] transfigured so that he was supposed to be Jesus (compare 1 Cor.2:8: the Wisdom of God "which none of the archons of this aeon knew; for if they had known they would not have crucified the Lord of Glory"). Jesus [Christ] took the appearance of Simon and stood by to deride the archons. This looks like severely literal exegesis of Mark 15:21–24 (where Simon of Cyrene is named but then Jesus is not mentioned until after the crucifixion)[11] and Psalm 2:4: "He who dwells in the heavens will ridicule them and the Lord will mock them." As an incorporeal power and the Mind of the ungenerated Father, he transfigured himself as he wished, and ascended to the Father who sent him, deriding the archons because he could not be held and was invisible to all.

Gnostics must confess not the one who was really crucified (Simon of Cyrene) but the Christ who came in human form, was called Jesus, and was sent by the Father to destroy the works of the world-makers. Whoever confesses the Crucified is still a slave, but he who denies is freed from them and knows the plan of the Father. Only the soul can obtain salvation, for the body is perishable by nature. The Old Testament prophecies come from the archons who made the world, while the law comes specifically from their chief, the god of the Jews, who led the people out of the land of Egypt.

Basilides espoused a kind of Cynic morality, holding that one must despise the foods offered to idols, regard them as nothing and use them without the slightest fear, and treat sins such as debauchery with indifference. His followers also practise magic and invent names for the angels, claiming that some are in the first heaven, others in the second, and go on to give the names of the archons, angels, and powers of the 365 supposed heavens. They also say that the name under which the Savior descended and ascended is Caulacau – unintelligible Hebrew words (*Kau lakau*), hence mysterious, in an "oracle of the Lord" in Isaiah 28:10.[12] The person who has learned all these things will become invisible and intangible to the angels and their powers just as Caulacau was. "You must know everyone," they say, "but no one should know you." Here Basilides came close to the *Gospel of Thomas.* "Not many can know these things, but one out of a thousand and two out of ten thousand."[13]

Carpocrates and the Gnostics noted after him are not mentioned by Justin, and presumably Irenaeus has to follow special sources for them. Like other Gnostics, Carpocrates and his disciples say that the world and what is in it was made by angels much inferior to the ungenerated Father. Jesus, the son of Joseph, lived a virtuous life, and therefore the Father sent him a special power that enabled him to go above. Other souls can imitate him and become superior to Peter and Paul or even to Jesus himself. Unless they exercise absolute freedom and thus escape from the world, their souls will return to bodies.

Irenaeus ascribes a rather commonplace form of Gnosticism to the Asian Cerinthus.[14] The world was made by an inferior power that did not know the absolute Being above. Jesus, again the son of Joseph and Mary, was supremely virtuous and, after his baptism,[15] was deemed suited for the Christ to descend into him from above and empower him to proclaim the unknown Father and perform miracles. Finally the Christ flew away, remaining impassible, while Jesus suffered and was raised.

Irenaeus describes the Ebionites and the Nicolaitans as quite different from the Gnostics he has been discussing, though he claims, without evidence, that the Ebionites' views of "the Lord" are those of Cerinthus and Carpocrates. What he must mean is that they regarded Jesus as the son of Joseph (cf. 3.21.1). The most significant statement is that the Ebionites "*adorant* [supply "the temple in"] Jerusalem as the house of God." *Adorare* here means "pray toward," as in the usage of the second-century synagogue.

For the Nicolaitans Irenaeus relies exclusively on a brief notice in the Apocalypse of John (2:6,14–15) and, for the name Nicolaus, on Acts 6:5. His account does not come from Justin, who did not use Acts.

The mysterious Cerdo, at Rome under Hyginus, is called another descendant of Simon. For him the just God proclaimed by the law and the prophets was not the unknown good Father of Jesus. The sole reason for mentioning him is to provide the greater Marcion with an unreliable predecessor and connect him to Simon.

Marcion's own arrival from Pontus around 137 is also mysterious. Irenaeus may cast some light when he tells how Marcion interpreted Jesus' descent into Hades, where Old Testament saints rejected his offer of salvation and Old Testament sinners accepted it. This is essentially the doctrine of 1 Peter 3:18–20, in a letter sent to Pontus, the province from which Marcion went to Rome. Christ was

> put to death in the flesh but made alive in the spirit, in which he went and preached to the spirits in prison, who formerly did not obey, when God's patience waited in the days of Noah, during the building of the ark, in which a few, that is, eight persons, were saved through water.

The point is that Christ's preaching "in prison" (presumably in Hades) was addressed to the disobedient, not the saints like Noah. With the author of 1 Peter, Marcion believed that Cain and other Old Testament sinners were saved by the Lord when he descended into Hades. They ran to him and he took them into his kingdom, while none of the Old Testament saints shared in salvation. In the belief that their god was still testing them, they did not believe Jesus but remained in Hades (1.27.3). Irenaeus probably acquired this information about Marcion's doctrine from a famous letter of his.[16] Naturally when Marcion wrote his *Gospel* he revised Luke 13:28 so that "all the righteous" were within the kingdom of God rather than "Abraham and Isaac and Jacob and all the prophets."[17]

Toward the middle of the second century, however, the Christian view sharpened, perhaps in reaction against Gnostics. Justin, who did not use 1 Peter, claimed that Jews had cut out an important passage from the Greek text of Jeremiah: "The Lord God remembered his dead from Israel, those who had slept in the earth of dust, and he descended to them to proclaim his salvation to them."[18] Irenaeus uses this text: "The Lord, the Holy One of Israel, remembered his dead who had slept in the earth of dust, and he descended to them to proclaim his salvation to them and save them." "Jeremiah" agrees with the teaching of an earlier presbyter recalled by Irenaeus: Christ went down to preach to the righteous, the prophets, and the patriarchs.[19] Marcion's paradoxical view was not tolerated.

Marcion himself, developing a new version of a gospel and the Pauline epistles, had reached Rome under Hyginus and flourished under Anicetus. Literary heresies tended to flourish in the intellectual environment of Rome, the setting for the trilogy *Antitheses-Gospel-Apostle*, the book of *Syllogisms* by Apelles, and the syllogisms of the Adoptionists. Marcion was able to remain within the church until 144, when he was excommunicated under Pius, perhaps by a college of presbyters.[20]

In discussing Encratites and their denial of Adam's salvation, Irenaeus tells us something about Tatian, the first heretic to deny it.

> While he heard the teaching of Justin and stayed with him, he set forth no such doctrine, but after Justin's martyrdom he separated from the church. Lifted up and inflated by his claim to be a teacher, as if he were better than the rest, he created his own style of doctrine. Like the Valentinians he set forth a myth about invisible Aeons; like Marcion and Saturninus he called marriage corruption and debauchery, and finally he rejected the ultimate salvation of Adam.

The description of Tatian shows that Irenaeus knew his address *Against the Greeks*, in which he claimed that people said of him: "Tatian, beyond the Greeks and beyond the infinite multitude of philosophers, is innovating with barbarian doctrines."[21]

Later on Irenaeus says again that Tatian denied the salvation of Adam. "Becoming the synthesis of all heresies, as we have shown, he personally invented this doctrine. By thus adding something novel he was trying with words devoid of meaning to gain hearers devoid of faith."[22] This picture of Tatian's conceit and would-be innovation also comes from his address *Against the Greeks*, with its claim that people said how wonderful he was. The other points are derived from Tatian's more theological writings such as his treatise *On Perfection according to the Savior*, denounced by Clement of Alexandria.[23]

Irenaeus devotes a chapter (1.29) to a Greek version of the *Apocryphon of John*, preserved in four Coptic versions from Egypt. The first of these to be edited comes from a fifth-century Berlin papyrus that contains two other Gnostic works (part of the *Gospel of Mary* and all of the *Sophia of Jesus Christ*) and part of the non-Gnostic *Acts of Peter*.[24] This text is much the same as the one found in Codex III among the "Gnostic" papyri from Nag Hammadi, although Codex II and Codex IV contain a version with two long additions, the first with the names of 365 angels responsible for parts of the human body, the second with the descent of "the perfect Pronoia of the All" into the darkness below.[25] Irenaeus does not know this enlarged version but almost certainly used the shorter Greek *Apocryphon*.

An even stranger but similar system appears in the next chapter (1.30), with the Father of all called "First Man" and his Son-Thought called "Second Man," while below them is the Holy Spirit, called "First Woman." Christ is the "Third Male," son of the First and Second Men and First Woman. As the story develops it turns out to be a rewriting of Genesis on the basis of a highly distorted and sexualized version of the Christian story. A power that proceeded from the First Woman and was called Left or Prunicus or Wisdom or Male-Female, with a "watery body," produced a son Ialdabaoth, from whom proceeded in turn six other powers – from which ultimately the world and humanity came into existence. From that point these Ophites proceeded to retell the whole biblical story from their special viewpoint. A related sect claimed that the serpent of Eden was Wisdom, which gave Gnosis to men and was called more intelligent than any other being (Gen.3:1). Further proof? Our intestines, which give life, are shaped like a serpent.

Already in the New Testament Paul had cited what a Marcionite or Cainite would consider the Creator-god's words in Malachi 1.2–3: "Jacob I loved but Esau I hated" (Rom.9:13). The Epistle of Jude goes farther and refers to heretics who walk in the way of Cain, to those who perished in Korah's rebellion, and to Sodom and Gomorrah.[26] For the Cainite sect, as for Marcion, the sinners involved were the real saints of the Old Testament, for they resisted the Creator-god. Cain and the other Old Testament sinners came from the Absolute Sovereignty above. The Creator hated them but could not harm them, for they were protected by Sophia. The traitor Judas knew this and therefore brought about the mystery of the betrayal, as the Cainite *Gospel of Judas* shows.

Irenaeus has collected Cainite documents urging the destruction of the works of the Womb, the Creator of heaven and earth. Perfect Gnosis, they say, is the performance of unmentionable acts without fear (1.31.1–2).[27] Presumably he discusses the Cainites, self-evidently perverse, at the end of his account because he believes that to know Gnostic doctrine is to apprehend its falsity.

3

AGAINST THE VALENTINIANS

Irenaeus was alarmed by the various Gnostic teachers who had come to infest Rome. The first Gnostic, Simon Magus, lived there under Claudius Caesar, and much later a certain Cerdo came to Rome under Hyginus, ninth bishop, teaching that the God of justice announced by the Old Testament was not the unknown good Father of Jesus Christ. While his successor Marcion flourished a Gnostic woman named Marcellina won many converts.[1] The famous Gnostic teacher Valentinus also taught at Rome for decades.[2] Around the middle of the second century there was severe doctrinal trouble in the church at Rome.

Even in remote Lyons Irenaeus, friend of Rome, denounced the Gnostic heresy. He seems to have been concerned with the Valentinians because they were taking his own route westward from Asia. This was notably the situation of Mark the magician and his disciples, who led astray the wives of Christian hosts from Asia Minor to Gaul, "even in our regions by the Rhône." At least one of them returned to the church and spent the rest of her life in penitence.[3]

Irenaeus could not simply devote his talents to moral outrage, however, but had to explain why the Gnostics were wrong. His task was made easier because the Valentinians were relatively conventional and were trying to make their system relatively rational. Irenaeus had been able to read the "commentaries" by disciples of Valentinus, in which he found "the doctrine of those who teach error at the present time – I mean Ptolemaeus and his followers, whose doctrine is the "flower" of the school of Valentinus."[4] Using these commentaries, with an exact quotation of Ptolemaeus on John 1:1–14, meant that he could neglect the writings of other Valentinians closer to Christianity. He must have believed that the rational theology of Ptolemaeus would be easier to ridicule and contradict, though he neglected, or perhaps did not know, his *Letter to Flora* (cited by Epiphanius), which formally stood somewhat closer to Christian teaching.

Encounters with Valentinian exegetes disappointed him, however.

> When one and the same text has been read, all furrow their brows and shake their heads, saying, "This is a very profound word, and not all understand the greatness of the meaning it contains; therefore silence is the greatest thing for the wise." The Silence above must be expressed in the silence present among them. So they all go away, however many they are, giving birth to so many great thoughts from a single text and secretly taking their subtleties with them. If they ever agree on what was predicted in the scriptures, we ourselves will then refute them. Meanwhile, holding erroneous opinions they refute themselves, disagreeing over the same words.[5]

If they could be held to one system, no doubt they could be refuted.

PTOLEMAEUS' SYSTEM

Irenaeus' account of Valentinian doctrine therefore begins abruptly with the so-called "Great Notice" by Ptolemaeus, dealing with Gnostic cosmology. The one pre-existent Aeon, Pre-Beginning or Forefather or Depth, emitted a Beginning of all into his companion Thought/Grace/Silence, who then bore Mind/Only-Begotten/Father/Beginning. Truth was emitted with him to compose the first Tetrad: Depth, Silence, Mind, Truth. A series of emissions then began when Only-Begotten produced Logos and Life and they produced Man and Church, making up the Ogdoad, and then ten more. Man and Church emitted another twelve, the last of which was Sophia. These thirty Aeons made up the Pleroma.

Sophia "leaped forth" from her place with her consort Willed and experienced passion in her desire to comprehend the incomprehensible Father. She would have been dissolved had not Limit stopped her and made her return to herself, at the same time crucifying her Desire.[6] When Sophia was restored to the Pleroma, Only-Begotten emitted another pair, Christ and Holy Spirit, to teach how the Father is incomprehensible and what the nature of spiritual "rest" is.

Sophia's Desire, also known as Achamoth, was lost below, but Christ extended himself to her through the Cross and gave her shape as she suffered various emotions (1.4.2). Christ then returned to the Pleroma but sent the Paraclete, the Savior, to her. The Savior enabled her to shape three kinds of entities: material (from her passion), psychic (from her conversion), and spiritual (from her essential nature). Out of the psychic nature she fashioned the Demiurge, who preserved the image of Only-Begotten and was the maker of all psychic and material beings. He shaped seven heavens, which are angels, and dwells above them. He ignorantly thought he made them, but Achamoth projected them first.

There are also three classes of human beings: material (incapable of salvation); psychic (strengthened by works and mere faith, members of the church); and spiritual (who cannot decay or be harmed by material actions any more than gold is harmed in mud). "It is not conduct that leads one to the Pleroma, but the seed sent out from there as an infant and made perfect there." Only the spirituals will finally be given as brides to the angels of the Savior.

EXEGETICAL DETAILS

Ptolemaeus seemed especially dangerous because he distorted texts from the Lord's mysterious parables, the oracles of the prophets, and the words of apostles. Irenaeus has grouped the exegetical details together, with most of them coming from the synoptic gospels.[7] Wherever the Valentinians found thirties, as in the Savior's thirty years of private life (Luke 3:23) and his parable of the Laborers in the Vineyard, hired at the hours adding up to thirty (Matt.20:1–7), there were the thirty Aeons of the Pleroma above (1.1.3). The passion experienced in the Pleroma by the twelfth Aeon was concealed in the seemingly meaningless statement that the daughter of the chief of the synagogue, raised from the dead by the Lord, was 12 years old (Luke 8:41–42).

Paul spoke not of himself but in the person of Sophia's shapeless offspring. What could Paul possibly have meant when he wrote, "Last of all he appeared to me as to an abortion" (1 Cor.15:8)? This must mean that the Savior appeared to the shapeless Achamoth when she was outside the Pleroma. Again, since the Savior was incapable of suffering, his sayings in the gospel passion narrative were really expressed by Achamoth. He manifested her passions, not his, in his cry from the cross, "My God, my God, why have you abandoned me?" (Matt.27:46). She revealed her grief in "How sad is my soul" (Matt.26:38), her fear in "Father, if possible let the cup pass from me" (Matt.26:39), and her anguish in "I do not know what I shall say" (John 12:27).

Other mysterious sayings of Jesus about various kinds of disciples clearly pointed toward the Valentinian doctrine of the three races of men. The basic text was Matthew 8:19–22/Luke 9:57–62, where Jesus says to the first man he encounters, "The foxes have holes and the birds of the heaven have nests, but the Son of Man has nowhere to lay his head." The foxes and birds must be the lowest, "hylic" or material race, contrasted with the spiritual Son of Man. A second man implies that he will follow, but asks permission to say goodbye to those of his house. Since he is psychic, with free will but not stability, he chose not to follow. The Lord therefore replied, "Whoever has put his hand to the plow but looks back is not fit for the kingdom of heaven" (Luke 9:61–62). Another "psychic" man confesses performing the many duties of "justice" but refuses to follow the Savior because of his material wealth, which keeps him from becoming "perfect" (Matt.19:16–22). Finally, the Lord contrasted material with spiritual when he said, "Let the dead bury the dead, but you go and proclaim the kingdom of God" (Matt.8:22/Luke 9:60).

Naturally all three races can be found in the parable of the leaven which a woman hid in three measures of meal (Matt.13:33/Luke 13:20–21). She is the heavenly Sophia; the measures are spiritual, psychic, and earthly; the meal itself is the Savior. Ptolemaeus found that the Gospel speaks allegorically, but Paul spoke literally and precisely about "earthies" (= hylic or material), "psychics," and "spirituals" (1 Cor.15:48; 2:14–15).

Yet more speculatively, Ptolemaeus relates the words of Christ and stories about him to cosmic events in the world above. After Achamoth fell from the Pleroma, Christ (the merely psychic) gave her a shape and the Savior looked for her. This is expressed in his declaration that he came to "the lost sheep" (Matt.18:12–13/Luke 15:4–7). The woman who cleans her house and finds a lost drachma (Luke 15:8–10) is the Sophia Above, who is looking for her lost Enthymesis-Desire (Achamoth). Later, when everything has been purified by the coming of the Savior, she finds it, for Achamoth must be restored within the Pleroma. The Gospel tells how the prophetess Anna lived seven years with her husband and spent the rest of her life as a widow. Since she saw the Lord, recognized him, and spoke of him to all (Luke 2:36–38), she obviously is Achamoth, who saw the Lord with his companions for a moment and then remained in the Middle for the whole later period, waiting for him to come and establish her in her pair of Aeons. The Savior pointed to her name in his enigmatic statement, "Sophia was justified by her children" (Luke

7:35), as did Paul in these words, "We speak of Sophia among the perfect" (1 Cor.2:6). Paul also spoke of the pairs within the Pleroma when he spoke plainly about one such pair: "This mystery is great, but I speak of Christ and Church" (Eph.5:32) (1.8.4). The greatness of the mystery could thus be found in the more enigmatic sayings of Jesus in the synoptic gospels and confirmed from the language of Paul. Obviously what appealed to Gnostic converts was the theological synthesis of diverse scriptural passages, along with a secret pattern to hold them together.

VALENTINIAN MORALS

The church, unlike the Gnostics, also laid emphasis on Christian conduct, set forth for example in the moral codes used by Hermas, 2 Clement, and Justin. Irenaeus criticizes the sexual morality of the Valentinians (1.6.2–4), claiming that the Valentinian "spirituals" were so "perfect" that they could eat meat sacrificed to idols, and attend pagan festivals and gladiatorial shows. In any event, Gnostics steal other Christians' wives, for only the less exalted "psychics," ordinary Christians, have to obey the moral law.[8]

As we have seen, Irenaeus reserves his harshest criticism for the behavior of the Valentinian Mark. He also noted that Mark secretly put chemicals into his eucharistic cup to change the volume and the color of the wine, and charged him with combining the trivia (*paignia, ludicra*) of Anaxilaos with the wickedness of so-called magicians.[9] The elder Pliny says that the magician Anaxilaos played (*lusit*) with sulphur by putting some in a cup of wine, placing a hot coal beneath, and handing it around at dinner parties; its reflection cast a dreadful pallor on the guests' faces as if they were dead.[10] This kind of trick is what Irenaeus has in mind.

Perhaps more strikingly, Mark attracted rich and elegant women, often those who wore purple-edged robes, that is, the *toga praetexta* of the equestrian or even senatorial class. He could make one of them prophesy by sharing his grace with her so that she would say whatever entered her mind. At this point, Irenaeus declares, she would be bewitched and bewildered; her soul would be set on fire by the idea that she could prophesy, and her heart would pound much harder than it should. Her state strikingly resembles a case solved by his older contemporary Galen at Rome. The famous physician had decided that his patient's ailment was psychological rather than physical. When a visitor spoke of seeing a famous dancer at the theater, her expression and color changed, and Galen found that her pulse had become very erratic. For the next three days he had an assistant state that other dancers were to perform, but no pulse change resulted. Obviously, like Irenaeus' grace-filled woman, she was suffering from an infatuation.[11] Irenaeus says that women were accustomed to hand over their property as well as their persons to Mark. Galen's services were less expensive.

Irenaeus was sure that the Gnostics could not think straight because they themselves were mentally ill. "When sick people fall into delirium, the more they laugh and believe themselves healthy and do everything as if they were well or even more than well, the sicker they really are." When they try to count grains of sand, pebbles on the ground, waves in the sea, and stars in the sky – and to determine the cause of the number! – they are insane and stupid, just as if they had been struck by lightning.[12]

When he looks at Valentinian myths, such as the passions of the fallen Achamoth that produced matter, he is driven to irony.[13] He says the Gnostics rightly keep the story secret and reveal it "only to those capable of providing substantial payments for such great mysteries." After all, the mysteries were discovered "by the immense labor of these lovers of lies."

In addition, Irenaeus ridiculed the numerology of the Marcosians by constructing or borrowing an account of the possible meanings of the number five (2.25.1). To be sure, his own approach to the number of the Beast in Revelation 13 is quite similar to the Gnostic one, but it can be defended on the ground that the author himself had said there was a hidden meaning.

It is regrettable that he apparently did not encounter the Valentinian *Gospel of Truth* until he was writing his third book, for his criticisms already discussed do not really apply to it.[14]

VARIETIES OF VALENTINIAN SYSTEMS

Let us now look at their unstable teaching and how, when there are two or three of them, they not only do not make the same statements about the same things but give answers contradictory in content and expression alike.

Irenaeus' complaints about Gnostic inventiveness are not unlike what Galen said about non-Hippocratic physicians. "I always say that most of what is written by the younger physicians in their memoirs wastes our time and teaches nothing medical."[15] Both authors have a tradition to maintain against modern error.

The first among them, Valentinus, transferred the older doctrines from what is called the "Gnostic" sect and adapted them for his own school. He stated that there is an ineffable Duality consisting of the Inexpressible and Silence. Later this Duality emitted a second Duality, Father and Truth. This Tetrad bore as fruit Logos and Life, Man and Church, thus constituting the first Ogdoad. From Logos and Life ten powers were emitted, as we have said; from Man and Church were emitted twelve, one of which, leaving (the Pleroma) and falling into distress, made the rest of the creation. He has two Limits: one, between the Abyss and the Pleroma, separates the generated Aeons from the uncreated Father, while the other separates their Mother from the Pleroma. The Christ was not emitted by the Aeons of the Pleroma, but was borne by the Mother, when she was outside it, according to the memory she had of the powers above, though with a certain shadow. As this Christ was masculine, he cut off the shadow from himself and returned to the Pleroma. Then the Mother, abandoned with the shadow and emptied of spiritual substance, emitted another son: this is the Demiurge, omnipotent master of those beneath him. Along with him was emitted an Archon of the left, as in the system of those falsely called "Gnostics."

Jesus was sometimes said to be emitted by Theletos, the Aeon separated from their Mother and united with the others, sometimes by Christ, who ran upward again into the Pleroma, and sometimes by Man and Church. And the Holy Spirit was emitted by Truth for testing and fructifying the Aeons; it enters them invisibly, and by it the Aeons fructify the plants of Truth. Such is the doctrine of Valentinus.[16]

A disciple of his, Secundus (otherwise unknown),

teaches that the first Ogdoad includes a Tetrad of the right and a Tetrad of the left, and light and darkness; the Aeon that left the Pleroma and fell into distress did not come from the thirty but from their fruits.[17]

Another, a famous teacher of theirs, "spreads out" toward a Gnosis higher and more Gnostic and describes the first Tetrad thus:

There exists before everything a pre-unintelligible Pre-principle which I call Unicity. With this Unicity there coexists a Power which I call Unity. This Unity and this Unicity, being one, emitted without emitting a Beginning of all things, intelligible unengendered and invisible, the Beginning which language calls Monad. With this Monad coexists a Power of the same substance, which I call One. These Powers, Unicity, Unity, Monad, and One, emitted the rest of the Aeons.[18]

One might think the Gnostic quotation spoke for itself, but Irenaeus could not leave such Valentinians without producing a parody with a picture of the Great Cucumber and ironic use of long Homeric words.

There exists a certain royal Pre-principle, pre-unintelligible, pre-insubstantial and pre-prerotund, which I call Gourd. With this Gourd there coexists a Power which I call Supervacuity. This Gourd and this Supervacuity, being one, emitted without emitting a Fruit visible in all its parts, edible and sweet, which language calls Cucumber. With this Cucumber there is a Power of the same substance, which I call Melon. These Powers, Gourd and Supervacuity and Cucumber and Melon, emitted the whole multitude of Valentinus' delirious Melons.

The parody owes some of its force to the Gnostics' love of transforming history into nature, here specifically vegetable nature.[19]

4

CHRISTIAN BOOKS
AND TRADITIONS

Irenaeus insists that scripture is the basic authority, not Gnostic exegesis, for the latter is built on shifting sand. Gnostic exegetes neglect word-order and context and rely on isolated words and passages. They interpret the clear and obvious by the dark and obscure, out of the most mysterious passages of parables and allegories, adapting ambiguous expressions to their own fictitious creation. You cannot explain one ambiguity through another, he insisted. He suggests ironically that the Gnostics rightly reserved their exegesis for those able to pay for it, since it had cost them such an immense effort to produce it.[1]

THE OLD TESTAMENT

Minimal acquaintance with Hebrew

Irenaeus believed that the Old Testament was a Christian book, for Moses mentioned the pre-existent Son of God in Hebrew at the beginning of Genesis: *Bereshith bara Elohim basan benuam samenthares.* Somehow he had the impression that this means, "Son (*bara*) in the beginning (*bereshith*); God (*Elohim*) established then the heaven (*ha-shammayim*) and the earth (*ha-arets*)."[2] Whether or not he got this from an exegetical tradition, *bara* really means "created" and is not the same as *bar*, "son."

He tells how the Ophite Gnostics used their own limited knowledge of Hebrew for analyzing inspiration, since they believed that each of the seven planetary angels bore a Hebrew name of God and chose his own herald to glorify him. One would expect, therefore, that they would correlate their theory with the usage of such names by the various prophets. They could have found a point of departure in Exodus 6:3, where God says to Moses, "I am Yahweh. I appeared to Abraham, to Isaac, and to Jacob, as El Shaddai, but by my name Yahweh I did not make myself known to them." These Gnostics did not use exactly this correlation, however. They held that the chief angel was Ialdabaoth, the creator, redeemer, and legislator who inspired Moses, Joshua, Amos, and Habakkuk. The second, Iao, inspired Samuel (cf. 1 Sam.1:20), Nathan (2 Sam.7:3–5), Jonah (1:1), and Micah (1:1). The third, Sabaoth, inspired Elijah, Joel, and Zechariah. Though the name Sabaoth does not occur from Genesis to Judges, the prophet Elijah does refer to Yahweh Sabaoth occasionally (1 Kings 18:15; 19:10,14) and Sabaoth is named in Joel 2:2–11 and 4:14, Yahweh Sabaoth frequently in Zechariah.

The major inspiration of the major prophets was Adonai ("the Lord"), who revealed his presence in key passages in Isaiah (6:1), Jeremiah (1:6), Ezekiel (2:4), and Daniel (1:2). Eloeus or Elohim supposedly inspired Tobias and Haggai, but while the name occurs frequently in Job, it does not appear in these prophets. The correlation of Horeus or Oreus with Micah is probably due to God's being called Ôr (light) in Micah 7:8 (and Isaiah 10:17) but the correlation with Nahum does not make sense. Astaphaeus does not seem a meaningful choice in regard to Esdras and Zephaniah, unless perhaps it is a variant of Elyon, frequent in 1 Esdras. Though some of these choices fail because of the ineptitude of either Gnostic or anti-Gnostic writers or scribes, there are still enough correlations to show that the idea had a semi-rational base. (1.30.10–11)

Irenaeus himself claims that the word *Eloe* in Hebrew means "true God" and *Elloeuth* means "what contains all." *Adonai* sometimes means "unnameable" and "admirable," he says, and sometimes with a double delta and an aspiration it means "He who separates the earth from the water so that the water cannot rise up against it." Similarly *Sabaôth* with omega in the last syllable means "voluntary"; with omicron it means "first heaven." Just so, Iaôth with omega means "fixed measure," while with omicron it means "He who puts evils to flight" (2.35.3). All this is extremely unlikely.

Finally, Irenaeus' account of Hebrew (really Aramaic or Syriac) words used in Marcosian rites is eccentric. He quotes some of their formulas in "Hebrew" but does not notice that his "translations" do not fit them. His first "Hebrew" text, according to Graffin, should read "in the name of Sophia, Father and Light, called Spirit of holiness, for the redemption of the angelic nature" (1.21.3).[3] Though some terms are the same, Irenaeus obviously mistranslates: "I invoke what is above every power of the Father and is called Light and Spirit and Life," adding "for you have reigned in a body." Another Greek fragment refers to "Jesus the Nazarene [see below] in the zones of the light of Christ, who lives through the Holy Spirit for the angelic redemption;" here Holy Spirit and angelic redemption recur from the "Hebrew." What Irenaeus says is the translation of the second "Hebrew" fragment is not such, and the real translation is found in the "response of the initiate." The original reads thus: "I am anointed and redeemed from myself and from all judgment in the name of Iao; redeem me, Jesus the Nazarene." The response is translated as follows: "I am confirmed and redeemed and I redeem myself from this age and everything with it, in the name of Iao, who redeemed himself for redemption in the living Christ." To sum up: the first "Hebrew" text is for an initiator, as the Greek translations indicate, while the second is for the person initiated. Confusion may have arisen because alternative formulas were listed. In any event, Irenaeus could not make sense of the "Hebrew" words. Even his explanation of "Mammon" is wrong.[4] Indeed, the Gnostics themselves probably criticized his mistranslations of their liturgical texts, as Hippolytus seems to indicate.[5]

His errors fit well with his almost complete ignorance of contemporary Judaism. He knows that Jews do exorcisms in the name of the one God (2.6.2), though they still persecute the church (4.21.3) and have lost eternal life by killing the Lord (4.28.3). He may even have discussed some points with them, for he believes that to them the law is like a myth because they do not have a Christian interpretation of it (4.26.1). The law really speaks symbolically when it calls unclean the animals that chew the cud (and therefore have good works) but do not have a cloven hoof (Lev.11:4). These animals symbolize the Jews themselves, who have the oracles of God in their mouth but are not founded on the Father and the Son and therefore easily slip, since they are less stable than the cloven-hoofed (5.8.3). Certainly Irenaeus was farther from Judaism than Justin, for example, had been.

GREEK VERSIONS

Irenaeus believes that the Old Testament was miraculously preserved in Hebrew and miraculously translated into Greek. Second Esdras told him that long after the books had been burned in 587 BC, God inspired Esdras to rewrite them all.[6] As for the Greek version, Irenaeus begins his account with a matter-of-fact historical setting and proceeds to miracle. Ptolemy son of Lagos wanted the best books for his library at Alexandria, and when he asked Jerusalemites for their scriptures in Greek they sent seventy linguists to him. To find out if they were concealing the truth hidden in the scriptures, he had them produce seventy independent translations. Every item turned out to be the same, thus proving the divine inspiration of the Greek version. Irenaeus rejected the translation of Isaiah 7:14 made by Theodotion and Aquila, calling both of them proselytes to Judaism,[7] and relied on a simple form of the Hellenistic Jewish tradition that necessarily devalued the Hebrew text.[8] His story of the translation is nonsensical, even though the author of the *Exhortation* ascribed to Justin claims to have visited the translators' cells. A real translator like Origen neglected the legend. Another, Jerome, ridiculed it.[9] Augustine, below Jerome's level, found it edifying as he defended the Septuagint against Jerome's recent translation from Hebrew.[10]

Like other patristic authors, Irenaeus fully accepted the authority of the Septuagint. The idea that the canon should be confined to Hebrew books never occurred to him.[11] He therefore used 1-2 Esdras,[12] as well as 1 Enoch,[13] Baruch (ascribed to Jeremiah)[14] and the Greek additions to Daniel.[15]

THE NEW TESTAMENT

The four Gospels

On the gospels Irenaeus seems to combine what Papias said about Matthew and Mark[16] with further Ephesian tradition about John. Matthew set forth a gospel among the Hebrews, written in their language, at the time when Peter and Paul were preaching the gospel at Rome and founding the church there. (In other words, the tradition of the Roman church is just as ancient as this earliest Gospel.) After the deaths of these apostles, Mark, disciple and interpreter of Peter, transmitted his oral preaching in writing. Papias' comments on Luke and John, if any, have not survived. Irenaeus claimed that Paul's companion Luke set forth Paul's Gospel in a book, and John, the Lord's disciple who reclined in his bosom, produced the Gospel while living at Ephesus in Asia (3.1.1). Irenaeus' hero Polycarp told more about John, who in his old age encountered the heretic Cerinthus at the baths in Ephesus and immediately left, saying, "Let us escape in case the bath falls in, because Cerinthus, enemy of the truth, is inside." (This tells us nothing about what either John or Cerinthus taught.) In Irenaeus' judgment the Ephesian church, founded by Paul and preserved by John, is a reliable witness to the tradition of the apostles (3.3.4) though his exegesis of John 8:57 ("you are not yet 50 years old") leaves much to be desired. He is convinced that Luke cannot have meant to say that Jesus was baptized in his thirtieth year, because unless he reached "the most necessary and honorable period of his life" he could not have had disciples. John certifies that he was over 40 but under 50. "All the presbyters of Asia who were with John the Lord's disciple testify that John delivered the same tradition to them, for he remained with them until the reign of Trajan" (2.22.4–5). Irenaeus' doctrine of recapitulation assured him that in order to save men of all ages Jesus had to "recapitulate" the life of humanity and pass in five stages from infant to child to adolescent to manhood and finally advanced age. His analysis of ages is like what we find in Hippocrates, for whom each of the ages mentioned by Irenaeus occupies some multiple of seven years. One is a child from 1 to the loss of teeth at 7, a boy to puberty at 14, a lad till the trace of a beard comes at 21, a young man until the whole body is grown at 28, then a man from 29 to 49; an elderly man lasts only until 56, and after that becomes an old man.[17] Jesus could not have become really mature before reaching 49. Since Irenaeus explicitly dated the birth of Jesus around the forty-first year of Augustus, he cannot have had in mind the real beginning of that emperor's reign in January 27 BC, but must have backdated it to the death of Julius Caesar in 44. If then Jesus was born in about 3 BC he would have reached 49 during the reign of Claudius (41–54), and that is where Irenaeus set his death in his later *Demonstration*.[18]

Irenaeus uses further unconvincing analogies to show that there must be exactly four Gospels as compared with the Gnostics' many books. He begins with natural history (four regions and four principal winds in the world), then turns to theology. For equilibrium the church has to rest on four columns. According to Psalm 79:2, the Logos is seated on the Cherubim, which have four faces and thus point to the four evangelists. Only heretics employ individual Gospels; thus Ebionites used Matthew, Marcion used Luke, Docetists used Mark, and Valentinians used John. Such individual emphases are wrong; instead, all must be synthesized.[19]

Irenaeus had a rather full collection of the letters of Paul, not quite identical with the one used by Marcion but now including the Pastoral Epistles to Timothy and Titus. The title of his own work echoed 1 Timothy 6:20, "knowledge falsely so called," and his first quotation was from 1 Timothy 1:4.[20] He also explicitly named the epistles to Timothy when he showed that Paul mentioned Linus, bishop of Rome.[21] Paul's advice to Titus, moreover, gave him basic counsel against heretics. "After a first and a second warning, avoid the heretic, knowing that such a man is perverted and when he sins is self-condemned" (Tit.3:10–11).[22] He apparently refers to Galatians 5:21 as scripture when he says that "the scriptures affirm that 'those who perform [forbidden acts] will not inherit the kingdom of God.'"[23] On the other hand he rejected the Pauline authorship of Hebrews, as did Marcion.[24] Among the Catholic Epistles he made use of 1 Peter as from Peter, perhaps also of 2 Peter 3:8,[25] and of 1–2 John as one letter by John.[26] The Apocalypse written down by John, he says, was seen "not long ago but nearly in our own times, at the end of the reign of Domitian." The book contains the enigmatic number of the Beast (Revelation 13:18), mistakenly given as 616 in some manuscripts, though the correct reading, 666, appears in the oldest manuscripts and is attested by "those who saw John face to face."[27] There seem to be no traces of James or Jude. The anti-heretical Jude would have been useful had he known it.[28]

Scholars sometimes claim that Irenaeus' stand on the New Testament books was decisive for Christian theology. This seems unlikely in view of his devotion to older teaching, as well as the very similar collection in use by his older contemporary Theophilus of Antioch.[29]

AFTER THE NEW TESTAMENT

In discussing apostolic tradition Irenaeus speaks of the successors of Peter and Paul at Rome, as well as those "to this day" who succeeded Polycarp, appointed bishop of Smyrna by apostles in Asia, and those in "the church of Ephesus, founded by Paul, with John continuing with them until the times of Trajan."[30] He accepts traditions from the apostles but rejects the Gnostics' "infinite multitude of apocryphal and bastard scriptures," along with their story about the boy Jesus and the mystical meaning of the letters A and B.[31] He either rejects or does not know the Gnostic claim to possess traditions from the apostles.

He cannot have known that some of the Marcosian formulas are close to the *First Apocalypse of James* found at Nag Hammadi,[32] or that a saying he ascribes to Basilides appears in a "gospel" from the same collection).[33] For him it was enough to see that they were heretical. He mentions various apocryphal books used by the Gnostics, only to reject them absolutely.[34]

Papias from Hierapolis in Phrygian Asia

Christians circulated information about the origins of their literature so that they could exclude alien books, such as "apocryphal" gospels, epistles, acts, and apocalypses, from their collections. Toward the end of the first century (or a little later) the Asian Papias of Hierapolis supplied "tradition" on this point, discussing his memories and even going back to Mark's memories of what Peter taught. Papias considered himself a literary historian, not a critic. He began his book with a positive statement about the tradition from the presbyters and added criticism of rival traditions.

> For I did not, like the many, delight in those who say much but in those who teach the truth [as contrasted with the content of the authentic tradition] nor in those who mention outside commandments, but in those who mention the [inside] commandments given by the Lord to faith, and derived from the truth itself.

He himself had collected oral tradition at Hierapolis.

> If anyone ever came who had followed the presbyters, I asked about the words of the presbyters – what Andrew or Peter or Philip or Thomas or James or John or Matthew, or any other of the Lord's disciples, said, or what Aristion and the presbyter John, the Lord's disciples, were saying.

"Presbyters" appear to be the equivalent of "Lord's disciples," as may be implied by 2–3 John, while the reference to Andrew, Peter, and Philip suggests that Papias was acquainted with John 1:44–45, where all three appear.[35]

His oral tradition was better than books. "I did not suppose what came from books would help me as much as what was from a living and enduring voice."[36] In spite of his rhetorically balanced phrases, however, Papias tells us next to nothing about his sources and their value. To judge from his eschatological traditions, one might suppose he uncritically recorded tradition, whatever it might be, or perhaps he critically recorded tradition in support of his millenarian views.

How reliable were Papias' presbyters? They related an over-vivid legend about the death of Judas, not to mention some unlikely words

CHRISTIAN BOOKS AND TRADITIONS

of Jesus about the fantastic productivity of vines and plants in the age to come. Eusebius refers to these as "strange parables and teachings of the Savior and some other more mythical accounts." Papias explicitly claimed he had received these words from presbyters who had seen "John the Lord's disciple."[37] For Irenaeus and Papias, as well as this John (the John of Revelation?), Jesus was a teacher of Jewish apocalyptic eschatology, much closer to the Apocalypse than to the Fourth Gospel, and he insisted that Jesus predicted enormously productive harvests. A vine was going to produce 2,500,000,000,000,000,000,000 (2.5 sextillion) *metretatai* of wine (100 sextillion litres). When one of the saints picks a bunch, another bunch will cry to him, "I am better, pick me, and bless the Lord through me!" Similarly the grain of wheat will produce 10,000 sheaves, each sheaf with 10,000 grains, and each grain with five choinixes (at about a litre apiece) of good flour,[38] and similarly in proportion for other fruits, seeds, and grasses. All the animals would have a vegetarian diet and live in peace and harmony with one another, subject to humanity. The traitor Judas remained incredulous and asked, "How can God create such fruits?" but the Lord answered, "They who live then will see it" (5.33.3–4). Papias obviously believed that these events would take place in the near future. Such credulous acceptance of tradition led Eusebius to call him "feeble in intelligence," and to quote only Papias' comments on the evangelists.[39] In fact, the measures of production come from the late first-century Jewish *Apocalypse of Baruch* (29.5), not from Jesus, and they have nothing to do with John the Lord's disciple.[40]

Polycarp of Smyrna in Ionian Asia

Irenaeus' strongest witness to tradition was Polycarp, disciple of apostles, who lived with many who had seen our Lord and was appointed bishop of the church in Smyrna by apostles. As we have seen, Irenaeus regarded Polycarp as the most important living link between Christ and himself.

Polycarp's letter to the Philippians presents the character of his faith and his preaching of the truth. It refers to the incomparable wisdom, example, and teaching of "the blessed Paul," and frequently echoes his letters, especially the Pastoral Epistles, though it does not refer to John.[41] Polycarp stood so close to the Pastoral Epistles ascribed to Paul that Von Campenhausen ascribed them to Polycarp himself.[42] His letter to the Philippians is essentially pastoral, not theological, and it comes not from a monarchical bishop but from

"Polycarp and the presbyters with him." Indeed, the term "bishop" does not appear in it, even though Bishop Ignatius called him "bishop of the church of the Smyrnaeans."

Though Polycarp does not refer to John, he may well know 1 John (4:2–3; 3:8).

> Everyone who does not confess that Jesus Christ came in flesh is an Antichrist, and whoever does not confess the testimony to the cross is of the devil, and whoever twists the oracles of the Lord to his own lusts and says there is neither resurrection nor judgment is Satan's firstborn.

Such an echo of the Epistle suggests that he knew the Gospel as well, even though there is no trace of it in his letter. The expression "oracles of the Lord" recalls Papias' *Dominical Oracles*, while "Satan's firstborn" is abuse Polycarp applied to Marcion in person.[43]

The confusion about John as apostle, disciple, or presbyter arises from the existence of 2(–3) John, handed down with 1 John and therefore with other Johannine literature, addressed by "the presbyter" to his readers. Irenaeus himself cites 1 John and then, referring back to the same epistle, quotes from 2 John (1.16.3; 3.16.5,8). But though both Papias and Polycarp traced their traditions back to a certain John it is not clear how he was related to the extant Johannine literature, even though in Irenaeus' view Gospel, Epistle (1–2), and Apocalypse came from him.

Other Presbyters (of Asia?) or Pothinus(?)

In his fourth book against heresies (4.27.1–32.1) Irenaeus set forth the apostolic teaching of a presbyter whom he had seen.[44] This person showed that the same God made both covenants in spite of the moral problems raised by Old Testament personages such as David and Solomon and by Christ's work when he descended into Hades; by the frequent transgressions of the Hebrew people and Paul's teaching about them; by the hardening of Pharaoh's heart and the despoiling of the Egyptians, not to mention Lot, whose wife became a pillar of salt. He insists that

> we must not reproach the patriarchs and prophets for the faults for which the scriptures themselves blame them . . . but must rather give thanks to God because their sins were remitted at the coming of our Lord; for they themselves give thanks and rejoice

for our salvation.[45] As for the acts that the scriptures do not blame but are content to report, we must not become accusers of them, for we are not more zealous than God nor can we be above our Master.

(The topic leads into an unusual digression on economics:

> The houses we inhabit, the clothing we wear, the utensils we use, and whatever serves our daily life come from what as pagans we acquired by avarice or from pagan parents or relations or friends who got it by injustice – not to mention what we acquire now living in faith.

Irenaeus, or his teacher, also noted that "thanks to the Romans, the world is at peace, so that we may use the roads without fear and sail wherever we will.")

Because of such ambiguities we must seek for the figurative meaning of the text. In other words, a text describing morally questionable acts encourages us to look for a non-literal meaning, "for no act described in the scriptures without criticism lacks significance" (4.31.1). Christians sharing this faith must "attentively read the scriptures," as the apologists Tatian and Theophilus said they did before conversion, not by themselves but, as Irenaeus urges, "with the presbyters in the church, with whom is the apostolic teaching" (4.32.1). Scripture-reading in isolation is ineffective because the reader may not raise or solve the problems correctly.

Irenaeus even possessed a Christian poem directed at the Valentinian magician Marcus, against whom "the divinely inspired Elder and herald of truth cried out" (1.15.6).

From Rome: Clement, Hermas, and Justin

At Rome Irenaeus found two other early Christian writings treated as authoritative. He probably does not refer to them as "scripture" when he calls each *graphé*. In each instance the word may simply mean "writing" (3.3.3; 4.20.2).[46] One was the letter of Clement to the Corinthians. In a list of early bishops of Rome Irenaeus explained that Clement was an eyewitness of the apostles (certainly some Clement is mentioned in Philippians 4:3), whose teaching still resounded in his ears, while their tradition was before his eyes (1 Clement 5:3: "Let us set before our eyes the good apostles"). Clement wrote from Rome to Corinth to put down the dissension among Christians there and, says Irenaeus, recalled them to the apostolic tradition about

> one God Almighty, Creator of heaven and earth, who fashioned the human race, brought about the deluge, called Abraham, brought the people out of the land of Egypt, spoke with Moses, gave the law, sent the prophets, and prepared fire for the devil and his angels (3.3.3).

This description owes little to Clement's letter, much to Irenaeus' own rule of faith. His teacher Polycarp had paid more attention to the text of 1 Clement, frequently echoing it in his own letter.

Early in the second century an ex-slave at Rome named Hermas produced a collection of revelations entitled *Shepherd* and consisting of *Visions, Mandates,* and *Similitudes* or *Parables*. It is not clear just when he wrote his three books. The so-called Muratorian fragment says that his brother Pius was bishop of Rome, but the fragment is very late and not very reliable. A vision telling Hermas to read his book of visions with "the presbyters in charge of the church"[47] must be early, when no monarchical bishop held office. The same vision refers to Clement, probably the author of the epistle, as secretary for the external affairs of the Roman church, and thus points toward the maintenance of tradition at Rome.

What Irenaeus valued in Hermas was his faith in one God the Creator. This is what Hermas wrote: "First of all, believe that God is one, who created and completed everything, contains everything, and alone is contained by nothing" (4.20.2).[48] The formula thus begins with biblical faith but moves toward semi-philosophical theology.

Irenaeus also knew works by Justin, a recent and reliable teacher and martyr at Rome, and used not only his *Apology* but also his early work *Against all Heresies*, now lost, for pre-Valentinian sects. This was a text, as Justin indicates in the *Apology*, in which he attacked at least the heretics Simon and Menander, both like himself originally from Samaritan towns or villages, and Marcion, still at work in Rome.[49] Irenaeus took over and developed his idea that heresy began with Simon and Menander, and also referred to a whole treatise by Justin against Marcion. "Justin well said, 'I should not have believed the Lord himself had he proclaimed a God other than the Creator'" (4.6.2). Presumably the quotation ends here, as Eusebius suggests,[50] and Irenaeus' reference to recapitulation is his own, as is the reference to eternal fire in the next quotation (5.26.2). This deals with Satan.

Justin well said that before the Lord's advent Satan never
ventured to blaspheme God, because he still did not know about
his own condemnation, concealed in parables and allegories, but
after the Lord's advent he learned clearly from the words of
Christ and the apostles that eternal fire has been prepared for
him [Matt.25:41].

The reference to eternal fire for Satan is probably Irenaeus' own
contribution, as it is in his "summary" of 1 Clement.

Irenaeus may well have learned from Justin that Revelation was
written by "John, one of the apostles of Christ." Papias, another
possible witness, is not said to have discussed authorship.[51]

Justin's authority was weakened by the heresy into which his pupil
Tatian fell, but Irenaeus insists that he was not responsible for any of
Tatian's errors (1.28.1).

From Antioch: Ignatius and Theophilus

What Irenaeus knows about Ignatius is much less significant.
Ignatius was a bishop from Antioch whose vivid letters usually insist
on episcopal authority and anticipate his own death in the arena at
Rome, consumed by wild animals.[52] Since he supposed that the
Roman church was influential enough to prevent his death, he urged
the Romans not to intervene. From his letter to Rome, though
without naming him, Irenaeus cited the vivid language used by "one
of our people, condemned to the beasts for his testimony to God."
The passage speaks of his prospective sacrifice as "Christ's wheat,
ground by the teeth of wild beasts to become the pure bread of God"
(5.28.4). Irenaeus makes no use of Ignatius' doctrine of the episcopate.

A later bishop of Antioch, Theophilus (around 180), used rhetorical analysis of Logos as human thought within, speech as expressed
outside, to analyze the divine Logos (*To Autolycus* 2.105 22).
Irenaeus rejected the use of such terms about God, and also corrected
Theophilus' language about God's two "hands," his Word and his
Wisdom.[53] (It seems unlikely that Irenaeus knew Philo of Alexandria,
uncertain that Theophilus did so.[54])

5

GREEK EDUCATION
AGAINST GNOSTICISM

WHAT GREEK EDUCATION INVOLVES

When discussing Gnostic claims to "knowledge," Irenaeus treats of
the arts and sciences to be found in the curriculum of a Graeco-Roman
school that would be merely preparatory to rhetoric. Some fields
involve theory, such as music, arithmetic, geometry, and astronomy,[1]
while others are practical: medicine, pharmacy; painting, portrait
sculpture (working in bronze and marble); agriculture (horses, flocks);
nautical, gymnastic, hunting; war, and kingship (2.32.2). Jerome
provides a similar list: grammar, rhetoric, philosophy, geometry,
dialectic, music, astronomy, astrology, medicine, all based on doctrine,
method, and experience. Beyond these are manual skills: farming,
stone-cutting, carpentry, metallurgy, forestry, woolworking and
fulling, etc.[2] Irenaeus does not mention Jerome's first three (grammar,
rhetoric, philosophy), but he obviously has them in mind. Indeed, his
criticism of the Gnostics resembles the conventional Sceptical attack
on grammarians in Sextus Empiricus, who alleges that

> the art of grammar cannot deal with all the forms of speech in the
> poets. [To do so] is absolutely impossible, since on the poets
> there is discourse about the gods and about virtue and the soul,
> concerning which the grammarians have no expert knowledge.[3]

The grammarians of Sextus were implicitly making the same claim to
expert knowledge as were the Gnostics of Irenaeus.

Origins of Valentinian theories in poetry

A poet of the Old Comedy, Aristophanes,[4] spoke with much
more probability and elegance about the genesis of everything in

41

a theogony. According to him, from Night and Silence was emitted Chaos, then from Chaos and Night, Eros; from Eros came forth Light, then all the rest of the first generation of gods. After this the poet introduced the second generation of gods and the making of the world; then he tells of the shaping of mankind by the second gods. From this, the Valentinians shaped their myth like a natural history, simply changing the names of the gods and showing the same beginning and emission of everything. For Night and Silence they name Abyss and Silence; for Chaos, Mind; for Eros, by which according to the comic poet all the rest were set in order, they have introduced the Logos. In place of the first and greatest of the gods they imagined the Aeons, in place of the second gods they tell of the activities of their Mother outside the Pleroma, calling her "Second Ogdoad," to whom they ascribe the making of the world and the fashioning of mankind just as the poet did, and claiming that they alone know ineffable and unknown mysteries. In reality they transfer to their own system what is said in theaters everywhere by actors with splendid voices, or rather they use the same plots and simply change the names (*Heresies* 2.14.1).

Menander, favorite of the New Comedy, serves as another stick to beat Valentinians. "They seem to me to have applied to this Aeon the passion of the personage [Thrasonides] in the comic poet Menander who loves but is hated" (2.18.5). The reference is to the hero in the play *Misumenos*, of which extensive papyrus fragments have turned up.[5] Stoics drew moral lessons from Menander's treatment of the conflict between love and hate. Zeno in his *Republic* and Chrysippus in his treatise *On Love* used the example of Thrasonides, who "had his mistress in his power but kept away from her because she hated him." This showed that "love is based on friendship and is not sent by the gods." Epictetus criticizes Thrasonides for his emotions: he is the slave of desire, sends gifts to the woman he hates, and is elated when only moderately successful.[6] Thus Irenaeus need not have seen the *Misumenos* when repeating what moralists said about it.

Irenaeus does not care for tragedy and finds "much tragedy and fantasy" in the Valentinian myths. Indeed, the Gnostic story is more extreme than the "Iou, iou" and "Pheu, pheu" and every other exclamation and expression of grief found in tragedy.[7] The passion of Sophia apart from her consort is the basis of "the whole composition of their 'tragedy.'" He compares the Gnostics to people who blind themselves, and later makes the allusion explicit by referring to "the Oedipus of tragedy."[8] This does not show that he was close to the tragedies themselves.

... and Philosophy

> Not only do they put forward as their own what is found with the comic poets, but they collect what has been said by all the people who do not know God and are called philosophers; they have woven together a kind of cento out of many wretched pieces and prepared a false surface with subtle speech. The doctrine they present is new because it has been elaborated recently with a new art, but it is really old and worthless, since it was stitched together from old doctrines smelling of ignorance and lack of religion.

To prove his point Irenaeus reinterprets a textbook on Presocratic philosophers' opinions about basic principles (2.14.2): Thales – water (the Valentinian Abyss), Homer – Oceanus and Tethys (Abyss and Silence), Anaximander – the Infinite (Abyss and Aeons), Anaxagoras – seeds fallen on the earth from the sky (seeds of the Mother). It was more difficult to show the influence of Democritus, Epicurus, Plato and the Stoics on the Gnostics, but Irenaeus tried hard (2.14.3–4).

But they do not know what they are talking about

In regard to "nature," he read in the same textbook of philosophical opinions ("doxography") that the philosophers usually disagreed with one another; he could therefore conclude that they knew nothing about the subjects discussed. He criticized them for their physics and modestly claimed that "many things will escape our knowledge."[9] While Job 38 had made the point much more vividly, Irenaeus used the school text to discuss four geographical topics: why the Nile rises, where migratory birds go in winter, why the tides rise and fall, and what lies beyond the ocean. Then he turned to weather phenomena: the causes of rain, lightning, thunder, the blowing of winds, the collections of clouds and fog and winds, snow and hail, etc., and the formations of clouds and fog. He ended with astronomy and metallurgy: causes of the phases of the moon and the differences in waters, metals, stones, etc. Only God knows the answers. From a different point of view Seneca lists phenomena with

43

unknown causes and suggests that they be passed over as "neither possible nor useful to know."[10] The argument is not philosophical, for Irenaeus also points out that his Gnostic opponents do not know how many hairs they have on their head or how many sparrows they will catch in a day.[11]

An anonymous philosopher knew the truth

More positively, a text from the Presocratic philosopher Xenophanes provided a cornerstone of Irenaeus' anti-Gnostic theological system. He cites it five times, without naming Xenophanes. Sextus Empiricus quoted the original, also anonymously: "All of him [God] sees, all thinks, and all hears."[12] Diogenes Laertius explained that "the substance of God is spherical, in no way resembling man. He is all seeing and all hearing (though not breathing); he is all Mind and Thought and eternal."[13] Even Pliny the Elder, relying on a philosophical mediator, cited the text (anonymously) as "all Mind, all Sight, all Hearing, all Soul, all Spirit, all himself."[14] Irenaeus too uses nouns, and naturally leaves out the spherical. God "is all Mind, all Spirit, all Mentality, all Thought, all Word, all Hearing, all Eye, all Light, and entirely the source of every good thing – as religious and pious men rightly say of God."[15] He thus appeals to a supposed consensus including Christians and devout pagans like Plato. After Irenaeus this theological opinion enjoyed considerable success. Within a few years Clement of Alexandria states that "the Son of God is all Mind, all Paternal Light, all Eye," and then adds "seeing all, hearing all, knowing all." Later he says that God is "all hearing, all eye."[16] Other Greeks who cite the formula from Irenaeus include Cyril of Jerusalem and Theodoret. The Latin writer Novatian of Rome and three later authors from Gaul reflect continuing use of Irenaeus.[17]

In Irenaeus' view the Creator predisposed us to be "religious." He regarded Plato as more religious than Marcion, for he held that God is both just and good.[18] Though Gnostics call themselves religious, it is truly religious to study what can be known, and a simple presbyter is better than a blasphemous sophist or heretic. The Presocratic Anaxagoras, the "atheist," was irreligious, and so are Gnostic heretics.

Against Gnostic emanation doctrines, he repeats that "God is all Thought, all Will, all Mind, all Light, all Eye, all Hearing, the source of all good things." He is contrasting the true doctrine of God with that of Ptolemaeus, who differentiates the aeonic "dispositions" of Thought and Will, which unite and produce other aeons. Such confusion also appears in the all too human Zeus of Homer, whose cares keep him from sleep as he wants to honor Achilles and make a multitude of Greeks perish (*Iliad* 2.1–4, really Trojans). The true God is quite different from these.[19]

Again, Irenaeus claims that Gnostics create the emanations of Aeons "in accordance with human psychology" (*ab hominum adfectione*), as does anyone who compares the generation of the Logos with the human expression of a word. Presumably he has Theophilus, bishop of Antioch, in mind as well as the Gnostics. The comparison cannot be allowed, for God is all Mind, all Word, all Vision, all Hearing.[20] Once more against the emanations but in more detail, he says that God is "all Mind, all Word, all operative Spirit, all Light, always identical with and like himself (as it is useful for us to think of God and as we learn from the scriptures)."[21] What he earlier ascribed to "religious men" he now believes he finds in the Bible, presumably because God is Word, Spirit, and Light in the Johannine literature.[22]

Finally he uses the text to contrast the perfect Creator-god with imperfect created humanity and its progress and growth (Luke 2:40,52) toward God. "God is perfect, equal to himself and uniform; he is all Light, all Mind, all substance (*hypostasis*), the source of all good things."[23] It is significant, as J. H. Lesher notes after Werner Jaeger, that Xenophanes does not offer any argument to support this statement or his other theological comments. After all, another fragment points out that "men *cannot* have knowledge of divine attributes and activities."[24] Therefore when Irenaeus ascribes his doctrine both to religious men and to the scriptures he is appealing to "consensus," not logic.

6

RHETORIC IN THEOLOGY

Does the word "biblical" explain the work of Irenaeus as he wrote against the manifestly non-biblical Gnostics? Certainly he thought the Bible was his primary source. Yet the Bible does not have a single theology, and one must work hard in order to find one or impose one on it. Irenaeus did not use the Bible alone but relied on "tradition," which included the efforts of apostles and their disciples, as well as disparate Asian presbyters like Papias and Polycarp, and also the Romans Clement and Justin Martyr. He says nothing about what the 90-year-old bishop of Lyons taught, though the acts of the martyrs show that some local Christians were concerned with abstinence from meat and other foods, a topic on which Irenaeus simply quotes the "western" text of Acts 15:20,29 against meats offered to idols, fornication, and blood.[1] Perhaps they were following their bishop's guidance. On the other side Irenaeus certainly excluded Gnostic writings, as well as what we call "the apocryphal New Testament," and such authors, apparently Alexandrian, as Barnabas. We need not set Irenaeus against his predecessors at Lyons. After all, Lawlor and Oulton suggest that Pothinus "was probably an emigrant from Asia" and (possibly) "saw St. John in his childhood, and knew Polycarp in later life."[2] Irenaeus did not invent his tradition, but he certainly employed a method of correlation in order to pull together the ideas of the authorities he accepted. Perhaps he could have found such a method in philosophy, but he did not consider it the most useful tool for second-century theology. The method he used was based on the rhetorical schools, I suspect, as in fourth-century Antioch.[3]

There Irenaeus had learned to deal with Greek literature, tackling questions still found in the numerous *Progymnasmata* by teachers like Theon and Hermogenes. He treated problems of authorship like the one he discusses on the book of Acts, and chronological problems such as the age of Jesus. In regard to both topics he rates his synthetic method more highly than mere historical details, as we shall see.

Irenaeus shows that he knew rhetorical modes of expression when in the preface to his treatise he insists on his lack of skill in the technique. "We are not accustomed to writing nor have we studied the art of rhetoric," he says.

> You will not expect from us, who live with the Celts and most of the time use the language of barbarians, either the art of rhetoric which we did not learn, or the skill of a writer which we have not exercised, or elegance of language or persuasion which we do not know.[4]

Schoedel adduces parallels from Plato's praise of unadorned truth "not cosmetized with words and phrases," Lysias's contrast of "artifice and alacrity" with the speaker's inexperience; Isaeus's contrast of "able speakers and clever plotters" with his inexperienced self; and especially the contemporary rhetor Hermogenes, advising the speaker to say he is inexperienced.[5] Indeed, Irenaeus' older contemporary Theophilus began his address *To Autolycus* by attacking "fluent speech and euphonious diction."

In spite (or because) of such criticisms, Irenaeus took terms from his rhetorical studies for describing key theological ideas. Indeed, the very title of his work bears rhetorical overtones: "Detection and Refutation of the Knowledge Falsely So Called." The rhetorical prefaces placed before each book show clearly that "detection" meant finding out the Gnostic secret teaching. Book I was devoted to detection, Books II–V to refutation.[6] As the Archbishop of Quebec once pointed out to me, the Marcionite Apelles, who wrote *Syllogisms*, was zealous for the "refutation and detection" of the Old Testament.[7] The terms were there to be used by anyone concerned with literary matters.

Irenaeus took three more words with primary literary meanings from "secular" writers, and like other Christians proceeded into theology with them. These terms were *hypothesis, oikonomia,* and *anakephalaiôsis,* all used in the old grammatical scholia on the *Odyssey.*[8]

HYPOTHESIS

The first is *hypothesis,* the presentation (sometimes in a summary) of a plot or structure intended by an author such as Homer.[9] The historian Polybius refers to his proposed subject as "our hypothesis." In his

Progymnasmata the rhetorical analyst Theon speaks of the "hypotheses" of political speeches. This is the primary meaning for the word as discussed by Sextus Empiricus. He tells us that

> it refers to the "argument" or "plot" of a drama, as we say that there is a tragic or a comic "hypothesis," and certain "hypotheses" of Dicaearchus of the stories of Euripides and Sophocles, meaning by "hypothesis" just the argument of the drama.

So it is that "hypotheses" for plays by Sophocles and Euripides turn up in Oxyrhynchus papyri of the second and third centuries. The Christian Theophilus speaks of the first creation story as "the first presentation (*hypothesis*) in the narrative of the origin of the world."[10]

The basic meaning of *hypothesis* for Irenaeus is clear from his polemical usage.

> After collecting scattered texts and names they [the Gnostics] transfer them . . . out of their natural meaning to a meaning contrary to nature, acting like those who propose random hypotheses for themselves and try to treat them from the Homeric verses, so that the untutored may suppose that Homer composed verses on this completely novel subject and that many readers may be led astray, through the well ordered sequence of the verses, to ask if Homer wrote them. Here is how, with verses from Homer, one could describe Heracles as sent by Eurystheus to the dog in Hades. Nothing keeps us from using such an example, since it involves the same argument in both cases.

Suffice it to say that Irenaeus then cites five unrelated verses from the *Odyssey* and five from the *Iliad* to prove his point. "What simpleton," he asks,

> would be taken in by these verses to suppose that Homer composed them in this way? One who knows his Homer will recognize the verses but not the subject matter. He knows that one of the verses deals with Odysseus, another with Heracles, another with Priam, another with Menelaos and Agamemnon. If anyone takes these verses and restores them to their original setting, he will make the system disappear.

Similarly the Christian "rule of truth," the real "hypothesis" of scripture, will demolish the exegesis of the Gnostics. "Setting each word in its context and adjusting it to the body of truth, he will strip it of their fiction and show their inconsistency."[11] *Hypothesis* thus means the same thing in the Bible as in Homer, and Irenaeus uses it to attack Valentinian exegesis of the Bible.[12]

Irenaeus' rule of faith or truth is the same as the *hypothesis* of the scriptures. It starts with belief in one God, maker of heaven and earth and everything in them. After Hermas he insists that Christians must "believe that there is one God, who created and completed all things and made everything exist out of the non-existent, he who contains all and alone is contained by none."[13] With the apologists Irenaeus insists upon God's absolute supremacy in creation. The *hypothesis* more fully includes "one God almighty, Creator of heaven and earth, the fashioner of man, who brought about the deluge and called Abraham and brought the people out of the land of Egypt, who spoke with Moses, who gave the law and sent the prophets, who prepared fire for the devil and his angels" (Matt.25:41). We have seen Irenaeus ascribing this to Clement when writing to the Corinthians to restore their faith and proclaim the tradition he had recently received from the apostles.[14] Since Clement did not so write, his name reveals the synthesizing strength of Irenaeus' hypothesis.[15]

OIKONOMIA

Oikonomia is the "arrangement" of a poem or the purpose and direction of the plot. Diodorus Siculus speaks of the importance of good arrangement both in business matters and in writing history, while Dionysius of Halicarnassus insists on the arrangement of ideas as against random presentation. He says that Xenophon deserves praise both for his subjects and for their arrangement. Lucian refers to arranging subject matter.[16]

Irenaeus says that the saving plans (*oikonomiai*) proclaimed through the prophets included

> the coming and the birth from the Virgin and the suffering and the resurrection from the dead and the ascension into the heavens of the beloved Christ Jesus our Lord in the flesh; and his coming from the heavens in the glory of the Father to "recapitulate all things" (Eph.1:10) and raise up all flesh of all humanity ... so that he may make a just judgment among all men, sending into everlasting fire the spiritual powers of evil and the angels who transgressed and fell into rebellion and the impious ...

among men, but bestowing life and immortality upon the just and securing everlasting glory for them.[17]

This is another synthesis based on the tradition but bearing the marks of Irenaeus' special emphases. We cannot tell whether he imposed two favorite terms on this summary or derived them from it. The story of the *oikonomiai* of Jesus comes from the Gospel of Luke, which Irenaeus uses literary criticism to defend. The "we-passages" in Acts, confirmed by 2 Timothy 4:11, show that its author was inseparable from Paul, while Colossians 4:14 adds that he was Paul's "beloved" friend.[18] Once more, rhetorical proof joins hands with theology.

ANAKEPHALAIÔSIS

The third important term was *anakephalaiôsis*, the summary or recapitulation of a narrative. We have just seen it related to the *oikonomiai* about Jesus. For Dionysius of Halicarnassus such an *anakepalaiôsis* is a "concluding summary," while in a rhetorical preface to his last book Theophilus says, "I will not shrink from summing up for you ... the antiquity of our writings." For Clement of Alexandria (who knew Irenaeus' work) Christ's crown of thorns "recapitulates" Moses' vision of the Logos in the burning (thorn) bush.[19] Irenaeus quotes Justin at one point (Eusebius gives the Greek) but it is unlikely that the quotation ran on to include recapitulation, Irenaeus' own word.[20] His context is strictly literary when he asserts that the evangelist John "sums up" the account in his prologue (John 1:1–13) by saying that the Word became flesh (1:14).[21]

More often Irenaeus converts grammar into theology, as he does in an argument in which he does not use the term "recapitulate" but obviously has it in view.[22] He claims that as a teacher Jesus must have had the age of a teacher. He "did not abolish in his person the law of human growth, but sanctified every age by the resemblance we have with him." Since he came to save through himself all who are reborn, he passed through every age, and among infants was an infant sanctifying others; among children a child, sanctifying others and also becoming for them a model of piety and justice and submission (Luke 2:41–52); among young men a young man, becoming a model to young men and sanctifying them for the Lord. Thus also he was an elder among elders, in order to be a perfect teacher in all, sanctifying the elders and becoming a model for them. Finally he came even to death, that he might be "Firstborn from the dead, holding the primacy in all things" (Col.1:18) and "Prince of life" (Acts 3:15), preceding all.

The Valentinians appealed to the "acceptable year of the Lord" mentioned in Luke 4:19 to show that Jesus preached for one year and suffered in the last month of it. They denied that he reached advanced age and guided all men by his teaching. But how could he have taught, Irenaeus asks, when he was younger than a master?[23] It is true that at his baptism he was about 30 (Luke 3:23), but that is the age of a young man, extending to the fortieth year, while from the fortieth to the fiftieth one declines into seniority, the age at which our Lord was teaching. The point is made in John 8:56–57, where Jesus says to the Jews, "Your father Abraham rejoiced to see my day, and he saw it and was glad," and they replied to him, "You are not yet fifty years old, and have you seen Abraham?"

> Such a reply is properly addressed to a man already past forty and without reaching fifty is close to it. But to a man only thirty it would be said, "You are not yet forty years old."

The Jews gave an approximate age, whether from the census rolls or a guess.

> It would have been completely irrational for them to lie about twenty years when they wanted to show he was later than the time of Abraham. Therefore the Lord was not far from fifty, and that is why the Jews could say to him, "You are not yet fifty years old, and have you seen Abraham?" (*Heresies* 2.22.6)

The gospel point is confirmed by the tradition of "all the presbyters who met in Asia with John the Lord's disciple" and received this information before he died in the reign of Trajan. Some of them saw not only John but also other apostles, heard these things from them, and attest the fact.

Proof that Irenaeus knew what he was doing comes from his *Epideixis* (74), where he carefully notes that Pilate was "the governor of Claudius Caesar" and thus allows time for Jesus, born in the 41st regnal year of Augustus,[24] to reach 50 not in the fifteenth year of Tiberius (AD 28–29) but about the sixth or seventh year of Claudius (46–47).

FROM RHETORIC TOWARD THEOLOGY

Some of Irenaeus' key theological terms, we have claimed, originated in grammar and rhetoric. For him their meaning is not restricted by their origins but is transposed into a theology strongly influenced by Paul's contrasts between Adam and Christ, such as "As in Adam all die, even so in Christ shall all be made alive" (1 Cor.15:22); and "The first man Adam became a living soul; the last Adam, a life-giving Spirit" (15:45).[25] Just as the Valentinians found, and reinterpreted, their Pleroma in the epistle to the Ephesians,[26] so Irenaeus found divine plan and recapitulation in the same letter, where we read that God set forth his purpose in Christ "as a plan (*oikonomia*) for the fullness (*pleroma*) of time, to recapitulate all things in him" (Eph.1:10). In Irenaeus' scheme the disobedience of Adam was especially important. He was made in the image and likeness of God and lost both when he fell (3.18.1) or, according to another passage, retained the image but lost the likeness (5.6.1). Christ, the creative Word, restored one or both to human beings by the gift of the Spirit and made them immortal.

Presumably Irenaeus himself recovered Paul's word *oikonomia* for Christian theology, in discussion with Valentinians, who also used it. Though it occurs eleven times in the writings of Justin, it was not a key term for him. For Irenaeus its most important meaning must be "dispensation" or "ordering."

The emphasis on "recapitulation" is undoubtedly Irenaeus' own. He used it as the key to at least four events in the history of salvation, referring to God's series of covenants with humanity: first in the time of Adam, second in the time of Noah, third in the time of Moses, and fourth, "which renews man and recapitulates everything in itself, that which by the Gospel raises men and wings them for the celestial kingdom" (3.11.8). This must be the incarnation of the Word, by which he redeemed and restored humanity by himself recapitulating all the stages of human life. The disobedience of Adam and Eve had resulted in their expulsion from Eden, to which humanity could be restored only when the Virgin Mary undid the fall of Eve and Christ reversed the fall of Adam. Thus Justin already described Eve as "an uncorrupted virgin who conceived the word from the serpent and bore disobedience and death," while "the virgin Mary conceived faith and joy when the angel Gabriel spoke to her . . . and she answered, "May it be to me according to your word.'"[27] For Irenaeus, Mary recapitulated and reversed the work of Eve, and he went so far as to say that "as the human race was subjected to death by a virgin, it was freed from it by a virgin" (5.19.1; 3.22.4). Hitchcock claims that here Irenaeus "allows the antithesis to get the better of his doctrine."[28] It might be better to call recapitulation responsible.

While Paul had simply contrasted the new with the old, Irenaeus adds covenants to indicate gradual progress in God's dealings with his people. There is even something like a fifth covenant, for the end will recapitulate the beginning. The creation of matter will be recapitulated by the restoration and increase of matter. Animals and men alike will live in peace, as they once did. Since he had found sayings of Jesus about the literal fulfillment of prophecies about the end, he insisted on such a fulfillment,[29] and faced the scorn of the church historian Eusebius. Irenaeus must have been led astray by Papias, who did not understand that the apostles spoke mystically and symbolically.[30] Papias was not, however, the only source of Irenaeus' doctrine. The apologist Justin had insisted on the orthodoxy of the doctrine that Jerusalem was to be restored as the capital of the saints' thousand-year kingdom.[31] The *Sacra Parallela* ascribed to John of Damascus (eighth century) are still willing to provide an excerpt from *Heresies* 5.36, but the millenarian chapters 32–36 are entirely absent from two significant Latin manuscripts of *Heresies*.[32] Obviously, as the Sources Chrétiennes editors maintain, they were suppressed, perhaps in the fifth century – though not in the East. The principal opponents of the older view were the Gnostics and, later, the Christian Platonists of Alexandria, whose opinions Eusebius shared.

As Irenaeus developed some key structures in his theology he relied on terms which he knew came from grammar and rhetoric and proceeded to use them partly with their original connotations, partly in the richer context of New Testament ideas, especially derived from the apostle Paul. Sometimes he got into difficulties when he allowed the literal literary meanings to overshadow theology. It is undeniable, however, that the terms served as structural beams in his theological thought. He was treating the *hypothesis* as the plot of the whole sacred story from creation to the coming of God's kingdom, while his *oikonomiai* are the subplots included in the plot as a whole. One might even call them "chapters." And *anakephalaiôsis* explains why the events repeat one another, as well as why the story involves not progress but restoration. It is always going back as well as forward. These are the key terms of a theology not philosophical but historical, recalling the *Heilsgeschichte* of half a century ago. Like that understanding, it offers the prospect of fresh insights into the biblical story from the creation to redemption and the new creation.

TRANSLATION AGAINST HERESIES

On the Detection and Refutation of the
Knowledge Falsely So Called

PREFACE TO BOOKS I AND II

Pr. 1 Some persons reject the truth and introduce false statements and "endless genealogies, which provide questions," as the Apostle says, "rather than the divine training that is in faith" (1 Tim.1:4).[1] They combine plausibility with fraud and lead the mind of the inexperienced astray and force them into captivity. They falsify the words of the Lord and make themselves bad interpreters of what was well said. Thus they overthrow many and on the pretext of "knowledge" (*Gnosis*) divert them from the one who founded and arranged this universe, as if they could show something higher and greater than the God who made heaven and earth and everything in them. By persuasion and rhetoric they attract the simple to pursue the quest and wickedly destroy them, inculcating blasphemous and impious ideas about the Creator in people unable to distinguish false from true.

Pr. 2 Error is not shown forth such as it is, for fear that when stripped it may be recognized, but is fraudulently adorned with persuasive attire and appears more true than the truth itself, ridiculous to say, thanks to this external appearance to the eyes of the ignorant – as was said by one of our betters: "The precious stone emerald, of great price in the eyes of some, is devalued by glass artfully polished, as long as no one is present who can test it and prove the existence of fraud. And when bronze has been mixed with silver, who can readily verify it if he is no expert?" We do not want people snatched away by our fault like sheep by wolves when deceived by the outer covering of sheepskin (Matt.7:15), wolves from whom the Lord warned us to keep away, those who speak like us but think otherwise. Therefore, after reading the commentaries of those who call themselves disciples of Valentinus, and meeting some of them and having fully understood their teaching, I considered it necessary to show you, beloved, their portentous and profound mysteries, which "not all understand" (Matt.19:11), because not all have lost their brains! Thus you will know the doctrines and will make them manifest to all who are with you and instruct them to avoid the "abyss" of unreason and blasphemy against God. As well as we can, we will briefly and clearly report the teaching of those who teach this error at the present time – I mean Ptolemaeus and his followers, whose doctrine is the "flower" of the school of Valentinus;[2] and we will set it forth briefly and plainly, and in accord with our moderate ability will provide opportunities to refute them, showing that their statements are absurd, inconsistent, and discordant with the truth. We are not accustomed to writing nor have we studied the art of rhetoric, but love encourages us to show you and all with you things thus far hidden but now by God's grace brought to light. "For there is nothing hidden that will not be revealed, nor secret that will not be known" (Matt.10:26).

Pr. 3   You will not expect from us, who live with the Celts and most of the time use the language of barbarians,[3] either the art of rhetoric which we did not learn, or the skill of a writer which we have not exercised, or elegance of language or persuasion which we do not know. You may, however, accept with love what we have written for you with love, simplicity, and truth, and without technique, and yourself develop it, being more capable than we are. After receiving "seeds" from us you will make what we have expressed to you in a few words "bear fruit" abundantly, in the breadth of your spirit, and will powerfully express to those with you what we have inadequately told you.   And in response to the request you once made when seeking to learn their doctrine, we have zealously labored not only to show it to you but also to provide you with the means of proving it false, and thus you will successfully serve others according to the grace given you by the Lord, so that men may no longer be taken captive by their persuasive talk. The following is their doctrine.

BOOK I

The "Great Notice" of Ptolemaeus: Emanations

1.1   In the invisible and unnameable heights there was a perfect Aeon, prior to all. This Aeon is called Pre-Beginning and Pre-Father and Abyss. Since he was incomprehensible and invisible, eternal and unbegotten, he was in silence and in rest for unlimited ages. With him was Thought, also called Grace and Silence. When this Abyss wanted to emit a Beginning of all, he set it like a seed in the womb of his companion Silence. When she received this seed she became pregnant and generated Mind, similar and equal to the one who emitted him, alone comprehending the greatness of the Father. This Mind they call Only-Begotten and Father and Beginning of all; with him was emitted Truth, to compose the first and primary, indeed Pythagorean Tetrad: Abyss and Silence, then Mind and Truth.

This Only-Begotten, sensing the purpose for which he was emitted, himself emitted Logos and Life, Father of all later than himself, and the Beginning and Formation of the Pleroma. From Logos and Life were emitted, by pairing, Man and Church, and this is the firstborn Ogdoad, the root and substance of all, called by four names by them: Abyss, Mind, Logos, and Man. Each of these is male-female: first the Pre-Father united by pairing with his Thought, which they also call Grace and Silence; then the Only-Begotten, that is, Mind, with Truth; then Logos with Life; and Man with Church.

1.2   Then all these Aeons, emitted for the glory of the Father, desiring in turn to glorify the Father by something of their own, made emissions in pairs. Logos and Life, after emitting Man and Church, emitted ten more aeons, called Mythical and Mingling, Ageless and Union, Self-Grown and Pleasure, Immovable and Compound, Only-Begotten and Bliss. These are the ten Aeons emitted by Logos and Life.

Man with Church emitted twelve Aeons, with the following names: Paraclete and Faith, Paternal and Hope, Maternal and Love, Everlasting and Understanding, Ecclesiastical and Blessedness, Willed and Sophia (Wisdom).

The thirty Aeons of the Pleroma

1.3 These are the thirty Aeons of their error, enveloped in silence and unknown. This is their invisible and spiritual Pleroma, with its triple division into Ogdoad, Decad, and Dodecad. For this reason, they say, the Savior (they refuse to call him Lord) spent thirty years without doing anything in public (Luke 3:23), thus revealing the mystery of these Aeons. Also the parable of the Laborers sent to the Vineyard clearly signifies these thirty Aeons. Certain laborers were hired at the first hour, others at the third, others at the sixth, others at the ninth, others at the eleventh. Added together, these hours, 1+3+6 +9+11, give a total of thirty (Matt.20:1–7). And these are the great and wonderful hidden mysteries which they themselves "fructify," not to mention all the other words of the scriptures which they have been able to adapt and assimilate to their fiction.

2.1 Thus, they say, their Pre-Father was known only to Only-Begotten, that is, Mind, while being invisible and incomprehensible to all the other Aeons. According to them, only Mind took pleasure in seeing the Father and rejoiced in contemplating his immeasurable greatness. He considered sharing with the other Aeons the greatness of the Father, revealing his size and nature, and how he was without beginning and uncontainable and not visible; but Silence kept him from this by the will of the Father, for she wanted to bring all the Aeons to the thought and the desire of searching for this Pre-Father. And the rest of the Aeons similarly desired, with a desire more or less quiet, to see the one who emitted their seed and to meet the root without beginning.

The fall of Sophia

2.2 But the last and youngest Aeon of the Dodecad emitted by Man and Church, that is, Sophia, leaped forth and experienced passion outside the embrace of her consort Theletos. This passion had arisen among the Aeons about Mind and Truth, but it was concentrated in the Aeon Sophia, now altered by it. She was moved by love or audacious yearning, because unlike Mind she did not have communion with the perfect Father. Her passion was a search for the Father, for she wanted to comprehend his greatness. As she could not do so, for it was impossible, she struggled violently because of the greatness of the Abyss and its unsearchable character and her caring love for the Father. As she always pressed on (Phil.3:13), she would finally have been swallowed by his sweetness and dissolved in the universal Substance if the Power which consolidates the Aeons and keeps them outside the inexpressible Greatness had not met her. They call this Power Limit. It stopped her and consolidated her; with difficulty she returned to herself (Luke 15:17), now believed that the Father is incomprehensible, and put off her previous Desire with its accompanying passion, now with wondering admiration.

2.3 Some of the heretics thus imagine the passion and conversion of Sophia. Because she had undertaken something impossible and incomprehensible, she gave birth to a shapeless substance such as a woman normally produces. When she looked at it, first she was sad because of the incomplete character of her offspring; next she feared that it might disappear; then she was beside herself and confused, seeking the cause as well as the way in which she could hide what was born. After experiencing these passions she accepted conversion and tried to run back to the Father. In her weakness she supplicated the Father, and the rest of the Aeons, especially Mind, asked along with her. From all this, they say, the substance of matter took its origin, from ignorance, sadness, fear, and perplexity.

2.4 The Father through Only-Begotten then further emitted Limit in his own image, without a pair but male-female. Sometimes they speak of the Father with his consort Silence, sometimes they make him neither male nor female. To Limit they give the names Cross, Redeemer, Emancipator, Delimiter, and Guide. By this Limit, they say, Sophia was purified, consolidated, and restored to her consort. When her Desire had been separated from her with its passion by Limit, she remained within the Pleroma, but her Desire with its inherent passion was separated, crucified, and expelled from the Pleroma by Limit. Desire had a spiritual substance, since it was the natural movement of an Aeon, but it was a formless and shapeless substance because Sophia understood nothing, and therefore her fruit was weak and female.

2.5 After Desire was banished from the Pleroma and her Mother was reintegrated in her pair, Only-Begotten emitted another pair, in accordance with the providence of the Father, so that none of the Aeons might again experience such an emotion. These were Christ and Holy

61

Spirit, emitted to fix and consolidate the Pleroma, to teach the incomprehensibility of the Father and the nature of spiritual "rest."

Mysterious exegesis

3.1 [The Valentinian myth] was not clearly expressed in the scriptures, since "not all understand" (Matt.19:11) their Gnosis, but was indicated mysteriously by the Savior when he spoke in parables to those able to understand in this way. The thirty Aeons were indicated by the thirty years (Luke 3:23) when the Savior did nothing in public, and by the parable of the laborers in the vineyard (Matt.20:1–7). Paul too, they say, frequently mentions Aeons, even preserving their hierarchy when he says, "In all the Aeons of Aeons" (Eph.3:21). And we ourselves allude to these Aeons, when in the Eucharist we refer to "the Aeons of Aeons," and wherever Aeon or Aeons are named they want them to refer to those.

The Gnostic method

3.6 This is what they say about their Pleroma and the formation of their Aeons, eager to adapt things well said to things they have badly invented. They try to draw their proof not only from the Gospels and the writings of the Apostle, changing the interpretations and twisting the exegesis, but also from the law and the prophets. Since they encounter many parables and allegories which can be taken in various ways, they adjust what is ambiguous to their fiction through exegesis and lead captive, far from the truth, those who do not preserve a firm faith in one God the Father Almighty and in one Jesus Christ the Son of God.

The salvation of the fallen Sophia

4.1 Shapeless, ugly Desire, also known as Achamoth, was lost below, but Christ extended himself to her through the Cross and gave her shape as she suffered grief, fear, perplexity, and ignorance, though sometimes, oddly enough, she laughed. Christ then returned to the Pleroma but sent the Paraclete, the Savior, to her. The Savior made it possible for her to shape three kinds of entities: material (from her passion), psychic (from her conversion), and spiritual (from her essential nature). From the psychic nature she fashioned the Demiurge, who preserved the image of Only-Begotten and was the maker of all psychic and material beings. He shaped seven heavens, which are angels, and dwells above them. He thought he made them, but Achamoth projected them first. In his ignorance he thought he was alone.

Irenaean irony

4.3 What now? It is tragic to see each one pompously explaining the passion and element from which matter derived its origin. I think they are right when they do not want to teach this to everyone in public, but only to those capable of providing substantial payments for such great mysteries. For they do not speak of things like those our Lord mentioned, "Freely you have received, freely give" (Matt. 10:8), but hidden, marvelous, and deep mysteries, discovered by the immense labor of these lovers of lies. Who would not spend his whole fortune to learn that from the tears of Desire, the Aeon in passion, originated seas and springs and rivers and everything wet? And from her laughter, light? And from her perplexity and anguish, the corporeal elements of the world?

4.4 I too wish to contribute to their "fruit-bearing." For since I see that some waters are sweet (springs, rivers, rains, etc.) while seawater is salt, I realize that all these cannot come from the tears of Achamoth, since the property of tears is salt. So it is evident that the salty waters are the ones that come from tears. But I suppose that Achamoth, being in agony and great hesitation, also sweated. Therefore according to their argumentation one must suppose that springs and rivers and any other sweet waters originated from her sweat. For it is not likely that since tears are of one property both salt and sweet waters come from them. It is more likely that some are from tears, others from sweat. But since in the world there are waters both warm and acrid, you should understand what she was doing and from what member she emitted these. "Fruits" of this kind are entirely suited to their argument.

The three elements or classes

6.1 There are three elements. One, material, which they also call "left," will necessarily perish because incapable of receiving any breath of imperishability; another, psychic, which they call "right," is in the middle between spiritual and material and will go where it makes a turn; and the spiritual has been sent forth so that joined with the psychic it will receive formation, instructed with it during its life. This, they say, is "salt" and "the light of the world" (Matt.5:13–14). The psychic needed teaching for the senses. This is why, they say, the world was made and why the Savior came to save this psychic element, since it possessed free will. For, they say, he assumed the first fruits of what he was going to save: from Achamoth, the spiritual; from the Demiurge he was clothed with the psychic Christ; finally, from the divine plan he was surrounded by a body possessing psychic substance but prepared with ineffable skill to be visible, tangible, and capable of suffering. He received nothing material, for the material is not capable of being saved. The final consummation will take place when everything spiritual has been shaped and made perfect by Gnosis, that is, the men who have perfect Gnosis about God and have been initiated into the mysteries of Achamoth. These men are themselves, they say.

Imperfect psychic Christians versus perfect Gnostics

6.2 On the other hand, the psychics are trained in psychic teaching, those men who are made firm through works and mere faith and do not have perfect Gnosis. These men, they say, are we who belong to the church. That is why good behavior is necessary for us, and otherwise we cannot be saved, but they are definitely saved not by works but because they are spiritual by nature. Just as what is material cannot share in salvation, for it is not receptive of it, they say; so again what is spiritual cannot undergo perishability, whatever acts it experiences. For as gold deposited in mud does not lose its beauty but preserves its own nature because mud cannot harm gold, so they themselves, they say, no matter what material acts they experience, cannot be harmed or lose the spiritual substance.

6.3 Therefore the "perfect" among them fearlessly perform all the forbidden acts, of which the scriptures affirm that "those who perform them will not inherit the kingdom of God" (Gal.5:21). They eat foods indiscriminately and think they are in no way defiled by them. They are the first to meet on every festival of the gentiles celebrated in honor of the idols, so that some of them do not abstain from the murderous spectacles of fights with wild beasts and gladiatorial combats, hateful to God and men. Some are insatiable slaves of carnal pleasures, and they say they pay the tribute of carnal to the carnal and of the spiritual to the spiritual.

Some secretly corrupt the women who learn this doctrine from them, as many of those persuaded by them have frequently confessed, along with their other errors, after returning to the church of God. Others, proceeding openly and without shame, have become infatuated with certain women and have stolen them from their husbands, then married them. Still others after a chaste beginning, pretending to live with women as with sisters, in time have been unveiled, when the sister was made pregnant by the brother.

6.4 [They claim that] whoever is "in the world" (John 17:11) and does not love a woman and unite with her does not come "from the truth" (18:37) and will not pass "into the truth" (16:13); but if he who is "of the world" (8:23) unites with a woman, he will not pass into the truth because he has united with this woman with lust.

Three classes of human beings

7.5 There are also three classes of human beings: spiritual, psychic, and material, after the fashion of Cain, Abel, and Seth, from whom come the three natures, no longer in an individual but in the human race. The material element will go to corruption. The psychic element, if it chooses the better, will repose in the place of the Middle; but if it chooses the worse it will go to recover what it will have come to resemble. As for the spiritual elements that Achamoth has sown from then until now in just souls, after they have been instructed and nourished there, for they were sent forth as very small, after being judged worthy of "perfection" they will be given as brides (they say) to the angels of the Savior, while their souls will eternally rest in the Middle with the Demiurge. The souls themselves, they say, are subdivided into two categories, those by nature good and those by nature bad, and the good are those receptive of the seed while the others by nature can never receive it in any way.

Gnostic exegesis

8.1 Such is their doctrine, which the prophets did not proclaim, the Lord did not teach, and the apostles did not transmit. They boast that they have known it more abundantly than anyone else. While citing texts from unwritten sources and venturing to weave the proverbial ropes out of sand, they try to adjust, in agreement with their statements, sometimes parables of the Lord, sometimes prophetic sayings, and sometimes apostolic words, so that their fiction may not seem without witness. They contradict the order and the continuity of the scriptures and, as best they can, dissolve the members of the truth. They transfer and transform, making one thing out of another, and thus lead many astray by the badly constructed phantom that they make out of the Lord's words they adjust.

King into dog or fox

It is as if someone destroyed the figure of a man in the authentic portrait of a king, carefully created by a skillful artist out of precious stones, and rearranged the stones to make the image of a dog or fox, declaring that this badly composed image is that good image of the king made by the skillful artist. He shows the stones arranged by the first artist for the image of the king but badly transferred by the later one into the image of a dog, and by the appearance of the stones deceives the simple, that is, those ignorant of the king's image, and persuades them that this ugly image of a fox is the good image of a king. In the same way these people compile old wives' tales and then, transferring sayings and words and parables, want to accommodate the words of God to their fables.

Texts for events outside the Pleroma

8.2 Here are the texts that they try to apply to the events outside the Pleroma. The Lord, they say, came to his passion in the last times of the world to show the passion in the last of the Aeons and to make known by its end what the end of the production of Aeons was. The 12-year-old girl, daughter of the ruler of the synagogue, whom the Lord stood beside and raised from the dead (Luke 8:41–42), was a figure of Achamoth, whom their extended Christ shaped and led to understand the Light which had abandoned her. The Savior manifested himself to her as she was outside the Pleroma in a state of abortion, as Paul declared in his first letter to the Corinthians: "Last of all, he appeared to me also as to an abortion" (1 Cor.15:8). This coming to Achamoth by the Savior escorted by contemporaries is similarly revealed by Paul in the same letter: "A woman ought to have a veil on her head because of the angels" (11:10). And Moses made known, by covering his face with a veil (2 Cor.3:13), that when the Savior came to her Achamoth put a veil on her face because of reverence. As for the passions experienced by Achamoth, the Savior, they say, underwent them. Thus when he cried out on the cross, "My God, my God, why have you abandoned me?" (Matt.27:46), he revealed that Sophia had been abandoned by the Light and stopped by Limit in her rush forward; he revealed her grief when he said, "How sad is my soul" (Matt.26:38); her fear when he said, "Father, if possible let the cup pass from me" (Matt.26:39); and her anguish similarly: "I do not know what to say" (John 12:27).

8.3 The Lord, they teach, set forth the three races of men (Matt.8:19–22 = Luke 9:57–62): the material in his response to the man who said, "I will follow you," when Jesus replied, "The Son of Man has nowhere to lay his head"; and the psychic, in what he said to the one who said, "I will follow you, but let me go and say goodbye to those of my house." The Lord replied, "No one who has put his hand to the plow but looks back is fit for the kingdom of heaven" (Luke 9:61–62). This man was from the Middle, and so was the one who confessed having achieved the manifold duties of justice but then refused to follow, overcome by wealth that kept him from becoming perfect (Matt.19:16–22). They say this man was of the psychic race. Finally, he indicated the spiritual when he said, "Let the dead bury their dead, but you go and proclaim the kingdom of God" (Matt.8:22 = Luke 9:60), and saying to Zacchaeus the tax-collector, "Hasten to come down, for I must stay in your house today" (Luke 19:5). And the parable of the leaven that a woman is said to have hidden in three measures of meal (Matt.13:33 = Luke 13:20–21), shows forth the three kinds of men. The woman is Sophia; the three measures of meal are the three kinds of men, spiritual, psychic, earthly; and the meal itself is the Savior. And Paul spoke plainly about earthly, psychics, and spirituals. In one place, "As the earthly, so also the earthly ones" (1 Cor.15:48). Again, "The psychic man does not receive the things of the Spirit," and again, "the spiritual examines all" (2:14–15). According to them, "the psychic does not receive the things of the Spirit" refers to the Demiurge, who being psychic knows neither the Mother, who is spiritual, nor her seed, nor the Aeons in the Pleroma. Paul further affirms that the Savior received the first-fruits of what he was going to save: "If the first-fruit is holy, so is the lump" (Rom.11:16). The first-fruit, they teach, is the spiritual, and we are the lump, that is, the psychic church, whose lump they say the Savior assumed and raised with him, for he was the leaven.

8.4 That Achamoth wandered outside the Pleroma and was shaped by Christ and sought by the Savior, they say he revealed when he said he had come to the lost sheep (Matt.18:12–13; Luke 15:4–7). They say the lost sheep is their Mother, from whom they claim the church here below was sown. The wandering is its straying outside the Pleroma, experiencing all the passions from which they say matter was made. The woman who cleans her house and finds a lost drachma (Luke 15:8–10) they explain as the Sophia Above, who has lost her Desire (Achamoth) and later, when everything has been purified by the coming of the Savior, will find it again, for, according to them, she must be restored within the Pleroma. They say that "Symeon, who took Christ in his arms and gave thanks to God and said, "Lord, now let your servant depart in peace according to your word'" (Luke 2:29) is a figure of the Demiurge, who at the Savior's coming learned about his change of abode and gave thanks to Abyss. As for the prophetess Anna, who in the Gospel is said to have lived seven years with her husband and the rest of her life as a widow, until she saw the Savior, recognized him, and spoke of him to all (2:36–38), she obviously signifies Achamoth, who saw the Lord with his companions for a moment and then remained in the Middle for the whole later period, waiting for him to come back and establish her in her pair. The Savior indicated her name when he said, "Sophia was justified by her children" (7:35), as did Paul in these words, "We speak of Sophia among the perfect" (1 Cor.2:6). The say that Paul also spoke of the pairs within the Pleroma when he spoke plainly about one such pair: speaking of the marriage that is in this life, he wrote, "This mystery is great, but I speak of Christ and Church" (Eph.5:32).

Exegesis of the Prologue of John's Gospel

8.5   They also teach that John the Lord's disciple pointed to the first Ogdoad and the generation of all and they speak thus. He set forth the "Beginning," first made by God, also called "Son" and "Only-Begotten God," in whom the Father emitted everything in seminal fashion. By this Beginning, says John, was emitted the Logos and, in him, the whole substance of the Aeons, which the Logos himself later fashioned. Since John is speaking of the first genesis, he rightly starts his teaching with the Beginning or Son and by the Logos. He speaks thus: "In the Beginning was the Logos, and the Logos was toward God, and the Logos was God; this Logos was in the Beginning, toward God." First he differentiates three terms: God, Beginning, Logos; then he unites them, in order to show not only the emission of both Son and Logos but also the unity between them and with the Father. For in the Father and from the Father is the Beginning, and in the Beginning and from the Beginning is the Logos. Therefore John well said: "In the Beginning was the Logos." The Logos was in fact in the Son. "And the Logos was toward God." For that was the

Beginning. "And the Logos was God." Just so, since what is born of God is God. "This Logos was in the Beginning toward God." He reveals the sequence of emissions. "Everything was made by him, and without him nothing was made." In fact, for all the Aeons after him the Logos was the cause of formation and generation. But John continues, "What was made in him is Life." He thus points to a pair, for he says that everything was made through him, but "Life," in him. This, made in him, is closer to him than what was only made through him; it is united to him and bears fruit through him. Since John continues, "And the Life was the Light of Men," by saying "Men" he speaks of "Church" so that through one name he may set forth the communion of the pair; for from Logos and Life proceed Man and Church. John calls Life "the Light of Men" because they have been illuminated by it, that is, formed and made manifest. This is also what Paul says: "Everything made manifest is Light" (Eph.5:13). Therefore since Life manifested and generated Man and Church it is called their Light. By these words John clearly showed, among other things, the Second Tetrad: Logos and Life, Man and Church. He also indicated the First Tetrad. For speaking of the Savior, and saying that everything outside the Pleroma was formed by him, he says at the same time that this Savior is the fruit of the whole Pleroma. He calls him Light that shines in the darknesses and has not been seized by them because though it formed all the products of the passion it was ignored by them. This Savior John further calls Son and Truth and Life and Incarnate Logos. "We have seen his glory," he says, "glory as of the Only-Begotten, given him by his Father, full of Grace and Truth." And he says, "And the Logos became incarnate and dwelt among us and we saw his glory, glory as of the Only-Begotten from the Father, full of Grace and Truth" (1:14). So John carefully sets forth the First Tetrad, naming Father and Grace and Only-Begotten and Truth. Thus he spoke of the First Ogdoad, the Mother of all the Aeons, for he named Father and Grace, Only-Begotten and Truth, Logos and Life, Man and Church. This is what Ptolemaeus said.

A parallel in Homeric study

9.4 After collecting scattered texts and names they transfer them, as we said before, out of their natural meaning to a meaning contrary to nature, acting like those who propose random hypotheses for themselves and try to treat them from the Homeric verses, so that the untutored may suppose that Homer composed verses on this completely novel subject and that many readers may be led astray, through the well-ordered sequence of the verses, to ask if Homer wrote them. Here is how, with verses from Homer, one could describe Heracles as sent by Eurystheus to the dog in Hades. Nothing keeps us from using such an example, since it involves the same argument in both cases.

> Having thus spoken, he left groaning deeply (*Od.*10.76)
> The noble Heracles, witness of great deeds (*Od.*21:26);
> Eurystheus, born of Sthenelos the Perseid (*Il.*19.123),
> To lead from Erebos the dog of cruel Hades (*Il.*8.368).
> He left, like a fierce lion fed in mountains (*Od.*6.130),
> Through mid-city; his friends at once parted (*Il.*24.327).
> Old men and boys and unmarried girls (*Od.*11.38),
> Uttering laments as if he walked toward death (*Il.*24.328).
> Hermes went with him, and grey-eyed Pallas (*Od.*11.626),
> For he knew what grief agitated his brother (*Il.*2.409).

What simpleton would be taken in by these verses to suppose that Homer composed them in this way? One who knows his Homer will recognize the verses but not the subject matter. He knows that one of the verses deals with Odysseus, another with Heracles, another with Priam, another with Menelaos and Agamemnon. If anyone takes these verses and restores them to their original setting, he will make the system disappear. And thus whoever keeps the rule of truth, which he received through baptism, unchanged within himself, knows these names, phrases, and parables from the scriptures but does not recognize their blasphemous system. If he recognizes the stones [of the mosaic] he will not take the fox for the royal image. Setting each word in its context and adjusting it to the body of truth, he will strip it of their fiction and show their inconsistency.

The uniform faith of the church

10.1 The church, dispersed throughout the world to the ends of the earth, received from the apostles and their disciples the faith in one God the Father Almighty, "who made heaven and earth and sea and all that is in them" (Exod.20:11), and in one Christ Jesus, the Son of God, incarnate for our salvation, and in the Holy Spirit, who through the prophets predicted the dispensations of God: the coming, the birth from the Virgin, the passion, the resurrection from the dead, and the ascension of the beloved Jesus Christ our Lord in the flesh into the heavens, and his coming from the heavens in the glory of the Father to "recapitulate all things" (Eph.1:10) and raise up all flesh of the human race, so that to Christ Jesus our Lord and God and Savior and King, according to the good pleasure of the invisible Father, "every knee should bow, of beings in heaven and on earth and under the earth, and that every tongue should confess him" (Phil.2:10–11), and that he should render a just judgement on all and send to eternal fire the spiritual powers of iniquity, the lying and apostate angels, and men who are impious, unjust, iniquitous, and blasphemous, while on the contrary he should give life imperishable as a reward to the just and equitable who keep his commandments and persevere in his love (some from the beginning, others since their conversion), and surround it with eternal glory.

10.2 The church, having received this preaching and this faith, as we have just said, though dispersed in the whole world, diligently guards them as living in one house, believes them as having one soul and one heart (Acts 4:32), and consistently preaches, teaches, and hands them down as having one mouth. For if the languages in the world are dissimilar, the power of the tradition is one and the same. The churches founded in Germany believe and hand down no differently, nor do those among the Iberians, among the Celts, in the Orient, in Egypt, or in Libya, or those established in the middle of the world. As the sun, God's creature, is one and the same in the whole world, so the light, the preaching of truth, shines everywhere and illuminates all men who wish to come to the knowledge of truth. And none of the rulers of the churches, however gifted he may be in eloquence, will say anything different – for no one is above the Master (Matt.10:24) – nor will one weak in speech damage the tradition. Since the faith is one and the same, he who can say much about it does not add to it nor does he who says little diminish it.

What theological method can and cannot do

10.3 The fact that some people know more or less by insight does not result in changing the subject (*hypothesis*) and falsely imagining a God other than the Creator, Maker, and Sustainer of this universe, as if he were not sufficient for us, or another Christ or another Only Son. But knowledge lies in (a) the more complete investigation of everything said in parables and its adaptation to the argument of truth; (b) telling in detail the action and plan of God for humanity; (c) setting forth God's long-suffering toward the apostasy of the rebellious angels as well as the disobedience of men; (d) stating why one and the same God made some things temporal, others eternal, some celestial, others earthly; (e) understanding why God, being invisible, appeared to the prophets, not in one form but variously; (f) indicating why many covenants were handed down to the human race, and teaching the character of each one; (g) investigating why "God consigned all things to unbelief that he might have mercy on all" (Rom.11:32); (h) giving thanks for why "the Word" of God "became incarnate" (John 1:14) and suffered; (i) proclaiming why the advent of the Son of God took place in the last times, that is, why the Beginning appeared at the end; (j) investigating whatever is contained in the scriptures about the end and things to come; (k) not being silent about why, when the gentiles were without hope, God made them joint heirs incorporate, sharers with the saints (Eph.3:6); (l) announcing how "this mortal flesh will put on immortality and this perishable, imperishability" (1 Cor.15:54); (m) proclaiming how "the not-people became a people and the non-beloved beloved" (Hos.2:25) and how "the children of the one abandoned have become more than the children of her who had a husband" (Gal.4:27).

On these matters and others like them the Apostle shouted, "Oh, the depth of the riches and wisdom and knowledge of God! How inscrutable are his judgements and his ways cannot be investigated" (Rom.11:33). He did not imagine or blaspheme that above the Creator and Demiurge there is a 'Mother' of him and of them, the Desire of an Aeon that went astray, nor did he falsely state that above her is a Pleroma which would contain sometimes thirty Aeons, sometimes innumerable multitudes of Aeons. Thus these masters, truly destitute of divine understanding, express themselves, while the whole church has one and the same faith in all the world, as we have said.

Varieties of systems after Valentinus

11.1 Let us now look at their unstable teaching and how, when there are two or three of them, they not only do not make the same statements about the same things but give contradictory answers in content and expression alike. The first among them, Valentinus, transferred the older doctrines from what is called the "Gnostic" sect and adapted them for his own school. He stated that there is an ineffable Duality consisting of the Inexpressible and Silence. Later this Duality emitted a second Duality, Father and Truth. This Tetrad bore as fruit Logos and Life, Man and Church, thus constituting the first Ogdoad. From Logos and Life ten powers were emitted, as we have said; from Man and Church were emitted twelve, one of which, leaving (the Pleroma) and falling into distress, made the rest of the creation. He has two Limits: one, between the Abyss and the Pleroma, separates the generated Aeons from the uncreated Father, while the other separates their Mother from the Pleroma. The Christ was not emitted by the Aeons of the Pleroma, but was borne by the Mother, when she was outside it, according to the memory she had of the powers above, though with a certain shadow. As this Christ was masculine, he cut off the shadow from himself and returned to the Pleroma. Then the Mother, abandoned with the shadow and emptied of spiritual substance, emitted another son: this is the Demiurge, omnipotent master of those beneath him. Along with him was emitted an Archon of the left, as in the system of the falsely called "Gnostics."

Jesus was sometimes said to be emitted by Theletos, the Aeon separated from their Mother and united with the others, sometimes by Christ, who ran upward again into the Pleroma, and sometimes by Man and Church. And the Holy Spirit was emitted by Truth for testing and fructifying the Aeons; it enters them invisibly, and by it the Aeons fructify the plants of Truth. Such is the doctrine of Valentinus.

11.2 Secundus teaches that the first Ogdoad includes a Tetrad of the right and a Tetrad of the left, and light and darkness; the Aeon that left the Pleroma and fell into distress did not come from the thirty but from their fruits.

Fantastic language

11.3 Another, a famous teacher of theirs, "stretches out" toward a Gnosis higher and more Gnostic and describes the first Tetrad thus: There exists before everything a pre-unintelligible Pre-principle which I call Unicity. With this Unicity there coexists a Power which I call Unity. This Unity and this Unicity, being one, emitted without emitting a Beginning of all things, intelligible unengendered and invisible, the Beginning which language calls Monad. With this Monad coexists a Power of the same substance (*homoousios*), which I call One. These Powers, Unicity, Unity, Monad, and One, emitted the rest of the Aeons.

11.4 Iou iou! Pheu pheu! This exclamation of tragedy ought to be expressed over such a fabrication of names and such great audacity as he shamelessly gives names to his lying inventions. For when he says, "There exists before everything a pre-unintelligible Pre-principle which I call Unicity" and "With this Unicity there coexists a Power which I call Unity," he admits clearly that whatever he has said is fiction and that he imposes on the fiction names that no one one else ever set. Without his boldness, today the "truth" would not have a name, according to them.

It deserves parody

But then, nothing keeps another who writes on the same subject from defining the terms thus: There exists a certain royal Pre-principle, pre-unintelligible, pre-insubstantial and pre-prerotund, which I call Gourd. With this Gourd there coexists a Power which I call Supervacuity. This Gourd and this Supervacuity, being one, emitted without emitting a Fruit visible in all its parts, edible and sweet, which language calls Cucumber. With this Cucumber there is a Power of the same substance, which I call Melon. These Powers, Gourd and Supervacuity and Cucumber and Melon, emitted the whole multitude of Valentinus' delirious Melons. For if one must accommodate ordinary language to the first Tetrad and if each one chooses the terms he wants, who would keep him from using these last terms, much more worthy of credence, in ordinary usage, and known by all?

Further ridiculous examples

11.5 Others among them again have given the first and primal Ogdoad the following names: first the Pre-beginning, then the Unintelligible; third the Inexpressible, fourth the Invisible. From the Pre-beginning was emitted, in the first and fifth place, the Beginning; from the Unintelligible was emitted, in the second and sixth place, the Incomprehensible; from the Inexpressible was emitted, in the third and seventh place, the Unnameable; from the Invisible was emitted, in the fourth and eighth place, the Unengendered, with which the first Ogdoad is completed. These Powers pretended that they existed before Abyss and Silence, in order to appear more perfect than the "perfect," more Gnostic than the Gnostics. One could rightly say to them, "Poor melons, who are vile sophists and not men" (cf. *Iliad* 2.235).

God is not like any of this

12.2 Do not these people seem to you, O beloved, to have envisioned the Homeric Zeus, sleepless because of cares, worried about how to honor Achilles and destroy a multitude of Greeks (*Iliad* 2.1–4), rather than the Lord of all? He is the one who considered doing something and at the same time accomplished what he considered; at the same time he willed and considered what he willed, and thinks when he wills and wills when he thinks, since he is all Thought, all Will, all Mind, all Light, all Eye, all Hearing, the source of all good things.

Mark the Valentinian magician

13.1 Another among them, named Mark, boasts that he is the corrector of the master. This man, highly skilled in magic tricks, through which he leads many men and not a few women astray to be converted to himself as to the most Gnostic and most perfect, and possessing the greatest power from the invisible and ineffable regions, is a true forerunner of the Antichrist. He combines the games of Anaxilaos with the wickedness of so-called magicians and is therefore considered a miracle-worker among those who have no sense or are demented.

Marcosian Eucharist, prophecy, and bridal chamber

13.2 Pretending to celebrate the Eucharist with a chalice of wine mixed with water, and prolonging the prayer of invocation, he makes the cup appear purple and red so that the Grace from the regions above all may be supposed to distill its blood in his chalice through his invocation, while those present experience a strong desire to taste from that cup so that in them too may flow what the magician calls Grace. Again, giving women mixed chalices he orders them to give thanks in his presence. That done, he brings forward another chalice, much greater than the one in which that woman led astray makes eucharist and, pouring from the smaller one made eucharist by the woman into the much larger one brought by him, straightway says this:

> May that incomprehensible and ineffable Grace which is before all things fill your inner man (Eph.3:16) and multiply its Gnosis in you, sowing the grain of mustard seed in good earth (Matt.13:31,8).

Saying such things and driving that unhappy woman mad, he shows forth marvels when the larger chalice is filled from the smaller one and overflows. And by other similar marvels he has led many astray and dragged them behind him.

13.3   He probably has an attendant demon through which he gives the impression of prophesying and makes those women he deems worthy prophesy too. For he busies himself especially with women, the most elegant and richest, who wear robes with purple borders.⁴ As he tries to seduce them he often says in flattery:

> I want you to share in my Grace, since the Father of all always sees your angel before his face (Matt.18:10). The place of Greatness is in us; we must establish ourselves in the One. Take Grace first from me and through me. Beautify yourself as a bride receiving her bridegroom (Rev.21:2), so that you may be what I am and I what you are. Establish in your bridechamber the seed of light. Take from me the bridegroom and receive him and be received in him. Behold, Grace has come upon you. Open your mouth and prophesy.

The woman replies thus: "I have never prophesied and I do not know how to prophesy." He makes invocations again to stupefy the one being seduced and says to her, "Open your mouth and say anything, and you will prophesy." Bewitched and bewildered by these words, her soul is set on fire by the idea that she will prophesy, and her heart pounds much harder than it should. She grows daring and speaks delirious words and whatever comes to mind, foolishly and boldly, in the heat of the empty spirit. (A better teacher than we are has said of such people, "A soul warmed by empty air is audacious and shameless.") From that moment she considers herself a prophetess. She gives thanks to Mark for sharing his Grace with her. She tries to repay him not only by the gift of her property – thus he has collected a great amount of wealth – but also by sharing her person in her desire to be united with him in everything so as to descend with him into the One.

13.4   He also tried to lead astray some of the most faithful women who possess the fear of God and cannot be seduced, by ordering them to prophesy, but they hissed at him and anathematized him and separated from such a detestable group. They knew that prophecy is not given to mankind by Mark the magician, but those on whom God has sent his grace from on high have prophecy given by God and speak where and when God wishes, not when Mark orders. The one who gives orders is greater and more powerful than the one ordered;

one is chief, the other is a subordinate. If then Mark or someone else gives orders, as all these people do in their banquets, playing at oracles, ordering one another to prophesy, and predicting according to their lusts, the one who gives orders will be greater and more powerful than the prophetic Spirit, though he is only a man; and this is impossible. But the spirits who are ordered by such people and speak when they desire it are feeble and powerless but bold and impudent, sent by Satan to seduce and destroy those who do not firmly keep the faith they have received from the beginning through the church.

13.5 The same Mark uses philtres and charms, if not with all women at least with some, so as to be able to dishonor their bodies. Once back in the church they have confessed that they were defiled by him in their bodies and that they felt a violent passion for him. A deacon of ours in Asia let Mark into his home, but fell into a disaster of this kind: his wife was beautiful and, corrupted in spirit and body by that magician, followed him for a long time. When the brethren were finally able to bring her back with great effort, she spent all her time in penitence, weeping and bewailing her seduction by the magician.[5]

13.6 And his disciples, wandering about in the same circumstances and seducing and corrupting many women, call themselves "perfect," as if no one can equal the greatness of their knowledge, not even if you should mention Paul or Peter or some other apostles, but they know more than all of them and alone have drunk the greatness of the knowledge of the inexpressible Power. They are on the height, above every Power; therefore they can do everything freely without any fear. Because of "redemption" they have become incomprehensible and invisible to the Judge. If anyone should arrest them, they stand before him, protected by "redemption," and say these words:

O Assistant of God and of the mystical Silence prior to the Aeons, you are the one through whom the Magnitudes who forever see the face of the Father (cf. Matt.18:10), using you as their leader and guide, draw their forms on high. That truly audacious Female fantasized because of the goodness of the Propator [the Abyss] and emitted these forms, none other than ourselves, as images of the Magnitudes, for she had the realities above present to her spirit as in a dream. Now the Judge is at hand and the herald orders me to make my defence. Do you, who know the nature of both of us, present to the judge the justification of our two cases as one.

When she hears these words the Mother covers them at once with the Homeric cap of Hades so that, becoming invisible (*Iliad* 5.845) they may escape from the Judge, and she immediately takes them into the bridal chamber and gives them to their spouses.

13.7 By saying and doing such things, even in our regions of the Rhône they have seduced a great number of women, who have their consciences cauterized (1 Tim.4:2) and some even confess publicly, while others importunately withdraw in silence, giving up hope for the life of God; while some have apostatized completely and others remain in suspense between the two, as the proverb puts it "being neither inside nor outside" and having the fruit of the seed of the sons of "knowledge."

Mark's revelation of origins

14.1 This Mark, who says that as the Only Son he was the womb and receptacle of the Silence of Colorbasus, sent into the world the seed deposited in him. The Tetrad from the highest invisible ineffable places came down to him in feminine form, since, he said, the world could not endure the masculine element she possesses, and she showed him who she was and told him alone the genesis of everything, which she had not revealed to any gods or men. She said this:

> When the Father who has no Father, inconceivable and insubstantial, neither male nor female, first wanted his ineffable element to be expressed and what was invisible in him to receive form, he opened his mouth and brought forth a Word like himself. This Word, staying with him, showed him what he was, appearing as the Form of the invisible. The enunciation of the Name took place thus: The Father spoke the first word of his Name, which was the Beginning, and it was one syllable with four elements; he added a second syllable, which likewise contained four elements; then he spoke the third, of ten elements; finally he pronounced the last, of twelve elements. Thus the enunciation of the Name was of thirty elements and four syllables. Each element has its own letters, its own character, its own resonance, and figures and images. None among them sees the form of which it is an element. They are not only ignorant of that, but each element does not know even the resonance of its neighbor but imagines that all its own resonance expresses the Whole. For each of them, being only a part of the

Whole, calls its own sound as if it were all, and does not stop resounding until they come in sequence to the last letter of the last element. Then (says the Tetrad) the restitution of all things will take place, when all things are converted into one letter and the same resonance, of which there is an image when we all say "Amen." These are the sounds which form the insubstantial and ungenerated Aeon, the forms which the Lord called "angels who forever see the face of the Father" (Matt.18:10).

14.3 After this exposition the Tetrad said:

I wish to show you the Truth herself, for I have made her come down from the higher abodes so that you may look upon her bare and contemplate her beauty, and also hear her speaking and marvel at her wisdom. See at the top her head, which is Alpha and Omega, her neck Beta and Psi, her shoulders and hands Gamma and Chi, her chest Delta and Phi, her diaphragm Epsilon and Upsilon, her back Zeta and Tau, her belly Eta and Sigma, her thighs Theta and Rho, her knees Iota and Pi, her legs Kappa and Omicron, her ankles Lambda and Xi, her feet Mu and Nu.

This, according to the magician, is "the body of Truth, the scheme of the Element, the character of the Letter." He calls the Element Man, and says he is the source of every word and the beginning of every voice, the expression of the Inexpressible, the mouth of silent Silence. "And this is his body. But as for you, follow the Tetrad, raise the thoughts of your spirit higher and hear the Logos, generator of itself and giver of the Father."

14.7 The first heaven sounds Alpha, the next Epsilon, the third Eta, the fourth (in the middle of the seven) has the power of Iota, the fifth Omicron, the sixth, Upsilon, and the seventh (the fourth from the middle), Omega. All the Powers, mutually embracing, sound forth and glorify the one by whom they were emitted, and the glory of the sound is sent forth to the Forefather. The sound of this glorification, carried to the earth, became the fashioner and generator of what is on earth.

14.8 He provides proof of this by citing newborn infants, whose soul, recently arrived from the womb, makes heard the sound of each of the vowels. As, then, the seven Powers glorify the Logos, so the soul of infants by lamenting and moaning glorifies Mark himself. This is why David said, "Out of the mouth of infants and those at the breast you have perfected praise" (Ps.8:1–2), and again, "The heavens declare the glory of God" (Ps.19:1). And therefore when the soul finds itself in sufferings and calamities for its purification, it says "O" as a sign of praise so that the soul above, recognizing its cognate, may send down help to it.

15.1 Mark uses the following names, expressing them seriously and with faith: Ineffable and Silence, Father and Truth. Of this Tetrad the whole number of letters is twenty-four, for Ineffable (*Arretos*) contains seven letters, Silence (*Seige*) five and Father (*Pater*) five and Truth (*Aletheia*) seven; all these letters added together, five twice and seven twice, reach the total of twenty-four. So also the second Tetrad, that is Logos and Life (*Zoe*), Man (*Anthropos*) and Church (*Ekklesia*), presents the same number of letters. The expressible name of the Savior, that is, Jesus (*Iesous*) is of six letters, but his inexpressible name is of twenty-four letters. "Son Christ" (*Uios Xreistos*) is of twelve letters, but what is inexpressible in Christ is of thirty letters. This is why Mark says he is Alpha and Omega, to show forth the dove (*peristera*), since the bird has this number.

15.3 From the Tetrad came forth the Aeons; in this Tetrad were Man and Church, Logos and Life. From these four Aeons, says Mark, emanated the "powers" which generated the Jesus who appeared on earth. The angel Gabriel took the place of the Logos, the Holy Spirit that of Life, the "power of the Most High" that of Man, and finally the Virgin took the place of Church. Thus according to Mark the man of the divine plan was generated by Mary; at his passage through the womb the Father of all chose him through the Logos for the knowledge of himself. When he came to the water there came down on him as a dove the one who ran back upward and completed the number twelve, and in him was found the seed of those sown with him and they came down and went up with him. This "power" that came down thus, according to Mark, was the seed of the Father, the seed which contained the Father, the Son, the ineffable "power" of Silence, known only by these, and all the Aeons. That is the Spirit which spoke by the mouth of Jesus, declaring himself the Son of Man and manifesting the Father, after having come down upon Jesus and being united with him. The Savior from the divine plan destroyed death, he says, and made known his Father, Christ. Jesus is the name of the man from the divine plan: he was in the likeness and image of the Man who was to come down in him. When he received him, he had in himself the very Man and the very Logos and the Father and the Ineffable, as well as Silence, Truth, Church, and Life.

Mark's mysticism and the history of the alphabet

15.4 That goes beyond the "Iou Iou and Pheu Pheu," and every other exclamation of grief in tragedy. Who, indeed, would not hate the evil inventor of such lies when seeing the idol of the Truth made by Mark and branded with the letters of the alphabet?

It is only recently (as they say, "yesterday or the day before") that the Greeks received an alphabet of sixteen letters from Cadmus; with the passage of time they discovered the aspirated consonants [Theta, Phi, Chi] and the double consonants [Zeta, Xi, Psi]. Finally Palamedes added the long vowels [Eta and Omega]. Therefore before all that took place among the Greeks Truth did not exist, for its body, according to you, Mark, is later than Cadmus and his predecessors, later than those who added the other letters, and later than yourself, for you alone have brought down the one whom you call Truth to the level of an idol.

The absurdity of the Marcosian system

15.5 Who will endure your talkative Silence, which speaks the Ineffable Aeon, describes the indescribable, claims that he who, you say, has no body or shape opened his mouth and emitted a Word, as if he were a living being composed of parts, and that this Word, like him who emitted it and forms the Invisible, is composed of thirty letters and four syllables? So because of his resemblance to the Logos, the Father of all, as you say, has thirty letters and four syllables. Furthermore, who will endure your enclosing in arrangements and numbers – thirty, twenty-four, or only six – the one who is the Creator and Demiurge and Maker of all, the Word of God, whom you cut up into four syllables and thirty letters; and reduce the Lord of all, who made firm the heavens, into the number 888 (as you did for the alphabet); and subdivide the Father himself, who encloses everything and is enclosed by no one, into Tetrad, Ogdoad, Decad, and Dodecad, by such multiplications describing what you say is the ineffable and inconceivable nature of the Father? The one you call incorporeal and insubstantial, you fabricate his substance out of many letters engendered the ones out of the others, lying Daedalus that you are and an evil maker of the supreme Power. You subdivide this substance that you call indivisible into mute consonants and vowels and semi-vowels, falsely attributing the mutes to the Father and his Thought; you thus have driven into the deepest blasphemy and greatest impiety all who believe you.

The old herald of truth denounced Mark

15.6 Therefore it was just and appropriate for your audacity that the divinely inspired old man, the herald of truth, cried out against you:

> Idol-maker and observer of monsters,
> Skilled in astrological and magical art,
> Through which you confirm your false teachings,
> Showing signs to those deceived by you,
> The workings of the apostate power,
> Which your father Satan always supplies to you,
> To achieve through the power of the angel Azazel,
> When he has you as forerunner of impiety toward God.

These are the words of the old man dear to God. But we shall try to set forth the rest of their mysteries briefly, since they are lengthy, and bring forth what has been long hidden into the light. For thus it will be easy for them to be refuted by all.

Biblical summary on Mark's theology

16.3 When you read all this, beloved, I know well that you will laugh hard at their pretentious foolishness. They are worthy of pity when they substitute the alphabet and the cold and artificial numbers for so great a religion, the greatness of the truly ineffable Power, and the great dispensations of God. All who separate from the church and adhere to these "old wives' tales" (1 Tim.4:7) are truly self-condemned (Tit.3:11). Paul orders us to "avoid them after a first and a second warning" (Tit.3:10). John the Lord's disciple condemned them still more severely, desiring us not even to greet them: "He who greets them participates in their evil works" (2 John 11). And rightly, for "there is no greeting for the impious, says the Lord" (Is.48:22). Impious beyond all impiety are these who say that the Creator of heaven and earth, the only almighty God above whom there is no other God, was emitted from a deficiency that proceeded from another deficiency, so that according to them he would be the product of a third deficiency. Rightly rejecting and anathematizing this notion, we must flee far from them and, the more they affirm and delight in their discoveries, the more we shall know that they are agitated by the most evil spirits of the Ogdoad. When sick people fall into delirium, the more they laugh and believe themselves healthy and do everything as if they were well or more than well, the sicker they really are. So it is with these people: the more they believe they have lofty thoughts and break down with bow-string stretched too tautly, the more unhealthy they are. The unclean spirit of ignorance comes forth and frees them not for God but for worldly questions, and it proceeds to take with it seven other spirits more evil than itself (Matt.12:43–45), and infatuates their thought to believe that they can discover what is above God, and after preparing them for their ruin deposits the Ogdoad [= 7 + 1] of the madness of evil spirits in them.

The heavens declare the glory of Gnosis

17.1 I wish to show you further how, according to them, the creation itself would have been made through the Mother after the image of invisible things by the Demiurge without his knowledge. First, they say, the four elements, fire, earth, water and air, were produced as an image of the superior Tetrad. Adding their operations, hot, cold, wet, dry, exactly portrays the Ogdoad. Then there are ten powers: first the seven spherical bodies called heavens, then the circle containing them, called the eighth heaven, and finally the sun and the moon. Since these are ten in number they are images of the invisible Decad emitted by Logos and Life. The Dodecad is indicated by the circle called zodiac, for the twelve signs of the zodiac most plainly indicate, as if in a picture, the Dodecad, daughter of Man and Church. And since the highest heaven is opposed to the rapid movement of all the stars, weighing them down with its mass and counterbalancing their speed by its slowness, so as to complete the whole cycle from sign to sign in thirty years, they say that the heaven is an image of Limit, which envelops their Mother who bears the thirtieth name. In turn, the moon, circling its heaven in thirty days, signifies the number of aeons through the thirty days. The sun, finishing its circular revolution in twelve months, signifies the Dodecad by these twelve months. The days too, measured by twelve hours, are the image of the invisible Dodecad. The hour itself, the twelfth part of the day, is divided into thirty degrees to be an image of the Thirty. The circle of the zodiac thus contains 360 degrees, each sign having thirty parts, and thus by the circle is preserved the image of the conjunction of the number twelve with the number thirty. Further, the earth is divided into twelve zones, and in each zone it receives straight down from the heavens a particular "power" and generates children like that power which has sent down its emanation. Thus, they say, the earth is a most obvious figure of the Dodecad and its children.

Humanity an image of the Pleroma

18.1 Modeled after the Power from above, man has within him a "power" coming from a single source. This "power" has its seat in the brain. From it flow four "powers" after the image of the Tetrad above: sight, hearing, smelling, taste. The Ogdoad is signified in man because he has two ears, two eyes, two nostrils, and dual tasting for bitter and sweet. Thus, they teach, the whole man is the complete image of the Thirty: in his hands, by his ten fingers, he bears the Decad, in his whole body, divided into twelve members, the Dodecad (they divide the body as they divide the body of Truth, mentioned above); as for the Ogdoad, inexpressible and invisible, they consider it hidden in the entrails ...

A false legend about the boy Jesus

20.1 Beyond that, they introduce an infinite multitude of apocryphal and bastard scriptures that they themselves have composed to stupefy the simple and those who do not know the authentic writings. For the same purpose they add this forgery: When the Lord was a boy learning the alphabet, his teacher said to him, as is customary, "Say Alpha," and he replied, "Alpha." But when the teacher ordered him to say Beta, the Lord replied, "First you tell me what Alpha is and then I will tell you what Beta is." They explain this reply as meaning that he alone knew the Unknowable, whom he showed forth in the figure of the Alpha.

Valentinian Gospel exegesis

20.2 They twist some of the content of the Gospels in this sense, for example what he said at the age of 12 to his mother: "Do you not know that I must be in what belongs to my Father?" (Luke 2:49): By that he was telling them, they say, about the Father whom they did not know; and for this reason he sent the disciples to the twelve tribes (Matt.10:5–6), announcing the God unknown to them. And to the man who said "Good Master" to him, he acknowledged the truly good God when he said, "Why do you call me good? A single one is good, the Father among the Heavens" (19:16–17 var.) They say that here the Aeons are called Heavens. And for this reason he did not answer those who asked him, "By what power do you do this?" but embarrassed them with his counter-questioning (21:23–27); they explain that by not replying he showed forth the ineffable character of the Father. And when he said, "Often they desired to hear one of these words, and they had no one to speak them,"⁶ the word "one" refers to the one true God whom they did not know. Further, when he was approaching Jerusalem and wept over it and said, "If you had known today what belongs to your peace, but it is hidden from you" (Luke 19:42), with the word "hidden" he referred to the hidden mystery of the Abyss. And again, when he said, "Come to me all you who labor and are burdened and learn from me" (Matt.11:28–29), he proclaimed the Father of Truth, for, they say, he promised he would teach them what they did not know.

20.3   Finally, as a proof of the foregoing and the final statement of their system, they bring forward this text: "I praise you, Father, Lord of the Heavens [Aeons] and the Earth [Achamoth], for you have hidden these things from the wise and revealed them to infants. Yes, Father, for such was your good pleasure. Everything has been delivered to me by my Father, and no one but the Son has known the Father, nor the Son but the Father and he to whom the Son has revealed it" (Matt.11:25–27). By these words, they say, he most plainly showed that before his coming no one clearly knew the Father of Truth. They claim that the Maker and Creator has always been known by all, but the Lord spoke these words of the Father unknown to all, whom they themselves proclaim.

Gnostic spiritual rites

21.3   Some of them use a bridal chamber and perform a whole mystery with profane invocations over the initiates; they call what is performed a "spiritual marriage," after the likeness of the pairs above. Others lead them to water and baptize them while saying,

> Into the name of the unknown Father of all,
> into Truth the Mother of all,
> into the one who came down into Jesus;
> for union, redemption, and the communion of the Powers.

Others also use Hebrew words in order to impress the initiates:⁷ *Basema cacabasa eanaa irraumista diarbada caeota bafobor camelanthi.*⁸ [Graffin's translation] "In the name of Sophia, Father, and

Light, called Spirit of Holiness, for the redemption of the angelic nature." Still others proclaim the "redemption" thus: "The Name hidden from every Deity and Lordship and Truth, which Jesus the Nazarene put on in the zones of the light of Christ, who lives through the Holy Spirit for the angelic redemption, the Name of the restoration:"

[Graffin's restoration] *Messia ufar magno in seenchaldia mosomeda eaacha faronepseha Iesu Nazarene*: "I am anointed and redeemed from my soul and from all judgment by the name of Iao; redeem me, Jesus of Nazareth."[9]

So the initiators speak, and the initiate then responds:

> I am confirmed and redeemed, and I redeem my soul from this age and everything from it, in the name of Iao, who redeemed his soul by redemption in the living Christ.[10]

Finally those present declare, "Peace be to all on whom this Name rests." Then they anoint the initiate with balsam, for they say this perfume signifies the good odor over all things.

21.4 Some of them say it is pointless to lead to water. They mix oil and water together, with formulas like those we mentioned, and pour it on the head of those being initiated, and this they claim as "redemption." They also anoint with balsam. Others, rejecting all these rites, say that the mystery of the ineffable and invisible Power should not be performed through created things, visible and perishable, nor that of unthinkable and bodiless realities through sensible and corporeal things. Perfect redemption is simply the Gnosis of the inexpressible Greatness, for the deficiency and passion took place out of ignorance. By Gnosis the whole state of ignorance will be dissolved, so that Gnosis is the redemption of the inner man. This redemption is neither corporeal, since the body is perishable, nor psychic, since the soul too comes from the deficiency and is like a dwelling for the spirit. Redemption must therefore be spiritual. By Gnosis the inner, spiritual man is redeemed, and for such persons the knowledge of everything is sufficient: such is the true redemption.

21.5 There are others who redeem the dead at their last moment, pouring oil and water on their heads, or the aforesaid ointment with water and the aforesaid invocations, so that they may become incomprehensible and invisible to the Archons and Powers and their inner man may ascend above the invisible regions, abandoning the body to the created universe and leaving the soul with the Demiurge. And they teach them to say when they come to the Powers after death:

I am a son from the Father, the pre-existent Father, and a son in the Pre-existent. I have come to see everything, all that is mine and that is not mine, not completely foreign but belonging to Achamoth, who is female and made them by herself but originated from the Pre-existent; and I am returning again to my own place from which I came.

By saying this he will escape from the Powers. He will come to those about the Demiurge and say to them

I am a precious vessel, more precious than the female who made you. If your Mother is ignorant of her origin, I know myself,[11] and know whence I come, and I invoke the imperishable Sophia which is in the Father, the Mother of your Mother [Achamoth] who has no Father or male companion. She, female from female, made you in ignorance of her Mother while supposing herself to be alone; but I invoke her Mother.

When they hear these words, the angels about the Demiurge will be greatly troubled and will blame their source and the race of their Mother, but the initiate will go toward his own places, rejecting his bond, that is his soul.[12]

Valentinian redemption versus the rule of truth

This is what we have found out about that "redemption" of theirs. Since they differ from one another in teaching and tradition, and those known to be more recent try to discover and fructify what no one ever thought of, it is hard to describe the doctrines of all of them. **22.1** But we hold fast the rule of truth, that there is one almighty God who founded everything through his Word and arranged it and made everything out of the non-existent (Hermas *Mandate* 1), as scripture says: "By the Word of the Lord the heavens were made firm and by the Spirit of his mouth all their power" (Ps.32:2), and further, "All things were made through him and without him nothing was made" (John 1:3). Nothing is excepted from this "all things."
Through him the Father made everything, visible and invisible, sense-perceptible and intelligible, temporal for God's plan or eternal. He did not make them through angels or powers separate from his will, for God has no need of anything at all; but by his Word and his Spirit he makes everything, disposes everything, governs everything, gives existence to everything. He made the world, for the world is

part of "all things." He fashioned man. He is the God of Abraham, the God of Isaac, the God of Jacob. There is no other God above him, nor a Beginning or a Power or a Pleroma. He is the Father of our Lord Jesus Christ, as we shall show. Holding fast to this rule, we can easily show that however varied and lengthy are the sayings (of the heretics) they have deviated from the truth. In fact, nearly all heretics, however many they are, say there is one God, but they change him by their perverse doctrine, being as ungrateful to him who made them as the pagans are through idolatry. They despise the work fashioned by God, rejecting their own salvation, these most bitter accusers and false witnesses. They will rise in the flesh, willing or not, to know the power of the one who raises them from the dead, but they will not be counted with the just because of their lack of faith.

The Valentinians' "source and root"

22.2 Since the refutation and overthrow of all the heretics is necessarily varied and lengthy, and since we intend to refute all in accordance with the character of each, we have considered it necessary first of all to make known their source and root, so that when you know their most sublime "Abyss" you may know the tree from which such fruits have flowed forth.

Simon the Samaritan magician

23.1 In his desire to contend with the apostles,[13] so that he might seem a celebrity, he looked more deeply into all magic, in order to drive the many into a stupor. He lived under Claudius Caesar, by whom he is said to have been honored with a statue because of his magic. He was therefore glorified by many as God, and taught that he himself was the one who appeared among the Jews as Son, came down in Samaria as Father, and arrived among the other nations as Holy Spirit. He was the Supreme Power, the Father above all, though he was willing to be called by all the names people call him.

23.2 Simon the Samaritan, from whom all the heresies originated, had subject matter of this kind for his sect. When he had bought a certain prostitute named Helen in Tyre, the city of Phoenicia, he took her about with him, saying that she was the first Thought of his mind, the Mother of all, through whom he originally conceived of making the angels and archangels by whom this world was made. This Thought, leaping forth from him and knowing what her Father wished, came down to the lower regions and gave birth to the angels and powers by whom this world was made. After she gave birth to them she was made captive by them because of envy, since they did not want to be considered the offspring of anyone. Simon was totally unknown by them, while his Thought was held captive by the powers and angels emitted by her and suffered complete degradation, so that she was enclosed in a human body and through the ages passed into other female bodies as from one vessel into another. She was in that Helen for whom the Trojan war was undertaken.

Therefore when Stesichorus cursed her in his poems he went blind, but later, when he repented and praised her in his "palinodes," he saw again. As she passed from body into body and always suffered degradation, she finally stood in a brothel. She is the "lost sheep" (Luke 15:4–6). Therefore he himself came, first to take her up and free her from her bonds and then to provide men with salvation by the Gnosis of himself. As the angels were misgoverning the world, since each desired the primacy, he came down to correct the state of affairs, transformed and disguised as various principalities and powers and angels, so that among men he appeared as a man, though not a man, and he was thought to suffer in Judaea, though he did not suffer. He said the prophets spoke their prophecies when inspired by the angels who made the world; therefore those who have set their hope on him and Helen should no longer be concerned with them, but as free people do whatever they will. People are saved by his grace, not by just works (Eph.2:8–9), for works are just not by nature but by convention, in accord with the decrees of the world-creating angels who lead mankind into slavery through such precepts. Therefore he promised to destroy the world and free those who are his from the control of those who made it.

23.4 The priests of their mysteries live in debauchery and practice magic, as much as each one of them can. They employ exorcisms, incantations, love-philters, charms, familiar spirits, dream-inducers, and every other magical practice. They venerate images of Simon as Zeus and Helen as Athena. They bear the name "Simonians" derived from the founder of the most impious doctrine, and from them originated the "knowledge falsely so called" (1 Tim.6:20), as can be learned from their assertions.

Menander, another Samaritan magician

23.5 Simon's successor, another Samaritan, was Menander, who also reached the pinnacle of magic and said that the First Power was unknown to all, while he himself was the Savior sent by the invisible powers for the salvation of humanity. The world was made by angels who (like Simon) he says were emitted by Thought. By the magic taught by him he provided a "gnosis" to overcome the angels who made the world. For his disciples receive resurrection through baptism into him and can no longer die but continue on, ageless and immortal.

Saturninus of Antioch

24.1 From these [Simon and Menander] Saturninus, from Antioch by Daphne, and Basilides took their points of departure but set forth different doctrines, the one in Syria, the other at Alexandria. Saturninus like Menander set forth one Father unknown to all, who made angels, archangels, principalities, and powers. By seven of these angels was made "the world and everything in it" (cf. Acts 17:24). Man too is the work of the angels, who could not retain a shining image that appeared downward from the Supreme Power because it immediately ran back upward. They exhorted one another, saying, "Let us make man after the image and the likeness" (cf. Gen.1:26). When what they made could not stand erect, because of the weakness of the angels, but wriggled like a worm, the Power from above took pity on it, for it was made in its likeness, and emitted a spark of life that raised the man, set him on his feet, and made him live. After death this spark of life runs back above to what possesses the same nature as its own, but the rest returns to the original elements.

24.2 The Savior was ungenerated, incorporeal, and shapeless. He was seen as a man only in appearance. The God of the Jews is one of the angels. When the Father wanted to destroy all the archons, the Christ came for the destruction of the God of the Jews and the salvation of those who believed him and have the spark of his life. The angels had fashioned two kinds of men, one bad, the other good, and since demons helped the worse, the Savior came for the destruction of evil men and demons but the salvation of the good.

They say marriage and generation are from Satan. Many of his followers abstain from meat and lead many astray through simulated continence of this kind. Some prophecies were spoken by the angels who made the world, some by Satan. This angel is the adversary of the world-makers, especially the God of the Jews.

Baslides of Alexandria

24.3 In order to seem to have discovered something rather deep and persuasive, Basilides extended the development of his doctrine to infinity. He postulated that Mind was first born from the ungenerated Father, from Mind Logos, from Logos Forethought, from Forethought Wisdom and Power, and from Power and Wisdom the powers, archons, and angels whom he calls first, who made the first heaven. Similarly other angels emanated from these and made another heaven like the first, and so on with copies of those above them to a total of 365; the year therefore has 365 days.

24.4 The angels who occupy the lower heaven seen by us made everything that the world contains and shared among themselves the earth and the nations on it. The chief of the angels is the one regarded as the God of the Jews. When he wanted to subject the other nations to his own people, the Jews, the other archons rose up against him and fought him, and therefore the other peoples rose against his people.[14]

But the ungenerated and unnameable Father saw their perversity and sent his First-Begotten Mind, called Christ, to liberate those who believe him from the power of those who made the world. He appeared on earth as a man to the peoples of the archons and worked miracles. Consequently he did not suffer, but a certain Simon of Cyrene was impressed into service and carried his cross for him, and he was crucified[15] by ignorance and error,[16] transfigured by him so that he was supposed to be Jesus. As for Jesus himself, he assumed the appearance of Simon and stood by to deride the archons.[17] Since he was an incorporeal power and the Mind of the ungenerated Father, he transfigured himself as he wished, and it was thus that he ascended to him who sent him,[18] deriding them because he could not be held and was invisible to all. Those who know this have been freed from the world-making archons. One must not confess the one who was crucified but the one who came in human form, appeared to be crucified, was called Jesus, and was sent by the Father to destroy the works of the world-makers by this plan. If anyone confesses the Crucified, he says, he is still a slave and under the domination of those who made bodies; but he who denies is freed from them and knows the plan of the unbegotten Father.

24.5 Salvation is only for the soul; the body is perishable by nature. The prophecies come from the archons who made the world, but the law comes specifically from their chief, that is, the one who led the people out of the land of Egypt. One must despise the foods offered to idols, regard them as nothing and use them without the slightest fear, treating other actions with indifference, including every kind of debauchery. These people also practice magic, incantations, invocations, and all the rest. They make up names for the angels, claiming that these are in the first heaven, those in the second, and go on to give the names of the archons, angels, and powers of the 365 supposed heavens. They also say that the name under which the Savior descended and ascended is Caulacau (Is.28:10).

24.6 The person who has learned these things and knows all the angels and their origins will become invisible and intangible to the angels and their powers just as Caulacau was. As the Son is unknown to all, so they will not be known by anyone but when they know all [the angels] and pass through all [their realms] they are invisible and unknown to all. "You must know everyone," they say, "but no one should know you." Therefore such people are ready to deny and indeed cannot suffer for the Name, since they resemble all. Not many can know these things, but one out of a thousand and two out of ten thousand. They say Jews no longer exist, Christians not yet. Their mysteries must not be divulged but held secret in silence.

24.7 They determine the positions of the 365 heavens as the astrologers do, and borrow the astrologers' "theorems" in order to adapt them to the nature of their own doctrine. Their chief is Abrasax, and therefore he bears the number 365.[19]

Carpocrates

25.1 Carpocrates and his disciples say that the world and what is in it was made by angels much inferior to the ungenerated Father. Jesus was the son of Joseph and was like all other men, though superior to the others because his soul, strong and pure, remembered what it had seen in the sphere of the ungenerated God. Therefore a power was sent him by the Father so that he could escape from the world-makers and pass through all of them and, freed in all, ascend to him. So it goes for those with dispositions like his. The soul of Jesus was brought up in the customs of the Jews but despised them; therefore it received powers through which it destroyed the passions found in men as punishments.

25.2 The soul which like that of Jesus can despise the world-making archons can similarly receive powers to perform the same actions. Therefore they reach such a pitch of pride that some of them declare themselves equal to Jesus, while others say they are stronger and still others claim to be superior to his disciples such as Peter and Paul and the other apostles – who are in no way inferior to Jesus. For their souls, coming from the same sphere and therefore similarly despising the world-makers, have been held worthy of the same power and return to the same place. If anyone despises what is here more than Jesus did he can be better than him.

25.3 They too work magic arts and use philters and charms and familiar spirits and dream-senders and the other infamies, saying that they have power to dominate the archons and makers of this world, and not only them but also all their works in it.

These people have been sent by Satan to the pagans in order to slander the divine name of the church, so that when men hear them spoken of in various ways and imagine we are all like them, they may turn their ears away from the preaching of the truth or, viewing their conduct they may blaspheme all of us, even though we communicate with them in nothing, neither doctrine nor morals nor daily life. But these people, who live in debauchery and profess impious doctrines, abuse the Name as a veil to cover their wickedness. "Their judgment is just" (Rom.3:8) and they will receive retribution worthy of their works from God.

25.4 They have become so insane that they say they can freely commit every sacrilege and impiety. Good and evil, they say, are merely matters of opinion. Souls in their transmigration must try out every possible way of living and acting. If anyone is not careful to perform all these actions in one lifetime – acts which it is not right for us to mention (Eph.5:12) or hear or even think of, and we would not believe that men living in the same cities as us would perform anything of the sort – according to their own writings their souls must try out every possible way of living so that when they depart they have nothing left to do; they must act so that nothing may be lacking in their freedom and they may not be compelled to enter bodies again. This is why, they say, Jesus spoke this parable: "While you are on the way with your adversary, act to be freed from him, for fear that he may deliver you to the judge and the judge to the officer, and he put you in prison. Verily, I tell you, you will not get out until you have paid the last quadrant."[20] The "adversary" is one of the angels who are in the world, the one named the Devil; he was made in order to conduct the souls of the dead of this world to the archon. This archon is the first of the world-makers. He delivers the souls to another angel, his officer, to enclose them in other bodies, for the prison is the body. "You will not leave there until you have paid the last quadrant" means that no one escapes the power of the world-making angels, but constantly transmigrates as long as he has not performed all the acts in the world. When not one is left, then his soul is freed for that god who is above the world-making angels. And thus all souls will be saved, whether they hasten to take part in all actions during a single coming or, transmigrating or inserted from one body into another, accomplish all kinds of actions, pay their debt, and are freed so that they no longer are in bodies.

25.5 Do they actually perform these irreligious, unjust, and forbidden acts? I would not believe it. In their writings, however, it is written thus and they themselves state it, saying that Jesus spoke privately in a mystery to his disciples and apostles and told them to transmit his secrets to those who were worthy and in agreement.[21] Salvation is achieved through faith and love,[22] and all the rest is a matter of indifference. It is called good or bad according to human opinion, but nothing is evil by nature.

25.6 Some of them brand their disciples on the back part of the right ear lobe. One of them named Marcellina came to Rome under Anicetus and caused the destruction of many. They call themselves Gnostics. They have images, some painted, others made of various materials, for, they say, a portrait of Christ was made by Pilate in the time when Jesus was with men. They put crowns on these and show them forth with images of the worldly philosophers, that is, Pythagoras, Plato, Aristotle, and others, and pay them the same honors as among pagans.

Cerinthus in Asia

26.1 A certain Cerinthus in Asia taught that the world was not made by the First God but by a certain Power far separated and distant from the Principality which is over all and ignoring the God over all. Jesus was not born of a virgin, for that is impossible, but was the son of Joseph and Mary by a generation like that of all other men, and he was better than them in justice, prudence, and intelligence. After his baptism the Christ came down into him in the form of a dove from the Principality which is over all and then he proclaimed the unknown Father and worked miracles. At the end the Christ flew away from Jesus, Jesus suffered and was raised, but the Christ remained impassible, being spiritual.

The Ebionites

26.2 Those who are called Ebionites agree that the world was made by the real God but as to the Lord they profess the same opinions as Cerinthus and Carpocrates. They use only the Gospel according to Matthew and reject the apostle Paul, whom they call an apostate from the law. They strive with excessive pedantry to expound the prophecies. They practice circumcision and persevere in legal customs and the Jewish way of life, so that they pray toward Jerusalem as if it were the house of God.[23]

The Nicolaitans

26.3 The Nicolaitans have as their master Nicolaus, one of the seven who first were ordained to the diaconate by the apostles (Acts 6:5–6). They live in promiscuity. The Apocalypse of John fully reveals who they are: they teach that fornication and the eating of meats offered to idols are matters of indifference (Rev.2:14–15). Therefore the scripture too says of them, "But you have this in your favor, that you hate the works of the Nicolaitans, which I also hate" (2:6).

Cerdo and Marcion

27.1 A certain Cerdo likewise began with the doctrine of the Simonians. He came to Rome under Hyginus, ninth to occupy the place of the episcopate by succession from the apostles, and he taught that the God announced by the law and the prophets was not the Father of our Lord Jesus Christ. The former was known; the second, unknown; one is just and the other is good.

27.2 For a successor he had Marcion, a man from Pontus who developed his teaching by impudently blaspheming the God announced by the law and the prophets, calling him the creator of evils, desirous of wars, inconstant in his thoughts and contradicting himself. As for Jesus, sent by the Father above the god who created the world, he came into Judaea in the times of the governor Pontius Pilate, procurator for Tiberius Caesar, manifest in human form to those who were in Judaea, abolishing the prophets, the law, and all the works of the god who made the world, whom Marcion called the Cosmocrator. Beyond that, he circumcised the Gospel according to Luke, taking out everything written about the birth of the Lord and removing many passages from his teaching, those in which he plainly acknowledged the Creator of this world as his Father. Thus Marcion persuaded his disciples that he was more truthful than the apostles who transmitted the gospel, and handed over to them not the gospel but a modest portion of the gospel. He also cut away the letters of the apostle Paul, suppressing all the texts in which the apostle plainly spoke of the God who made the world as the Father of our Lord Jesus Christ, as well as all those in which the apostle mentions the prophecies predicting the coming of the Lord.

27.3 He said there would be salvation only for souls that had learned his doctrine, while the body, as taken from the earth, cannot share in salvation. To his blasphemy against God he adds, as a true mouth of the devil, completely opposed to the truth, that Cain and those like him, the men of Sodom, the Egyptians and the like, the pagans who walked in every combination of evil, were saved by the Lord when he descended into Hades, for they ran to him and he took them into his kingdom; Abel, however, and Enoch and Noah and the rest of the righteous, Abraham and the patriarchs after him, with all the prophets and all who pleased God, did not share in salvation – as the serpent who was in Marcion proclaimed. These men, he says, knew that their god was always testing them, and in the belief that he was testing them then they did not run to Jesus and did not believe his proclamation, and therefore their souls remained in Hades.

Marcion is unique, but all come from Simon

27.4 But since this Marcion is the only one who openly dared to circumcise the scriptures and attack God more shamelessly than all others, we shall write against him separately, refuting him, with God's help, from his writings and from those words of the Lord and the Apostle which he respected and uses. For now we have to mention him so that you may know that all who in any way adulterate the truth and harm the church's preaching are disciples and successors of Simon the Samaritan magician. Although in their aim of deceiving others they do not confess the name of their teacher, his is the doctrine they teach. They set forth the name of Christ Jesus as an incitement, but in various ways introducing the impiety of Simon they cause the death of many, through the good name spreading their evil doctrine, and through the gentleness and modesty of this name presenting the bitter and malignant poison of the serpent who introduced apostasy.

28.1 Beginning with those we have just mentioned, there arose the many ramifications of the heresies because many, or rather all, among them want to be teachers and to leave the heresy in which they began and create one doctrine from another and then another from the previous one, declaring that they themselves invented whatever system they fabricated.

The Encratites and Tatian

Thus, for example, people called Encratites ("continent"), inspired by Saturninus and Marcion, have proclaimed abstinence from marriage, rejecting the ancient work of God and implicitly accusing him who made male and female for procreation (Gen.1:27–28), and they have introduced abstinence from what they call "animated," being ungrateful to the God who made everything. They also deny the salvation of the first-formed man. This last point was invented among them in our own time when a certain Tatian first introduced this blasphemy. While he heard the teaching of Justin and stayed with him, he set forth no such doctrine, but after Justin's martyrdom he separated from the church. Lifted up and inflated by his claim to be a teacher, as if he were better than the rest, he created his own style of doctrine. Like the Valentinians he set forth a myth about invisible Aeons; like Marcion and Saturninus he called marriage corruption and debauchery, and finally he rejected the salvation of Adam.

Barbelo-Gnostics

29.1 Beyond these people, a multitude of Gnostics has arisen out of the Simonians already mentioned, just as mushrooms come up from the earth. We are going to report their principal doctrines.[24]
Some say that there is a never-ageing Aeon in a Virginal Spirit called Barbelo, and in this Spirit an unnameable Father, who wanted to reveal himself to Barbelo. This Thought came forth and stood in his sight and asked for Foreknowledge. When Foreknowledge also came forth, they both requested Imperishability, and she came forth; then Eternal Life. Barbelo rejoiced in them and, looking toward the Greatness and delighting in the Conception, she bore a Light like it. This was the Beginning of the illumination and generation of all things.
When the Father saw this Light he anointed it with his own goodness so that it would be perfect. This is Christ ["anointed"], who then asked that a helper, Mind, be given him, and Mind came forth. Then the Father emitted Logos. Next there were unions of Thought and

Logos, Imperishability and Christ; Eternal Life was joined with Will and Mind with Foreknowledge. These emanations magnified the great Light and Barbelo.

29.2 Afterwards from Thought and Logos was emitted Self-Born as a representation of the great Light; it was greatly honored and all things were subjected to it (cf. Ps.8:6–7). With it was emitted Truth, and thus there was another pair, Self-Born and Truth. From the Light which is Christ and from Imperishability four luminaries were emitted to stand about Self-Born; again, from Will and Eternal Life four emissions took place to serve the four luminaries. These emissions were called Grace, Willing, Intelligence, and Thinking. Grace was united with the first great Light, Savior, also called Armozel; Willing with the second, called Raguel; Intelligence with the third, called David; Thinking with the fourth, called Eleleth.[25]

29.3 When all these had been established Self-Born also emitted the Perfect and True Man, also called Adamas because he is adamant, as are his origins. He was separated from the first Light by Armozel. Perfect Gnosis was emitted by Self-Born along with the Man, and was joined to him; from her he knows the one who is above all. Unconquered Power was given him by the Virginal Spirit in which all things rest to praise the great Aeon. Thus were revealed the Mother, the Father, and the Son: from the Man and Knowledge was born the Tree, itself also called Knowledge (Gen.2:9).

29.4 Then from the first angel with Monogenes (Self-Born) was emitted Holy Spirit, also called Sophia and Prunicus. When this Spirit saw that all the others had partners but she did not, she sought someone with whom to be united. When she found none, she stretched and looked down to the lower regions in the belief that she would find one there. Not finding one, she leapt back, wearied because she had made this effort without the approval of the Father. Afterwards, driven by simplicity and kindness, she generated a work in which were Ignorance and Presumption. This work is called Proarchon, the fashioner of this universe. He stole a great power from his mother and departed from her to the lower regions and made the firmament of heaven, in which he dwells. And since he is Ignorance he made the powers beneath him: angels, firmaments, and everything earthly. Then he was united with Presumption and generated Wickedness, Jealousy, Envy, Strife, and Desire. When they were generated, the Mother Sophia fled in grief and withdrew above, becoming the Eighth for those who count from below. When she withdrew, he thought he was alone, and therefore he said, "I am a jealous God and there is none but me" (Exod.20:5).[26] Such are the lies of these heretics.

Ophite Gnostics

30.1 Still others provide the following portentous account. There was a first Light in the power of the Abyss, blessed and imperishable and unlimited; this is the Father of All, called First Man. From him proceeded a Thought, the son of him who emitted it; this is the Son of Man, the Second Man.[27] Below them was the Holy Spirit, and under this Spirit were the separate elements, water, darkness, abyss, chaos; above these elements was borne the Spirit, called First Woman (Gen.1:2). Then the First Man exulted with his Son over the beauty of the Spirit, that is, the Woman, and he illuminated her; thus he generated from her an imperishable Light, the Third Male, called Christ, the son of the First and Second Man and of the Holy Spirit, the First Woman.

30.2 The Father and the Son then united with the Woman, whom they called also Mother of the Living (Gen.3:20). But she could not hold up or contain the greatness of the Light, which overflowed above the left-hand parts. And thus only Christ was their Son, as being on the right hand, and raised up above with his Mother into the imperishable Aeon. This is the true and holy Church, the convocation, association, and union of the Father of All, the First Man, and of the Son, the Second Man, and of Christ, their Son, and of the Woman we have mentioned.

30.3 Then the Power which flowed out of the Woman, with the moisture of light, left the domain of the Fathers and fell downward by her own will, having with her the moisture of light. This Power is called Left and Prunicus and Sophia and Male-Female. She came down all at once into the immobile waters and put them in motion, plunging boldly into them to the bottom, and took a body from them. Everything ran toward her moisture of light and adhered to it and imprisoned it on all sides; without this moisture of light she might have been completely absorbed and submerged by matter. While she was thus enchained and weighed down by the body of matter, she once came to herself and tried to escape from the waters and ascend to her Mother, but she could not, because of the heaviness of the body placed around her. She felt that her condition was very bad, and she planned to hide the light from above, for fear that it too, like her, would be harmed by the inferior elements. When she received power from the moisture of the light within her, she leapt forth and was raised into the height, and when she reached the height she extended herself and made this visible heaven, and she remained under the heaven she made, still having the form of a watery body. When she had felt desire for the light from above and had received a new power, she put off her body entirely and was freed from it. They call this body her son and they call her Woman from Woman.

30.4 Her son had an inspiration of imperishability that his Mother left him, because of which he was able to work.

Become strong, he himself emitted a son from the waters, without his Mother; for he did not know his Mother. His son, like his father, emitted another son; this third generated a fourth, the fourth a fifth, the fifth a sixth, and the sixth a seventh. Thus was finished the Hebdomad (cf. Gen.2:2), with the Mother occupying the eighth place, and as they have a hierarchy in origin so also they have a hierarchy of dignity and power.

30.5 Here are the names that they gave to what they invented. The first from the Mother is called Ialdabaoth; the one from him is Iao, from him Sabaoth, the fourth Adoneus [Adonai], the fifth Eloeus [Elohim], the sixth Horeus [Or, light], the seventh and last, Astaphaeus. These Heavens, Virtues, Powers, Angels, and Creators sit in order in the heaven, ranked by origins, while remaining invisible. They rule over celestial and terrestrial affairs. The first of them, Ialdabaoth, despised the Mother when without her permission he made sons and grandsons, that is, Angels, Archangels, Virtues, Powers, and Dominions. His sons had just come into existence when they turned against him to dispute the first place. Sad and despondent, Ialdabaoth looked down at the low-lying dregs of matter and consolidated his lust for it. From that, they say, a son was born, and this is Mind, with the twisted shape of a serpent (cf. Gen.3:1). From him came spirit and soul and everything worldly, and from him were born Oblivion and Malice and Jealousy and Envy and Death. The Father drove out this serpentine and twisted Mind of theirs for its prevarication when it had been with the Father in heaven and in paradise (cf. Gen. 3:14).

30.6 This is why Ialdabaoth exulted and boasted over everything below him and said, "I am Father and God and there is none above me" (Is.45:5–6; 46:9). But the Mother heard these words and cried out against him, "Do not lie, Ialdabaoth; above you are the Father of all, the First Man, and the Man, the Son of Man." All were disturbed by the new voice and the unexpected appellation and, while they asked whence the cry had come,[28] Ialdabaoth said to them, to turn them away and bring them to himself, "Come, let us make a man after the image."[29] When six Powers heard this, the Mother gave them the idea of a man in order to empty them of their original power through him. They came together and formed a man immense in breadth and length. When he could only writhe they brought him to their Father. Sophia effected this so that she might empty Ialdabaoth of the dew of light and so that the man, deprived of his power, could not stand erect against those who are above him. They say that when Ialdabaoth breathed into the man a breath of life (Gen.2:7) he inadvertently emptied himself of his power. Henceforward the man possessed mind and thought, and (they say) these are what are saved, and immediately he gave thanks to the First Man, abandoning those who made him.

30.7 Ialdabaoth jealously wanted to empty the man by means of the woman, and from his thought he drew out woman, but Prunicus seized her and invisibly emptied her of power. The others came up and, admiring her beauty, called her Eve, and desired her to generate sons from her, who they say are Angels. Their Mother then planned to seduce Eve and Adam through the serpent, so that they would transgress the commandment of Ialdabaoth. Eve readily believed him as if she heard from the Son of God, and she persuaded Adam to eat from the tree from which God said not to eat. When they had eaten, they say, they knew that Power which is above all and withdrew from those who made them. Prunicus, seeing that these had been overcome through their own creation, rejoiced greatly and again cried out that since the imperishable Father already existed, Ialdabaoth lied when he called himself Father, and since Man and First Woman already existed, he sinned when a made an imperfect copy.

30.8 Because of the Oblivion about him, Ialdabaoth paid no attention to these words and drove Adam and Eve out of paradise because they had transgressed his commandment. He had to generate sons for Adam out of Eve but did not achieve this, since her Mother acted against him in everything and secretly emptied Adam and Eve of their dew of light, so that the spirit from the Supreme Power might not receive curse or blame. They teach that thus emptied of the divine substance, they were cursed by Ialdabaoth and cast down from heaven into this world. The serpent who had acted against the Father was also cast down by him into this world, though he put under his control the angels who are here and generated six sons, himself being the seventh, in imitation of the Hebdomad about the Father. These, they say, are the seven cosmic demons, always hostile and resisting the human race since because of them their father was driven down below. 30.9 Adam and Eve formerly had light, luminous, and so to speak spiritual bodies, as they had been fashioned. But when they came here, the bodies became dark, fat, and idle. Even their souls became soft and languid because they had only the worldly breathing from the Maker – until Prunicus took pity on them and gave them back the sweet odor of the dew of light. Because of this they recognized themselves and knew they were naked and that their body was material. They knew that they bore death in themselves and were patient, knowing that they had been clothed with a body only for a time. Guided by Sophia, they found food and when filled they united carnally and generated Cain. But the fallen serpent and its sons immediately seized him, corrupted him, filled him with worldly oblivion, and sent him into stupidity and audacity, so that when he killed his brother Abel he was the first to reveal jealousy and death. After them, in accordance with the providence of Prunicus (they say) were generated Seth, then Norea; from whom the rest of mankind (they say) were generated, and sent by the lower Hebdomad into all malice and apostasy from the higher Hebdomad and into idolatry and universal contempt, while the Mother never stopped opposing the work of these powers and saving what was her own, the dew of light. They want the sacred Hebdomad to consist of the seven stars called planets, and they say that the serpent cast forth has two names, Michael and Sammael.

30.10 Ialdabaoth, angered by human beings because they did not worship him or honor him as Father and God, sent the deluge against them so that all would perish at once. Once more Sophia opposed him and those with Noah in the ark were saved because of the dew of light from her, and through her the world was again filled with human beings. Among them, Ialdabaoth chose a certain Abraham and made a covenant with him that if his seed would continue to serve him he would give them the earth as an inheritance. Later through Moses he brought forth from Egypt the descendants of Abraham, gave them the law, and made them Jews. From them the seven gods, also called the sacred Hebdomad, chose their own heralds to glorify each and proclaim him as God, so that the rest of mankind, hearing the glorification, might also serve those who were proclaimed by the prophets as Gods.

30.11 Thus they distribute the prophets: of Ialdabaoth, Moses and Joshua son of Nun and Amos and Habakkuk; of Iao, Samuel and

Nathan and Jonah and Micah; of Sabaoth, Elijah and Joel and Zechariah; of Adonai, Isaiah and Ezekiel and Jeremiah and Daniel; of Elohim, Tobias and Haggai; of Oraeus, Micah and Nahum; of Astaphaeus, Esdras and Zephaniah. Each of these prophets glorified his own Father and God, while Sophia spoke much through them (they say) about the First Man and the imperishable Aeon and that Christ who is above, recalling and reminding men of the imperishable light and the First Man and proclaiming the descent of Christ. The Archons were terrified by these and marveled at the novelty in what was proclaimed by the prophets. Prunicus worked through Ialdabaoth without his knowledge and effected the emissions of two men, one from the sterile Elizabeth (Luke 1:7), the other from the Virgin Mary (1:34–35).

30.12 Prunicus herself found rest neither in heaven nor on earth, but in affliction called the Mother to aid her. Her Mother, the First Woman, took pity on the repentance of her daughter and asked the First Man to send Christ to her as a helper, and he came down, sent to his sister and to the dew of light. Learning that her brother was coming down to her, the Sophia below [Achamoth] announced his coming through John and prepared a baptism of repentance (Luke 3:2–3,16) and formed Jesus in advance so that at his descent the Christ might find a pure vessel and that through her son Ialdabaoth the Woman might be proclaimed by Christ. The Christ then descended through the seven heavens, assimilated to their sons (they say), and gradually emptied them of power; the whole dew of light (they say) ran toward him. And when Christ came down into this world he first put on his sister Sophia and both exulted, taking their rest in each other; and they define them as the Bridegroom and the Bride (John 3:29). Jesus, because born of the Virgin by the work of God, was more wise, pure, and just than all other men (cf. Luke 2:40,52). Christ descended into him in the embrace of Sophia (3:22), and thus Jesus Christ came to be.

30.13 Many disciples of Jesus, they say, did not recognize the descent of Christ into him, but when Christ came down into Jesus he began to perform miracles and cures and proclaim the unknown Father and acknowledge openly that he was the Son of the First Man. In their anger the Archons and the Father of Jesus worked to kill him, and when he was being led to death, they say the Christ with Sophia withdrew into the imperishable Aeon, while Jesus was crucified. The Christ did not forget what was his own but sent from above a power into him which raised him in a body. They call this body psychic and spiritual, for he left his worldly elements in the world. The disciples saw that he had risen but did not recognize him (Luke 24:16), and did not even know by whose grace Jesus arose from the dead. And they say this was the greatest error among his disciples, that they thought he had risen with a worldly body, not knowing that "flesh and blood do not inherit the kingdom of God" (1 Cor.15:50).

30.14   They want to confirm the descent of Christ and his ascension from the fact that the disciples say that neither before the baptism nor after the resurrection from the dead did Jesus perform anything significant. These disciples did not know that Jesus was united to Christ, the imperishable Aeon to the Hebdomad, and they call the worldly body "psychic." After his resurrection Jesus remained on earth for eighteen months, and when intelligence descended in him he taught what was obviously true, and he taught these [secret] matters to a few of his disciples, who he knew were capable of under-standing such great mysteries (cf. Mark 4:11 and parallels), and thus he was taken up into heaven. There Jesus sits at the right hand of the Father Ialdabaoth to receive to himself, after they have put off the worldly flesh, the souls of those who knew him. He enriches himself, while his Father is in ignorance and does not even see him, for when Jesus enriches himself with holy souls the Father suffers a loss and diminishes, emptied of his power through the souls. For he will not possess the holy souls so as to send them back into the world, but only those which are from his substance, that is, from the "breathing." The final end will take place when the whole dew of the spirit of light is gathered together and taken into the Aeon of imperishability.

Miscellaneous sects

Such are the doctrines of these people, from which, like the Lernaean hydra, a beast with multiple heads, is generated the school of Valentinus. Some, however, say that Sophia herself was the serpent, and for this reason it rose against the Maker of Adam and insinuated Gnosis into men, and therefore the serpent was called "wiser than all others" (Gen.3:1). The position and shape of our intestines, through which food is brought in, shows hidden within us the generative substance with the form of the serpent.

31.1   Still others say that Cain came from the Absolute Sovereignty above, and Esau, Korah, and the men of Sodom, along with every person of this sort, have the same origin. They were hated by the Creator because though attacked they suffered no harm, for Sophia took to herself what was her own in them. The traitor Judas was the only one of the apostles who possessed this knowledge (cf. John 13:27). For this reason he brought about the mystery of the betrayal; through him all things on earth and in heaven were destroyed. They provide a work to this effect called the "Gospel of Judas."

31.2 I have collected writings of theirs in which they urge the destruction of the works of the Womb, calling the Creator of heaven and earth Womb. They cannot be saved unless they experience everything, as Carpocrates also taught. At each sinful and disgusting action an angel is present; the agent must act boldly and make the impurity fall upon the angel present in the act, saying to him, "O angel, I use your work; O power, I perform your operation." This is "perfect knowledge," to perform without fear such actions as may not even be named.

Conclusion of Book I

31.3 From such mothers and fathers and grandparents have come Valentinus and his disciples, as their own doctrines and systems show them to be. It was necessary to provide clear proof and bring their teachings to light. Perhaps some of them will repent and by returning to the only God, the Creator and Maker of the universe, can be saved.

BOOK II

SUMMARY OF BOOK I

Pr.1 In the first book, the one before this, we attacked the "Knowledge falsely so called" and showed you, beloved, the whole falsehood that was invented by the disciples of Valentinus in its many contradictory forms. We also set forth the opinions of those who lived earlier, showing that they disagreed with themselves as well as with the truth. We diligently described the views of Mark the magician, since he belongs among them, as well as his works; we reported the passages from the scriptures that they try to adapt to his fiction, and we carefully described the way they try to assert the truth through numbers and the twenty-four letters of the alphabet. We have related how they say that the created world was made after the image of their invisible Pleroma, and all that they think and teach about the Demiurge. We have revealed the doctrine of their ancestor, Simon the Samaritan magician, and all his successors, and we have also set forth the multitude of Gnostics descended from him. We have noted their differences, doctrines, and successions, have described all the heresies founded by them, and shown that all the heretics began from Simon and introduced their impious and irreligious doctrines into this world. We have revealed their "redemption," the way they initiate their adepts, their ritual formulas, and their mysteries. And we recalled that there is one God the Creator, not a "fruit of deficiency,"[1] and that there is nothing above him or beyond him.

SUMMARY OF BOOK II

Pr. 2 In this book we shall treat only what is useful for us and what time permits, and we shall refute their whole system through the major points. This is why, since it is a question of detecting and refuting their doctrine, we have given this very title to our work; for their hidden pairs have to be destroyed by stating and refuting them when brought to light, as well as the "Abyss," proving that it never existed and does not exist now.

1.1 We must begin with the primary and most important point, with God the Demiurge who made heaven and earth and everything in them, whom these blasphemers call "fruit of deficiency," and we shall show that there is nothing either above him or beyond him, and that he freely made everything, not moved by another but on his own initiative, since he is the only God and the only Lord and the only Creator and the only Father, the only one who contains all and provides being to all.

Divine transcendence

1.2 How could there be above this God another Pleroma or Beginning or Power or another God, when it is necessary for the God of all these to contain everything in his immensity and be contained by none? If there is something outside him, he is no longer the Pleroma of everything, nor does he contain everything; for to this Pleroma or the God above everything there will be lacking what they say is found outside him. That which lacks something or from which something has been withdrawn by someone is not the Pleroma of everything.

Furthermore, this being will have a beginning, a middle, and an end in relation to those outside him. If the end is in what lies below, the beginning is in those above. Similarly in the other directions it is necessary that he will know the same situation: he will be contained, determined, and enclosed by what is outside him. For the end which is below necessarily surrounds and encloses the being which is ended in it. Thus, then, their so-called Father of All, whom they also call Pre-existent or Pre-beginning, and their Pleroma with him, and Marcion's good God, will be contained, enclosed, and surrounded by another Principle, which is necessarily larger than it, since what contains is greater than what is contained; what is larger is also stronger and more the Lord; and what is larger and stronger and more the Lord will be God.

1.3 Since they say that something exists outside the Pleroma, into which they think that Power wandering from above came down, they must choose one of two views. Either this "outside" will contain the Pleroma and the Pleroma will be contained – otherwise there will not be something "outside," for if anything is outside the Pleroma the Pleroma will necessarily be within what they call outside the Pleroma, and the Pleroma, with the first God, will be contained by what is outside; or else the Pleroma and what is outside it will be immensely distant and separated from each other. But if they say this, there will be a "tertium quid," with this immense separation between the Pleroma and what is outside it, and this "tertium quid" will limit and contain the other two, and will be greater than both the Pleroma and what is outside it, since it contains both in its bosom.

Exegesis and theology

10.1 In their desire to explain the obscure passages of scripture (obscure not because they refer to another God but because they speak of the "economies" of God), they invent another God, weaving ropes from sand and developing a major question from a minor one. No question is resolved by another question. Intelligent people do not resolve one ambiguity through another, nor an enigma through a greater one. Such matters find resolutions out of what is evident, consistent, and clear.

Human and divine thought

13.2 The first movement of mind in relation to some object is called "notion." When this continues, strengthens, and possesses the entire soul, it is called "comprehensive thinking." In turn, this, when it spends much time on the same object and is so to speak tested, becomes "acceptance." This acceptance greatly amplified becomes "deliberation." When this deliberation grows and is amplified it becomes "interior discourse," from which comes the emitted word.

But all the movements we have mentioned are one and the same thing, taking their beginning from mind and receiving various names with growth. The human body too is sometimes that of a boy, sometimes that of a man, sometimes that of an old man, receiving names from its growth and continuity, not from any change of substance or loss of body. So it is with mental activities: one thinks of something and considers it; if one considers it, one reflects on it; if one reflects on it, one deliberates; if one deliberates, one holds an interior discourse; finally, one expresses this interior discourse. And the mind governs all these movements, as we have said; it remains invisible and by these movements emits the word from itself like a ray, but is not emitted by anything else.

13.3 If they had known the scriptures and had been taught by the truth, they would know that God is not like men (Num.23:19) and that God's thoughts are not like men's thoughts (Is.55:8–9). For the Father of all is at a great remove from human emotions and passions. He is unified, not composite, without diversity of members, completely similar and equal to himself, since he is all Mind, all Spirit, all Mentality, all Thought, all Word, all Hearing, all Eye, all Light, and entirely the source of every good thing – as religious and pious men rightly say of God.

13.4 But he is still above this and therefore ineffable. For he is rightly called all-embracing Mind, but unlike the human mind; and most justly called Light, but Light in no way resembling the light we know. Thus also in regard to all the other appellations the Father of all in no way resembles the weakness of humanity, and while he is given these names because of his love he is considered above them because of his greatness. If in the case of men the mind is not emitted and if he who emits the rest is not separated from the living subject, but only his movements and dispositions are evident outside, this is all the more true of the God who is all Mind and would never be separate from himself or be emitted as something is emitted by something else.

13.8 What has just been said about the emission of Mind also weighs against the followers of Basilides and the other Gnostics from whom the Valentinians received these beginnings of emissions, as we proved in the first book. We have plainly shown that the first emission of Mind is absurd and impossible. Let us see about the other emissions. From Mind, they say, Logos and Life were emitted as makers of this Pleroma. When they view the emission of Logos, that is, Word, in human fashion and make conjectures about God, they say as if making a great discovery that Logos was emitted by Mind. Everyone knows that this may rightly be said about men, but in the case of the God who is above all, since he is all Mind and all Logos, as we said before, and has nothing in himself either posterior or prior, but remains as a whole equal and similar and enduring as one, an emission of this kind could not ensue. Just as it is right to say that he is all Seeing and all Hearing – for as he sees he hears, and as he hears he sees – so it is also right to say that he is all Mind and all Logos, and in that he is Mind he is Logos, and his Mind is this Logos. In speaking thus one will remain subordinate to the Father of all but use more suitable terms than those who transfer the generation of the expressed word of men to the eternal Logos of God and give the expressions a beginning and a genesis as they would give it to their own word. But how will the Logos of God, or rather God himself, since he is Logos, differ from the word of men, if it has the same order and manner of generation?

Origin of Valentinian theories in poetry

14.1 A poet of the Old Comedy, Aristophanes,[2] spoke with much more probability and elegance about the genesis of everything in a theogony. According to him, from Night and Silence was emitted Chaos, then from Chaos and Night, Eros; from Eros came forth Light, then all the rest of the first generation of gods. After this the poet introduced the second generation of gods and the making of the world; then he tells of the shaping of mankind by the second gods. From this, the Valentinians shaped their myth like a natural history, simply changing the names of the gods and showing the same beginning and emission of everything. For Night and Silence they name Abyss and Silence; for Chaos, Mind; for Eros, by which according to the comic poet all the rest were set in order, they have introduced the Logos. In place of the first and greatest of the gods they imagined the Aeons, in place of the second gods they tell of the activities of their Mother outside the Pleroma, calling her "Second Ogdoad," to whom they ascribe the making of the world and the fashioning of mankind just as the poet did, and claiming that they alone know ineffable and unknown mysteries. In reality they transfer to their own system what is said in theaters everywhere by actors with splendid voices, or rather they use the same plots and simply change the names.

Origin of Valentinian theories in philosophy

14.2 Not only do they put forward as their own what is found with the comic poets, but they collect what has been said by all the people who do not know God and are called philosophers; they have woven together a kind of cento out of many wretched pieces and prepared a false surface with subtle speech. The doctrine they present is new because it has been elaborated recently with a new art, but it is really old and worthless, since it was stitched together from old doctrines smelling of ignorance and lack of religion.

Origin of Valentinian theories: Other examples

14.5 When they say that the Savior was made from all the Aeons, which set in him their "flower," they bring nothing new to the Pandora of Hesiod,[3] for what he says of her, they teach about the Savior, making him into a Pandora, as if each of the Aeons gave his best to him. They derived from the Cynics, since they share their opinions, their idea about the indifferent nature of foods and of various actions, and the notion that because of their excellent origin they cannot be defiled by anything at all. And they employ subtle investigations in the manner of Aristotle when they try to attack the faith.

14.6 They received their desire to make everything numerical from the Pythagoreans, who were the first to postulate numbers for the origin of everything and, as the beginning of the numbers, even and odd, from which they derive the perceptible and the intelligible.[4] They distinguish the beginnings of material substance from those of Mind and substantial reality, and from these kinds of principles everything was made, like a statue from bronze and formation. They have adapted this structure to what is outside the Pleroma. The Pythagoreans speak of the beginnings of Mind when the spirit, with an intuition of the original unity, seeks until in weariness it reaches the One and indivisible. The beginning of everything and the source of the universe is the One, from which proceed the dyad and tetrad and pentad and the rest. They apply these texts word for word to their Pleroma and their Abyss, and they try to introduce their pairs, starting from the One. Mark boasts of discovering something of his own that is newer than others, but he is setting forth the tetrad of Pythagoras as the origin and mother of everything.

Basilidians against Valentinians, both wrong

16.4 What the Valentinians criticize us for – remaining in the lower Hebdomad, not raising our mind on high or thinking of what is above (Col.3:2) because we do not accept their portentous sayings – the disciples of Basilides apply to them, claiming that they still wallow in things below, beneath the first and second Ogdoad, and imagine that beyond the thirty Aeons they have already found the Father above all, instead of raising themselves by intellectual research the Pleroma above the 365 heavens, or more than forty-five Ogdoads. But one might justly attack the Basilidians by inventing

4380 heavens or Aeons, since the days of the year have this many hours. And if someone adds to this figure the number of the hours of night, doubling the number, he will imagine that he has discovered an immeasurable production of Aeons against the Father above all. Considering himself the most "perfect" of all, he will criticize all for being incapable of rising into the height of the multitude of heavens or Aeons proclaimed by him but, being deficient, continuing in what is below or in the middle.

Did they imitate Menander?

18.5 It seems to me that they assigned to their Aeon the passion of the man who in the comic poet Menander is truly loving and hateful, for it is the image of an unfortunate lover that these writers of fiction had in mind, rather than that of a spiritual and divine substance.

False teaching on the spiritual seed

19.7 The falsity of their doctrine on the seed is more plainly proved, as anyone can understand, by their saying that "the souls that have the seed from the Mother are better than the others and for this reason were honored by the Demiurge and appointed princes, kings, and priests." For if that were true, the high priest Caiaphas would have been the first to believe in the Lord, along with Annas and the other high priests and the doctors of the law and the rulers of the people, since they were of the Mother's race, and even before them Herod the king. But neither he nor the high priests nor the rulers nor famous men of the people ran to the Lord but, on the contrary, the beggars sitting along the roads, the deaf, the blind, and those who were downtrodden and despised – as Paul says: "Look to your calling, brothers, there are not many wise among you, not many noble, not many powerful, but God chose the contemptible elements of the world" (1 Cor.1:26–27). The souls in question were therefore not better because of a seed deposited in them, nor for this reason were they honored by the Demiurge.

Valentinian use of Hesiod and Pindar

21.2 They have invented an Aeon formed out of all the Aeons and called "All" because it comes from all. This the poet Hesiod clearly designated, calling it "Pandora" because an excellent "gift from all," the Aeons, was gathered in it. In regard to the heretics, Hermes "set crafty words and a deceitful character in them,"[5] to lead stupid men astray and make them believe their fictions. For their mother, that is, Leto, moved them secretly, without the knowledge of the Demiurge, to pronounce profound and ineffable mysteries – to itching ears (2 Tim.4:3).

Their Mother expressed this mystery not only through Hesiod but also in the lyric poems of Pindar, expressing it very subtly in order to conceal it from the Demiurge. It was in the episode of Pelops, whose flesh, cut in pieces by his father [Tantalus], was collected, united, and compacted by all the gods, thus constituting a figure of Pandora.[6] Instigated by the Mother, they say the same as do the poets; they share their kind and their spirit.

Gospel chronology and "recapitulation"

22.3 One must marvel at how they claim to have discovered the "depths of God" but have not investigated in the gospels how many times the Savior went up to Jerusalem at Passover after his his baptism, in accordance with the custom for Jews of every region to meet in Jerusalem every year and there celebrate the paschal feast. First, when he made the water into wine in Cana of Galilee (John 2:1–11), he went up on the feast day of the Passover (2:13), when it is written: "Many believed in him, seeing the signs that he did" (2:23), as John the Lord's disciple states. Then he withdrew and is found in Samaria, when he disputed with the Samaritan woman (4:1–42), and at a distance cured the centurion's son with a word, saying, "Go, your son lives" (4:50). And after this again a second time he went up to Jerusalem for the feast of Passover (5:1), when he cured the paralytic who had lain by the pool for thirty-eight years, ordering him to arise, take up his bed, and go away (5:2–15). Then he withdrew across the sea of Tiberias, where when a great crowd followed him he filled all that multitude with five loaves, and twelve baskets of fragments were left (6:1–13). Then when he had raised Lazarus from the dead (11:1–44) and plots were made by the Pharisees, he withdrew to the city of Ephraim (11:47–54); and it is written that "six days before the Passover he came into Bethany" (12:1) from there, and from Bethany went up to Jerusalem (12:12), where he ate the Passover and suffered the following day. Everyone will agree that these three Passovers are not one year. If these people who boast that they "know" everything do not know that the month in which the Passover is celebrated, in which the Lord suffered, is not the twelfth but the first, they can learn it from Moses (Ex.12:12, etc.). Thus their interpretation of the year and the twelfth month is false, and they must reject either their interpretation or the Gospel; otherwise, how did the Lord preach for only one year?

Christ was not 30 but 49

22.4 And even if he was only thirty years old when he came to baptism, he had the perfect age of a master when he came to Jerusalem, so that he could rightly be called master by all. For he did not seem something other than he was, as the Docetists suppose, but what he was, he also appeared to be. As a master, he had the age of a master. He neither rejected nor went beyond the human condition and did not abolish in his person the law of human growth, but he sanctified every age by the resemblance we have with him. In fact, he came to save all men through himself: all, I mean, who through him are reborn into God, infants and children and boys and young men and elders. Therefore he passed through every age, and among infants was an infant, sanctifying infants; among children a child, sanctifying those who have this age and likewise becoming for them a model of piety and justice and submission (Luke 2:41–52); among young men a young man, becoming a model to young men and sanctifying them for the Lord. Thus also he was an elder among elders, in order to be a perfect master in all, not only in his interpretation of the truth but also in his age, at the same time sanctifying the elders and becoming a model for them. Finally he came even to death, that he might be "Firstborn from the dead, holding the primacy in all things" (Col.1:18), "Prince of life" (Acts 3:15), preceding all.

22.5 But they, in order to prove their fiction by what stands written, "to publish an acceptable year of the Lord" (Luke 4:19), say that he preached for one year and suffered in the twelfth month. Forgetting their own doctrine, they destroy his work and take from him the most necessary and honorable period of his life, I mean that of advanced age, in which he guided all men by his teaching. How did he have disciples if he did not teach? How did he teach when he did not have the age of a master? When he came to baptism he had not yet finished thirty years but was beginning to be about thirty – for so Luke indicated his years: 'Jesus was beginning at about thirty years' (3:23) when he came to baptism. But if from the baptism he preached only one year, he suffered after completing the thirtieth year, and was still a young man and had not yet reached advanced age. All will agree that the age of thirty is that of a young man and extends to the fortieth year, while from the fortieth to the fiftieth one declines into seniority. At this age our Lord was teaching, as the Gospel attests (John 8:56–57), and all the presbyters who came together in Asia with John the Lord's disciple attest that he delivered the same tradition to them; for he remained with them until the reign of Trajan. Some of them saw not only John but also other apostles and heard these things from them and attest the fact. Whose witness is more credible? Theirs or that of Ptolemaeus, who never saw the apostles and did not follow the traces of an apostle even in his dreams?

22.6 But even the Jews who then disputed with the Lord Jesus Christ most clearly indicated the same thing. For when the Lord said to them, "Your father Abraham rejoiced to see my day, and he saw it and was glad," they replied to him, "You are not yet fifty years old, and have you seen Abraham?" (John 8:56–57) Such a reply is properly addressed to a man already past forty and without reaching fifty is close to it. But to a man only thirty it would be said, "You are not yet forty years old." For if they wanted to convict him of lying they would have to avoid going beyond the age they saw he had. They gave an approximate age, whether they knew it from the census rolls or they guessed it as more than forty but certainly not thirty. It would have been completely irrational for them to lie about twenty years when they wanted to show he was later than the time of Abraham. Therefore the Lord was not far from fifty, and that is why the Jews could say to him, "You are not yet fifty, and have you seen Abraham?" Therefore he did not preach for one year, nor did he suffer in the twelfth month of the year. For the time from the thirtieth year to the fiftieth would never be one year unless these were great years of the length they attribute to their Aeons seated with Abyss in the Pleroma – of which the poet Homer said, himself inspired by the Mother of their error: "The gods, seated with Zeus, discussed together on a golden pavement" (*Iliad* 4.1).

Why years, months, days, hours?

24.5 Who will agree with them that the year has 365 days so that there may be twelve months of thirty days, with a figure unlike the reality? For them each Aeon is the thirtieth part of the entire Pleroma, while by their own admission the month is the twelfth part of the year. If the year were divided into thirty months and each month into twelve days, one could suppose that the figure was in harmony with their lie. On the contrary, their Pleroma is divided into thirty parts and a part of it into twelve, while the whole year is divided into twelve parts and each of these parts into thirty. Pointlessly the Saviour made the month as figure of the whole Pleroma and the year, the figure of the Dodecad in the Pleroma. It would have been far more appropriate to divide the year into thirty parts after the model of the whole Pleroma and the month into twelve parts after the model of the twelve Aeons in the Pleroma. They further divide the whole Pleroma into three, Ogdoad, Decad, Dodecad; but the year is divided into four parts: spring, summer, autumn, winter. Furthermore, the months that they call a figure of the Thirty do not have thirty days exactly: some have more, some less, because there is a surplus of five days. Even the days do not always have exactly twelve hours, but they increase from nine to fifteen hours and again decrease from fifteen to nine. So the months of thirty days were not made for the thirty Aeons, since they would have exactly thirty days, nor again the days of twelve hours to figure the Dodecad, for they would always have exactly twelve hours.

Problems of counting

26.3 What if someone, proud of his science and aware that the Lord said, "The hairs of your head are all counted" (Matt.10:30), should be curious to investigate the number of the hairs on each head and the reason why one has such a number and another something else? For all do not have the same number, and there are many thousands of different numbers, since one has a larger head and others a smaller one, or one has thick hair, another sparse, and others have only a few hairs. And when these people think they have found the number of hairs will they try to make it a testimony to the system they have invented? Or again if because of this saying in the Gospel, "Are not two sparrows sold for a penny? And not one of them falls to earth apart from the will of your Father" (Matt.10:29), someone should want to count the sparrows taken each day in the whole world or in each country and ask why such a number were taken yesterday, such the day before, another today, and then connect the number of sparrows with his system? Will he not deceive himself completely and drive into insanity those who agree with him, since men are always ready in such matters to suppose that they have discovered more than their teachers?

26.3 Someone may ask us if the total number of the things made and being made is known by God and if it is in harmony with his providence that each of them has received the number proper for itself. We shall agree with him that absolutely nothing of what has been made and is being made escapes from God's knowledge: by his providence each thing has received and receives appropriate form, order, number, and quantity. Absolutely nothing has been made or is being made without reason and by chance, but on the contrary everything has been made with a profound harmony and a sublime art, and there is a wonderful and truly divine Logos, which can discern all these things and set forth their causes. If we suppose that this man receives testimony and agreement from us, and goes on to count grains of sand and pebbles of the earth, as well as the waves of the sea and the stars of heaven, and discover the reasons for the numbers he believes he has found – will not this man be rightly considered as wasting his time and extravagant and crazy by all those who still have their good sense? And the more he is busy with questions like this, apart from other men, and imagines that he surpasses others by his discoveries, calling others as incompetent and laymen and "psychics" because they refuse to undertake such a vain task, the more he will really be insane and stupid, as if struck by lightning, yielding to God in no way; but through the Gnosis that he thinks he has found he changes God himself and shoots his thought above the greatness of the Creator.

Avoid such questions and trust God

28.2 If we cannot find the solutions for all the questions raised in the scriptures, let us not seek for another God than he-who-is, for this would be the worst impiety. We must leave such matters as these to the God who made it and correctly realize that the scriptures are perfect, since they were spoken by God's Word and his Spirit, while we, as we are inferior and more recent than God's Word and his Spirit, need to receive the knowledge of his mysteries. And it is not remarkable if we suffer this ignorance in spiritual and celestial matters and all those that have to be revealed, when even among matters before our feet – I mean those in this creation, which are touched and seen by us and are with us – many escape our knowledge and we entrust them to God; for he surpasses all.

What if we try to explain the cause of the rise of the Nile? We make many statements, perhaps persuasive, perhaps not, but what is true and certain and sure is God's concern. Also the habitation of the birds, who come to us in the spring and withdraw in the autumn, escapes our knowledge. And what explanation can we give of the rise and fall of the Ocean, since it evidently has a definite cause? Or say about the worlds beyond the Ocean?[7] Or what can we say about the origins of rain, lightning, thunder, clouds, fog, winds, and the like, and about the treasuries of snow, hail,[8] and similar phenomena, or the formation of clouds and fog, or why the moon waxes and wanes, or the cause of differences among waters and metals and stones and the like?[9] In all these matters we shall not be loquacious, seeking the causes of them. Only God who made them is truthful.

28.3 If, therefore, even in this created world there are matters reserved for God and others also coming under our knowledge, what harm is done if in questions raised by the scriptures (which are entirely spiritual) we resolve some by God's grace but leave others to God, not only in this age but in the age to come, so that God may be always teaching and man always learning from God? As the Apostle said, when the partial is destroyed these will continue: faith, hope, love (1 Cor.13:9–13). For faith in our Master will always remain firm, assuring us that he is the only true God, and that we should always love him, since he is the only Father, and that we should hope to receive and learn yet more from God, for he is good and has unlimited riches and a kingdom without end and immeasurable knowledge. If, then, as we have said, we leave certain questions to God, we shall preserve our faith and remain free from peril. All scripture, given us by God (2 Tim.3:16), will be found consistent. The parables will agree with the clear statements and the clear passages will explain the parables. Through the polyphony of the texts a single harmonious melody will sound in us, praising in hymns the God who made everything.

Answers known only to the Creator

If, for instance, someone asks us, "What was God doing before he made the world?" we shall say that the answer to that is in God's hands. All the scriptures teach us that this world was produced with God as its cause and that it had a beginning in time, but no scripture indicates what God would have done before this. So the answer to this question belongs to God, and one must not imagine foolish and stupid (cf. 2 Tim.2:13) and blasphemous emanations and, supposing you have found the origin of matter, reject the God who made everything.

28.4 Consider, you who invent such fables, that he whom you call

118

the Demiurge is the only one to be called, and really to be, God and Father; that the scriptures know only this God; that the Lord confesses him alone as his Father and knows no other, as we shall show by his own words. When, then, you make him a "fruit of deficiency" and a "product of ignorance," not knowing what is above him – and whatever else you say about him – consider the enormity of the blasphemy against him who is truly God. You appear to say seriously and honestly that you believe in God, but afterwards you cannot possibly set forth another God but pronounce that the one in whom you believe is "fruit of deficiency" and "product of ignorance." This blindness and stupidity comes when you fail to reserve anything for God but wish to proclaim the genesis and production of God himself and his Thought and Word and Life and Christ, all taken from no other source than human psychology. You do not understand that in the case of the human, a living being consisting of parts, one can differentiate, as we have done above, mind and thought: from mind thought, from thought reflection, from reflection word. In Greek, Logos as the directive faculty which elaborates thought is one thing, and another is the organ by means of which "word" is emitted. Sometimes man remains motionless and silent, sometimes he speaks and acts.

The transcendence of God

But since God is all Mind, all Word, all operative Spirit, all Light, always identical with and like himself (as it is right to think of God and learn from the scriptures), processes and distinctions of this kind do not exist in him. In fact, the tongue of man, being fleshly, cannot serve the speed of the human mind, which is spiritual, and hence our word is caught within and is produced outside not all at once, such as it was conceived, but in parts as the tongue is capable of serving.

28.5 God being all Mind and all Logos says what he thinks and thinks what he says; for his Reasoning is Logos and Logos is Mind and all-containing Mind is the Father himself. If then one speaks of the Mind of God and gives its own emission to the Mind, one calls him composite, since in this case God is one thing and the directing Mind is another. Similarly in giving the Word a third rank in emission from the Father (which would explain why the Word is ignorant of the Father's greatness) one deeply separates the Word from God. And indeed the prophet says of him, "Who will recount his generation?" (Is.53:8). But when you scrutinize his generation from the Father and transfer the expression of the human word, made with the tongue, to the Word of God, you yourselves rightly reveal that you know neither human nor divine matters.

28.9 But if some contentious person should contradict what we have said, as well as the word of the Apostle, "We know in part and we prophesy in part" (1 Cor.13:9); if he thinks that he does not know in part but possesses universal knowledge of all that exists; if he regards himself as a Valentinus, a Ptolemaeus, a Basilides, or one of those who say they have sought out the depths of God (1 Cor.2:10); he should not parade his vain boasting that he knows more than others about invisible and indemonstrable matters, but diligently seek out and learn from the "Father" and tell us the causes of things in this world we do not know, such as the number of the hairs of his head and of the sparrows caught every day and everything we cannot foresee, so that we believe him about greater matters as well. But if these "perfect" ones do not yet know what is to hand and under foot and in sight about earthly matters such as the disposition of the hairs of their head, how shall we believe them when they speak to us with specious arguments about spiritual and supercelestial matters, even those above God?[10] But we have said enough about numbers, names, syllables, questions about things above us, and their inappropriate exegesis of the parables. You will surely be able to say more about these matters.

Attack on Gnostic "miracles"

31.2 The followers of Simon and Carpocrates and any others said to work miracles, can be criticized thus: they do not act in the power of God nor in truth nor to benefit humanity, but to harm and deceive through magical tricks and every kind of fraud, doing more harm than good for those who believe them, since they lead them astray. They cannot give sight to the blind or hearing to the deaf nor drive demons away (except those they introduce themselves, if they do), nor cure the weak and lame or paralytic or those harmed in some other part of the body, as often happens in sickness, nor restore good health to those made weak from an accident. Even less have they ever raised a dead man as the Lord did, and the apostles by prayer, and in our brotherhood very often because of need. When the whole local church asked with fasting and much prayer, "the spirit returned" (Luke 8:55) to the dead man and the man was given to the prayers of the saints. But they do not even believe that this is possible. For them, resurrection from the dead is the knowledge of what they call the truth.

Gnostic ignorance of the arts and sciences

32.2 Further, when they call themselves bound to accomplish all deeds and all actions so as to achieve them all in one life, if possible, and thus reach perfection, they are never found even trying to do what relates to virtue and involves labour and glorious deeds and efforts in the arts, approved as good by all. For if they ought to experience every work and activity, first they ought to learn all the arts, whether theoretical or practical or learned through labour and meditation and perseverance – for example, every form of music and arithmetic and geometry and astronomy, and all the other theoretical disciplines. They should also study the whole of medicine and the science of pharmacy and all the disciplines developed for human health, and painting and sculpture and working in bronze and marble and other arts like these, as well as every form of agriculture and the care of horses and of flocks and herds, and the mechanical arts, which are said to involve all the others; and navigation, gymnastics, hunting, military science, kingship – without counting all the others. If they worked their entire lives they could not learn a ten-thousandth part of them.

Spiritual gifts of Christians

32.4 But if they say the Lord has done [his miracles] merely in appearance we shall take them back to the prophetic writings and show from them that all these things had been predicted of him, and that they really happened, and that he alone is the Son of God. Therefore his real disciples have received grace from him and use it in his name for the benefit of other men, as each has received the gift from him. Some really and truly drive out demons, so that often those who have been cleansed of evil spirits believe and are in the church, and some have foreknowledge of the future, and visions and prophetic speech, and others lay their hands on the sick and make them well, and as we said (31.2), even the dead have been raised and have remained with us for many years.[11] Why should I say more? It is impossible to tell the number of the gifts which the church throughout the world received from God in the name of Jesus Christ, crucified under Pontius Pilate, and uses each day for the benefit of the gentiles, neither deceiving nor making profit. For as it freely received from God, so it freely ministers (Matt.10:8).

The Old Testament prophets

35.2 As for the others who are falsely called "Gnostics," who say the prophets made their prophecies from various gods (1.30.11), they are easily refuted by the fact that all the prophets proclaimed one God and Lord as Creator of heaven and earth and everything in them, and that they announced the coming of his Son, as we shall prove from the scriptures themselves in the subsequent books.

Hebrew names of the one God

35.3 If anyone should oppose us because of the various Hebrew names placed in the scriptures, such as *Sabaoth* and *Eloe* and *Adonai*, etc., trying to prove from them that there are various Powers and gods, they must learn that all such terms are designations and terms for one and the same being. In fact, the word *Eloe* in Hebrew means "true God" and *Elloeuth* means "what contains all." *Adonai* sometimes means "unnameable" and "admirable," and sometimes with a double Delta and an aspiration (*Haddonai*) it means "He who separates the earth from the water so that the water cannot rise up against it." Similarly *Sabaôth* with Omega in the last syllable means "voluntary," while with Omicron it means "first heaven." Just so, *Iaôth* with Omega means "fixed measure," while with Omicron it means "He who puts evils to flight." And all the rest are appellations of one and the same being, such as "Lord of hosts," "Father of all," "God omnipotent," "Most High," "Lord of the heavens," "Creator," "Maker," etc. All these names belong not to different beings but to one and the same, the one God and Father who contains all and gives existence to all.

BOOK III

SUMMARY OF BOOKS I–II, PROSPECTUS FOR III

Pr. You asked me to bring to light the so-called secret doctrines of the disciples of Valentinus, show their diversity, and add a refutation of them. We therefore undertook to attack them, beginning with Simon, the father of all heretics, revealing their doctrines and successions and opposing all of them. Since the description required one book but the refutation required many, we sent you several books. The first contained the doctrines, usages, and way of life of all, while in the second what they wrongly taught was refuted and overturned and laid bare and shown forth such as it is. In this third book we shall add proofs from the scriptures, so that you may lack nothing of what you asked from us and even, beyond your expectation, may receive from us the means of refuting and overturning all who in any way teach error. Grace in God is rich and without grudging; it gives more than anyone asks of it. Remember, then, what we said in the first two books, and by adding this to them you will have from us a most complete argumentation against all heretics, and you will fight against them with confidence and determination on behalf of the only true and life-giving faith, which the church received from the apostles and transmitted to its children.

The evangelists

The Lord of all gave his apostles the power of the Gospel, and by them we have known the truth, that is, the teaching of the Son of God. To them the Lord said, "He who hears you hears me, and he who despises you despises me and Him who sent me" (Luke 10:16).
1.1 For we have known the "economy" for our salvation only

123

through those through whom the Gospel came to us; and what they then first preached they later, by God's will, transmitted to us in the scriptures so that would be the foundation and pillar of our faith (1 Tim.3:15). It is not right to say that they preached before they had perfect knowledge, as some venture to say, boasting that they are correctors of the apostles. For after our Lord arose from the dead and they were clad with power from on high (Luke 24:40) by the coming of the Holy Spirit (Acts 1:8), they were filled concerning everything and had perfect knowledge. They went forth to the ends of the earth, proclaiming the news of the good gifts to us from God and announcing heavenly peace to men (Luke 2:13–14). Collectively and individually they had the Gospel of God.

Thus Matthew published among the Hebrews a gospel written in their language, at the time when Peter and Paul were preaching at Rome and founding the church there. After their death Mark, the disciple and interpreter of Peter, himself delivered to us in writing what had been announced by Peter. Luke, the follower of Paul, put down in a book the Gospel preached by him. Later John the Lord's disciple, who reclined on his bosom (John 13:23; 21:20), himself published the Gospel while staying at Ephesus in Asia.

The apostolic tradition

3.1 Thus the tradition of the apostles, manifest in the whole world, is present in every church to be perceived by all who wish to see the truth. We can enumerate those who were appointed by the apostles as bishops in the churches as their successors even to our time, men who taught or knew nothing of the sort that they madly imagine. If however the apostles had known secret mysteries that they would have taught secretly to the "perfect," unknown to the others, they would certainly have transmitted them especially to those to whom they entrusted the churches. For they wanted those whom they left as successors, and to whom they transmitted their own position of teaching, to be perfect and blameless (1 Tim.3:2) in every respect. If these men acted rightly it would be a great benefit, while if they failed it would be the greatest calamity.

Apostolic succession at Rome

3.2 But since it would be too long, in a work like this, to list the successions in all the churches, we shall take only one of them, the church that is greatest, most ancient, and known to all, founded and set up by the two most glorious apostles Peter and Paul at Rome, while showing that the tradition and the faith it proclaims to men comes down through the successions of bishops even to us; thus we shall put to shame all who in any way, through infatuation or vainglory or blindness and a wicked doctrine, gather together wrongly. For it is necessary for every church – that is, the believers from everywhere – to agree with this church, in which the tradition from the apostles has always been preserved by those who are from everywhere, because of its more excellent origin.

3.3   After founding and building up the church, the blessed apostles delivered the ministry of the episcopate to Linus; Paul mentions this Linus in the letters to Timothy (2 Tim.4:21). Anacletus succeeded him, and after him, in the third place from the apostles, Clement received the lot of the episcopate; he had seen the apostles and met with them and still had the apostolic preaching in his ears and the tradition before his eyes. He was not alone, for many were then still alive who had been taught by the apostles. Under this Clement, when there was no slight dissension among the brethren at Corinth, the church at Rome wrote a most powerful letter to the Corinthians to reconcile them in peace and renew their faith and the tradition which their church had recently received from the apostles: one God Almighty, Creator of heaven and earth, who fashioned the human race, brought about the deluge, called Abraham, brought the people out of the land of Egypt, spoke with Moses, who gave the law, sent the prophets, and prepared fire for the devil and his angels.[1]

Those who wish can learn that the God proclaimed by the churches is the Father of our Lord Jesus Christ, and can understand the apostolic tradition by this letter, older than those who now teach falsely that there is another god above the Demiurge and Creator of all that exists. Evaristus succeeded this Clement; Alexander, Evaristus; then Xystus was appointed, sixth from the apostles; from him, Telesphorus, who achieved martyrdom most gloriously; then Hyginus; then Pius, whose successor was Anicetus. After Soter had succeeded Anicetus, now in the twelfth place from the apostles Eleutherus holds the episcopate. With the same sequence and doctrine the tradition from the apostles in the church, and the preaching of truth, has come down to us.

This is a complete proof that the life-giving faith is one and the same, preserved and transmitted in truth in the church from the apostles up till now.

Witness to tradition in Asia

3.4   And there is Polycarp, who not only was taught by the apostles
and conversed with many who had seen the Lord, but also was established by apostles in Asia in the church at Smyrna. We ourselves saw
him in our early youth, for he lived long and was in extreme old age
when he left this life in a most glorious and most noble martyrdom.
He always taught the doctrine he had learned from the apostles, which
he delivered to the church, and it alone is true. All the churches in Asia
bear witness to this, as well as the successors of Polycarp to this day,
and he was a witness to the truth of much greater authority and more
reliable than Valentinus and Marcion and the others with false opinions. For when under Anicetus he stayed in Rome he turned many
away from the heretics we have mentioned and brought them back to
the church of God by proclaiming that from the apostles he had
received this one and only truth transmitted by the church. Some
heard him say that John the Lord's disciple was going to the bath in
Ephesus when he saw Cerinthus inside and jumped out of the bath
without bathing, saying that he feared the bath would fall down since
Cerinthus, the enemy of the truth, was inside. And when Polycarp
himself once met Marcion, who ran to him and said, "Recognize us,"
he answered, "I do recognize you, firstborn of Satan." The apostles
and their disciples took great care not to communicate verbally with
any of those who adulterated the truth, as Paul too says: "After a first
and a second warning, avoid the heretic, knowing that such a man is
perverted and when he sins is self-condemned" (Tit.3:10–11).
There is also a very powerful letter of Polycarp, written to the
Philippians, from which those who desire and care for their salvation
can learn the nature of his faith and the preaching of the truth. In
addition, the church of Ephesus, founded by Paul, with John continuing with them until the times of Trajan, is a true witness to the tradition of the apostles.

The power of tradition

4.1   Since these proofs are so strong, one need not look among others
for the truth that is easy to receive from the church, for like a rich
man in a barn the apostles deposited everything belonging to the truth
in it so that whoever will might take the drink of life from it
(Rev.22:17). For it is the way of life, while "all" the others "are thieves
and robbers" (John 10:8). Therefore one must avoid them (Tit.3:10)

but love what belongs to the church and hold fast the tradition of truth. What then? If some question of minor importance should arise, would it not be best to turn to the most ancient churches, those in which the apostles lived, to receive from them the exact teaching on the question involved? And then, if the apostles had not left us the scriptures, would it not be best to follow the sequence of the tradition which they transmitted to those to whom they entrusted the churches?

Salvation by tradition not scripture

4.2 Many barbarian peoples who believe in Christ assent to this sequence, and possess salvation, written without paper or ink by the Spirit in their hearts, diligently observe the ancient tradition. They believe in one God, maker of heaven and earth and everything in them, and in Christ Jesus the Son of God, who because of his abundant love for the work he fashioned submitted to birth from the Virgin, in order himself through himself to unite man with God, and he suffered under Pontius Pilate and rose again and was taken up in glory, and will come in glory as Saviour of those who are saved and Judge of those who are judged, sending into eternal fire those who disfigure the truth and despise his Father and his own advent. Those who have believed this faith without letters are "barbarians in relation to our language" (2 Cor.14:11) but most wise, because of the faith, as to thinking, customs, and way of life, and they please God as they live in complete justice, chastity, and wisdom. And if someone told them, speaking in their own language, what has been invented by heretics, they would immediately shut their ears and flee far away, not even enduring to hear this blasphemous discourse.[2] Because of that ancient tradition of the apostles they do not admit even to thought any of the lying inventions of these people.[3] For among them there was neither a congregation nor a set doctrine.

Gnostic lack of tradition

4.3 Before Valentinus there were no disciples of Valentinus; before Marcion there were no disciples of Marcion; and none of the others enumerated above as holding evil doctrines existed before the mystagogues and discoverers of their perversity. For Valentinus came to Rome under Hyginus, flourished under Pius, and lasted until Anicetus. Cerdo, who was before Marcion, also lived under Hyginus, who was the eighth bishop. Though he often came into the church and did penance, he finished thus: sometimes teaching in secret, sometimes doing penance, finally convicted for what he wrongly taught and removed from the community of the brothers. Marcion, who succeeded him, flourished under Anicetus, the tenth to hold the episcopate. All the others who are called Gnostics originate from Menander the disciple of Simon, as we have shown, and each of them appeared as the father and mystagogue of the opinion he adopted. All these arose in their apostasy much later, in the middle of the times of the church.

Their criticism of the apostles

5.1 These vain sophists claim that the apostles hypocritically made their teaching according to the capacity of the hearers and gave answers according to the prejudices of the inquirers, speaking with the blind in terms of their blindness, to the sick in terms of their sickness, to those astray in terms of their wandering; to those who suppose that the Demiurge is the only God they proclaimed him, while to those who accept the unnameable Father they expressed the inexpressible mystery by parables and enigmas. Thus the Lord and the apostles expressed their teaching not truthfully but hypocritically, as each could hold it (cf. Matt.19:12).

The prayer of Irenaeus

6.4 I call upon you, Lord God of Abraham and God of Isaac and God of Jacob and Israel, you who are the Father of our Lord Jesus Christ, God who through the abundance of your mercy have been pleased with us so that we may know you (John 17:3), you who made heaven and earth and rule over all things, you who are the only true God (John 17:3), above whom there is no other God; you who through our Lord Jesus Christ gave us the gift of the Holy Spirit, now give to everyone who reads this writing to know that you are God alone and to be made firm in you and separate from every heretical doctrine, godless and impious.

Gnostics and "the God of this age"

7.1 They claim that Paul openly said in the second letter to the Corinthians, "Among whom the God of this age blinded the minds of unbelievers" (4:4), and that the God of this age is different from the one above every principality and power (cf. Eph.1:21; Col.1:16). We are not to blame if those who say they know mysteries above God do not even know how to read Paul. For, as we shall show from many other examples, Paul frequently uses transpositions of words (*hyperbata*). In accordance with this practice one reads: "Among whom God", then pausing for a brief interval and reading the rest together: "of this age blinded the minds of unbelievers" and finding the true meaning: "God blinded the minds of the unbelievers of this age." And the meaning is indicated by the pause. For Paul does not speak of a "God of this age," as if he knew another one above him, but confesses God as God and speaks of "the unbelievers of this age," so called because they will not inherit the age to come, that of imperishability (1 Cor.15:50). How God blinded the mind of unbelievers is what we shall show from Paul himself later in our discussion, so that for now we may not turn our attention too far away from our topic.

7.2 That the Apostle frequently uses transpositions because of the speed of his words and the impetus of the Spirit within him can be found in many other places. Thus he says in the letter to the Galatians, "What then is the law of works? It was established until the seed to which it was promised should come, ordained through angels by the hand of a mediator" (3:19). The real sequence is like this: "What then is the law of works? Ordained through angels, it was established by the hand of a mediator until the seed to which it was promised should come." A man asks, the Spirit answers. Again, in the second letter to the Thessalonians he says of the Antichrist: "And then will be revealed the Lawless One, whom the Lord Jesus will kill with the breath of his mouth and will destroy by the appearing of his coming, he whose coming will take place by the working of Satan with all power and signs and portents of falsehood" (2:8–9). The sequence of the words is like this: "And then will be revealed the Lawless One, whose coming will take place, by the working of Satan with all power and signs and portents of falsehood, he whom the Lord Jesus will kill with the breath of his mouth and will destroy by the appearing of his coming." For he does not say that the coming of the Lord will be by the working of Satan, but the coming of the Lawless One, whom we also call Antichrist. If then anyone does not pay attention to the reading and neglects to indicate by pauses the person of whom Paul wants to speak, he will read not only incoherence but blasphemy, as if the coming of the Lord would take place by the working of Satan. Just as in such cases it is necessary to indicate the transposition by the reading and keep the Apostle's meaning in order, so as above we do not read "God of this age" but we call "God" the one who really is God, and then we shall hear "the unbelievers and the blind of this age," so called because they will not inherit in the coming age, that of life.

God and Mammon

8.1 The prophets and the apostles never called "God" or "Lord" anyone but the true and only God ... The expression "You cannot serve two lords" is explained by the Lord himself when he says, "You cannot serve God and Mammon" (Matt.6:24), acknowledging God as God, and calling Mammon what he is. He does not call Mammon "lord" when he says, "You cannot serve two lords," but teaches the disciples who serve God not to be subject to Mammon or be dominated by him ... "Mammon" in the Jewish dialect used by the Samaritans means "greedy." In Hebrew as an adjective it is pronounced "Mamuel" and means "glutton." Using either translation, we cannot serve God and Mammon.

Is Jesus different from Christ?

9.3 Matthew (3:16–17) says of the baptism: "The heavens were opened and he saw the Spirit of God descending like a dove and coming upon him. And behold, a voice from heaven saying: 'You are my beloved Son in whom I am well pleased.'" For the Christ did not then descend into Jesus, nor was one the Christ, the other Jesus; but the Word of God, the Saviour of all who rules over heaven and earth, who is Jesus, as we have shown before, who took flesh and was anointed with the Spirit by the Father, became Jesus Christ. As Isaiah says, "A branch will come forth from the root of Jesse, and a flower will arise from its root; and the Spirit of God will rest upon him, the Spirit of wisdom and understanding, the Spirit of counsel and power, the Spirit of knowledge and piety, and the Spirit of the fear of God will fill him. He will not judge by appearance nor will he condemn by rumor, but he will render justice to the humble and condemn the great of the earth" (Is.11:1–4). Elsewhere Isaiah also announced his anointing and the reason for it.

Not one Gospel but the fourfold Gospel

11.7 Such are the first principles of the Gospel: one God, the maker of this universe, who was proclaimed by the prophets and gave the law through Moses. They proclaim the Father of our Lord Jesus Christ and know no other God or Father but him. The authority of the gospels is so great that the heretics themselves bear witness to them and each of them tries to confirm his own teaching out of them. Thus the Ebionites who use only the Gospel according to Matthew are proved by it not to think correctly about the Lord. Marcion, who circumcised the one according to Luke, is shown a blasphemer against the one real God out of what he still preserved. Those who separate Jesus from Christ, and think Christ lived without suffering and say that Jesus suffered, prefer the one according to Mark but if they read with a love of truth they can be corrected. And as to the disciples of Valentinus who use the one according to John most fully to demonstrate their pairs, this gospel reveals that they say nothing right, as we showed in the first book. Therefore, since those who contradict us bear witness to the gospels and use them, our proof derived from them is solid and true.

Why there are exactly four gospels

11.8 There cannot be either more or fewer gospels than there are. Since there are four regions of the world in which we exist, and four principal winds, and since the church, spread out over all the world has for a column and support (1 Tim.3:15) the Gospel and the Spirit of life, consequently it has four columns, from all sides breathing imperishability and making men live. From this it is evident that the Word, artisan of the universe, who sits above the Cherubim and encloses everything, when manifest to men gave us a fourfold Gospel, enclosed by one Spirit. Thus David, asking for his coming, says, "You who sit above the Cherubim, appear" (Ps.79:2). For the Cherubim have four forms (Ezek.1:6,10) and their forms are images of the constitution of the Son of God. "For the first animal," it says, "is like a lion," referring to the power, primacy, and royalty of the Son of God; "the second is like a young bull," indicating his function as sacrificer and priest; "the third has a face like that of a man," clearly describing his human coming; "the fourth is like a flying eagle," indicating the gift of the Spirit flying upon the church.[4]
The Gospels then are in accord with these animals on whom sits Christ Jesus. Thus the one according to John which tells of his primal, powerful, and glorious generation from the Father, speaks thus: "In the beginning was the Word and the Word was with God and the Word was God," and "Everything was made through him, and without him

was made nothing" (John 1:1,3). Therefore this Gospel is full of open declaration; such is its chief aspect. And that according to Luke, since it is of priestly character, begins with the priest Zechariah sacrificing incense to God (Luke 1:9), for the fatted calf was already prepared, to be sacrificed for the recovery of the younger son (15:23,30). Matthew tells of his human generation, saying "The book of the generation of Jesus Christ, the son of David, the son of Abraham" (Matt.1:1), and again, "The generation of Christ took place thus" (1:18). Therefore this Gospel is in human form and throughout the whole of it he remains a man of gentleness and humble thoughts (11:29). But Mark began from the prophetic Spirit coming to men from on high, saying, "The beginning of the Gospel, as it is written in Isaiah the prophet" (Mark 1:1-2), thus showing the winged image of the Gospel, and this is why he made a brief and rapid announcement, for this is the prophetic character. The same traits are found in the Word of God himself when speaking in his deity and glory to the patriarchs who lived before Moses; to those under the law he offered a priestly and ministerial order; and after this, becoming man for us, he sent the gift of the celestial Spirit on the whole earth, protecting us with his wings. What, then, the disposition of the Son of God was, such was the form of the animals; and what the form of the animals was, such was the character of the Gospel. Four forms of the animals; four forms of the Gospel; four forms of the activity of the Lord. This is why four covenants were given to the human race: the first before the deluge in the time of Adam; the second after the deluge in the time of Noah; the third is the legislation in the time of Moses; and the fourth, which renews man and recapitulates everything in itself, that which by the Gospel raises men and wings them for the celestial kingdom.

11.9 Since this is so, those people are vain, ignorant, and especially audacious when they reject the form of the Gospel and introduce a number of gospels either greater or smaller than those we have mentioned, some of them to appear to have found more than the truth, others in order to reject the "economies" of God. For Marcion, rejecting the whole Gospel or rather cutting himself off from the Gospel, boasts of having a part of this Gospel. Others, to reject the gift of the Spirit poured out in the last times on the human race by the will of the Father, do not accept the form of the Gospel according to John, in which the Lord promised to send the Paraclete (John 15:26), but drive out both the Gospel and the prophetic Spirit at the same time. They are truly unfortunate when they say there are false prophets and use this as a pretext to drive out prophetic grace from the church,[5] behaving like those who abstain from relations with the brethren because of people who come as hypocrites. Usually people of this sort do not accept the apostle Paul, for in the letter to the Corinthians he spoke precisely about spiritual gifts and knew men and women who prophesied in the church (1 Cor.14:1–40; 11:4–5). In all these ways they sin against the Spirit of God and fall into unforgivable sin (Matt.12:31–32). But Valentinians live apart from all fear, publish writings of their own composition, and boast of possessing more gospels than there are. They have reached such a pitch of audacity that they entitle their recently composed work *Gospel of Truth*, though it agrees in no way with the Gospels of the apostles. Thus with them not even the Gospel exists without blasphemy.

For if what they publish is the Gospel of Truth and if it differs from those the apostles have transmitted to us, those who wish can learn, as it appears from the scriptures themselves, that what the apostles transmitted is not the Gospel of Truth. In fact, we have abundantly shown that the Gospels are alone true and reliable and there cannot be more or fewer than those we have mentioned. For since God made everything with harmony and proportion, it was necessary for the form of the Gospel to be harmonious and in proportion.

After having thus examined the views of those who handed the Gospel down to us, in accordance with the very beginnings of the books, let us come to the other apostles and ask their opinion about God; after that we shall hear the very words of the Lord.

Luke agrees with Paul

13.3 Since there were those who called him to the apostles over a controversial question, Paul agreed and went up with Barnabas at Jerusalem to see the apostles, not without reason but so that the freedom of the gentiles might be confirmed by them. He says in the letter to the Galatians (2:1–2,5): "Then after fourteen years I went up to Jerusalem with Barnabas, taking also Titus. But I went up by a revelation and laid before them the gospel which I preach among the gentiles." And he says again: "We yielded[6] for the moment in subjection, so that the truth of the gospel might be preserved among you." If then one diligently investigates the time in which it is written in the Acts of the Apostles that he went up to Jerusalem because of this question, he will find the years Paul mentions in agreement. Thus the proclamation of Paul is in agreement and practically identical with the testimony of Luke concerning the apostles.

Luke wrote Acts

14.1 That this Luke was inseparable from Paul and was his collaborator in the preaching of the Gospel, he himself makes plain, not boasting but led by the truth itself. When Barnabas and John called Mark separated from Paul and embarked for Cyprus (Acts 15:39), "we came to Troas" (16:8), he says. And after Paul saw in a dream a Macedonian who said to him, "Paul, come into Macedonia and help us," he says that "immediately we sought to depart for Macedonia, understanding that the Lord called us to preach the Gospel there. So navigating from Troas, we sailed directly to Samothrace" (16:9–11). Then he carefully shows all the rest of their journey to Philippi and how they delivered the first sermon: "As we sat," he says, "we spoke to the women who had assembled" (16:13), and tells who and how many they were. And again he says, "But we sailed from Philippi after the days of unleavened bread and we came to Troas, where we stayed seven days" (20:6). And thus Luke reports in order all the rest of his voyage with Paul, with all possible care noting places, cities, number of days, until they went up to Jerusalem (20:7–21:16), and what happened to Paul there (21:17–23,35), how he was bound and sent to Rome (25–26), the name of the centurion who was in charge of him (27:1), the emblems of the ships (28:11) and how the ship was wrecked, and the island on which they were saved (27:27–44, 28:1), and how they were received humanely (28:2), while Paul cured the chief man of the island (28:7–8), and how they sailed to Puteoli and from there reached Rome, and how long they stayed in Rome (28:11–16, 30). Since Luke was present for all these events, he carefully recorded them. He cannot be described as a liar or a boaster, for all these facts hold together and he was prior to all who now teach something else and he knew the truth. That he was not only the companion but also the collaborator of the apostles and especially Paul, Paul himself made clear by saying in his letters, "Demas has left me and gone away to Thessalonica, Crescens to Galatia, Titus to Dalmatia; only Luke is with me" (2 Tim.4:10–11). This shows that he was always joined with him and never separated from him. And again in the letter to the Colossians he says, "Luke the beloved physician greets you" (Col.4:14). If that Luke, who always preached with Paul, whom he called "beloved," who announced the Gospel and was entrusted with the Gospel for us, learned nothing different from him, as we have shown by his words, how can these people who have never been joined with Paul boast that they have learned "hidden and ineffable mysteries"?

Paul's teaching was clear, not mysterious

14.2 Paul himself makes it clear that he taught in simple fashion just
what he knew, not only to his companions but to all who heard him.
For calling together in Miletus the bishops and presbyters from
Ephesus and the rest of the nearby cities (Acts 20:17) – since he
himself was hastening to Jerusalem to celebrate Pentecost (20:16) –
after attesting many things to them and telling what was to happen to
him at Jerusalem (20:18–24), he added:

> I know that you will not see my face again. I therefore testify to
> you this day that I am innocent of the blood of all. For I did not
> shrink from proclaiming the whole counsel of God to you.
> Watch over yourselves and over the flock in which the Holy
> Spirit set you as bishops to shepherd the church of the Lord,
> which he acquired through his own blood (20:25–28).

Then he said, indicating the evil teachers to come, "I know that after
my departure cruel wolves will come to you, not sparing the flock.
And from yourselves will arise men speaking perverse things in order
to draw away disciples after them" (20:29–39). "I have not held
back," he says, from proclaiming the whole purpose of God to you":
thus the apostles transmitted to all, simply and without holding back,
what they themselves had learned from the Lord. Thus Luke,
without holding back, transmitted to us what he had learned from
them, as he himself testifies, saying, "As those transmitted it to us
who from the beginning were eyewitnesses and servants of the
Word" (Luke 1:2).

Gnostic errors

16.8 Outside the "economy" are all those who on the pretext of
Gnosis suppose that Jesus is different from Christ, another is Only-
Begotten, still another is Word, and another is Savior, treating this last
as "the emission of the Aeons fallen into the decline," as these disciples of error say. On the outside they are sheep, for in their external
speech they resemble us since they say the same words, but inside
they are wolves, for their teaching is murderous, inventing many
gods and simulating many fathers, breaking up and dividing the Son
of God in many ways.

No 'Christ from above' but Jesus Christ

18.3 Who is he who thus shares with us in foods (cf. 1 Cor.10:16)? Is he the "Christ from above" invented by these people, the one who was extended on "Limit" and formed their "Mother"? Or the Emmanuel who is from the Virgin, who ate butter and honey and of whom the prophet said, "He is a man, but who will know him?" (Jer.17:9)? The same Christ was proclaimed by Paul: "I delivered to you first that Christ died for our sins according to the scriptures and was buried and rose the third day according to the scriptures" (1 Cor.15:3–4). Therefore it is obvious that Paul knew no Christ but the one who suffered and was buried and rose again, who was born, whom he called "man." For when he said, "If Christ is proclaimed as raised from the dead" (15:12), he adds, giving the reason for his incarnation: "Since by man came death, by man came also the resurrection of the dead" (15:21). And everywhere Paul used the name "Christ" in speaking of the passion of our Lord and his humanity and his being put to death; for example, "Do not destroy, by your eating, the one for whom Christ died" (Rom.14:15); and further, "But now you who were formerly far away have become near in the blood of Christ" (Eph.2:13); and again, "Christ redeemed us from the curse of the law, made a curse for us, since it is written, 'Cursed is every one who hangs on a tree'" (Gal.3:13; Deut.21:23); and again, "And the weak one perishes with your knowledge, the brother for whom Christ died" (1 Cor.8:11). These texts show that an impassible Christ did not come down into Jesus, but Jesus, since he was Christ, suffered for us, slept and rose again, descended and ascended (Eph.4:10), the Son of God become Son of man. This is what his name indicates, since the name "Christ" implies him who anoints, him who has been anointed, and the unction with which he is anointed. He who anoints is the Father; and the Son has been anointed in the Spirit, which is the unction; as the Word said through Isaiah (61:1), "The Spirit of God is upon me, because he anointed me," signifying the Father as anointing, the Son as anointed, and the unction which is the Spirit.

The Incarnation

19.1 Those who say he is a mere man begotten by Joseph remain and die in slavery to the primal disobedience, not yet mingled with the Word of God the Father nor sharing in freedom through the Son, as he himself says: "If the Son set you free, you are truly free" (John 8:36). Ignorant of him who is Emmanuel born of the Virgin (Is.7:14), they are deprived of his gift, which is eternal life (John 4:10,14); not having received the Word of imperishability, they remain in mortal flesh; they are debtors to death, not receiving the antidote of life.⁷ To them the Word says, speaking of his gift of grace, "I said, You are all gods and sons of the Most High, but you die like men" (Ps.82:6–7). He undoubtedly addresses those who do not accept the gift of adoption but despise the Incarnation, the pure generation of the Word of God, depriving man of his ascension to God and being ungrateful to the Word of God who became incarnate for them. For this the Word of God became man, and the Son of God Son of man, that man, mingled with the Word and thus receiving adoption, might become a son of God. We could not receive imperishability and immortality unless we had been united to imperishability and immortality. And how could we have been united with imperishability and immortality unless imperishability and immortality had first been made what we are, so that what was perishable might be absorbed by imperishability and what was mortal by immortality (1 Cor.15:53–54) "that we might receive adoption as sons" (Gal.4:5)?

19.2   This is attested by "Who will tell his generation?" (Is.53:8). For "he is man, but who will know him?" (Jer.17:9). The only one who knows him is the one to whom the Father in the heavens has revealed him (Matt.16:17), so that he understands that the Son of man (Matt.16:13), "born not of the will of the flesh nor of the will of man" (John 1:13), is "the Christ, the Son of the living God" (Matt. 16:16). We have shown from the scriptures that not one among the sons of Adam is properly called God or Lord. It is evident, however, to all who possess even a moderate bit of the truth, that unlike all men of the past the Christ is properly proclaimed as God, Lord, eternal King, Only-begotten, and incarnate Word, by all the prophets and apostles and the Spirit itself. The scriptures would not give this testimony to him if he were a mere man like all others. But because, alone among all, he had in himself this brilliant origin (Is.53:8) from the Father Most High, and because he also received the brilliant birth from the Virgin (Is.7:14), the divine scriptures testify to him in a double manner: as man he is without beauty and capable of suffering (Is.53:2–3) and sits on the foal of an ass (Zech.9:9), is given vinegar and gall to drink (Ps.69:21), is rejected by the people and goes down to death (Ps.22:7,16); on the other hand he is holy Lord, marvelous Counselor (Is.9:6), beautiful in appearance (Ps.44:3), mighty God (Is.9:6), and coming on the clouds as universal Judge (Dan.7:13,26). The scriptures predicted all this of him.

19.3 For as the Lord was man in order to be tested, so also he was Word in order to be glorified; the Word was quiescent so that he could be tested, dishonored, crucified, and die, and the man was absorbed when the Lord conquered, endured, showed his goodness, rose, was assumed into heaven. This is the Son of God, our Lord, who was the Word of God, and Son of man as born of Mary; he came from human beings and was a man, and had a human birth and became Son of man.

This is why the Lord himself gave us a "sign in the deep and in the height" without man's asking for it (Is.7:11–12); for man did not hope that a virgin could become pregnant as a virgin and bear a son, and that this offspring would be "God with us" (7:14) and would descend to the earth below (Eph.4:9) in search of the lost sheep (Luke 15:4–6) which was of his own fashioning (Gen.2:7), and would ascend to the height, offering and commending to the Father that man who had been found producing in himself the first-fruits of man's resurrection (1 Cor.15:20) so that as the head rose from the dead, so also the rest of the body of every man who is found in life will rise when the time of his condemnation for disobedience is past, knit together through its joints and ligaments and made firm by growth from God (Col.2:19), with each member having its own suitable place in the body (1 Cor.12:18). This is why there are many abodes with the Father (John 14:2), because there are many members in the body (1 Cor.12:12).

20.2 This, then, was God's generosity. He allowed man to pass through every situation and to know death and then come to the resurrection from the dead, and learning by experience that from which he had been liberated, might always be grateful to the Lord, having obtained the gift of imperishability from him, and might love him more, for "he to whom more is forgiven loves more" (Luke 7:42–43). He will know himself[8] as mortal and weak and will understand that God is immortal and powerful and can give the mortal immortality (1 Cor.15:53) and the temporal eternity. Thus he will understand all the other miraculous powers of God manifested to him and instructed by them will think of God how great he is. For the glory of man is God, and the recipient of God's activity and all his wisdom and power is man. As the physician is tested in the sick, so God is made manifest in men. This is why Paul says, "God assigned everything to disobedience so that he may have mercy on all" (Rom.11:32). He is not speaking of spiritual Aeons but of man, who after disobeying God and being cast out of immortality then obtained mercy (1 Pet.2:10) through the Son of God, receiving the adoption which is through him (Gal.4:4–5). When man without conceit and boasting holds a true opinion⁹ of the creatures and their Creator, who is the all-powerful God who gives existence to all, and remains in his love (John 15:9–10) and submission and thanksgiving will receive a greater glory from him, progressing until he becomes like the one who died for him. He was made "in the likeness of sinful flesh" to condemn sin and expel it, thus condemned, from the flesh (Rom.8:3) and also to call man to become like him, assigning him to God as imitator (Eph.5:1), raising him into the kingdom of the Father and giving him the ability to see God and comprehend the Father. This Word of God which dwelt in man was made Son of man to accustom man to perceive God and to accustom God to dwell in man, according to the good pleasure of the Father.

Incarnation as recapitulation: Christ and Mary

21.9 And he recapitulated in himself the work originally fashioned, **21.10** because, just as through the disobedience of one man sin came in, and through sin death prevailed (Rom.5:12,19), so also through the obedience of one man justice was brought in and produced the fruit of life for the men formerly dead. And as the first-fashioned Adam received his substance from earth uncultivated and still virgin ("for God had not yet rained and man had not worked the earth", Gen.2:5) and was fashioned by the hand of God (Ps.119:73), that is, by the Word of God, for "everything was made through him" (John 1:3) and "the Lord took dust from the earth and fashioned man" (Gen.2:7), thus the Word, recapitulating Adam in himself, from Mary still virgin rightly received the generation that is the recapitulation of Adam. If then the first Adam (1 Cor.15:45) had had a man for father and had been born of the seed of a man, the heretics could rightly say that the second Adam (15:47) was generated by Joseph. But if the first Adam was taken from the earth and fashioned by the Word of God, it was necessary that the Word himself, working in himself the recapitulation of Adam, possessed a like origin. One might object, why did God not take dust anew and why did he make what he fashioned proceed from Mary? So that there would not be another fashioning nor another work fashioned to be saved but that the same being might be recapitulated, with the likeness preserved. **22.2** Why would Christ have come down into her if he was to receive nothing from her? And if he had received nothing from Mary he would never have taken foods derived from the earth; after fasting forty days like Moses and Elijah he would not have felt hunger because his body needed food; John his disciple would not have written of him: "Jesus sat, wearied from the journey" (John 4:6); nor would David have proclaimed, "They have added to the pain of my wounds" (Ps.69:26); he would not have wept over Lazarus (John 11:35); he would not have sweated drops of blood (Luke 22:44);[10] he would not have said, "My soul grieves" (Matt.26:38), nor would blood and water have come forth from his pierced side (John 19:34). All these are signs of the flesh taken from the earth, which he recapitulated in himself, saving what he had formed.

22.3 This is why Luke presents a genealogy of seventy-two generations from the birth of our Lord back to Adam (Luke 3:23–38), linking the end to the beginning and indicating that he is the one who recapitulated in himself, with Adam, all the nations and languages and generations of men dispersed after Adam. Therefore Paul calls Adam the "figure of the one to come" (Rom.5:14) because the Word, Fashioner of all, preformed in Adam the future divine plan for humanity around the Son of God, since God first predestined the psychic man, obviously, to be saved by the spiritual. Since he who would save pre-existed, what would be saved had to come into existence so that the saving one would not be in vain.

The role of the Virgin Mary

22.4 Like the Lord, the Virgin Mary is also found obedient when she says, "Behold your servant, Lord, may it be for me according to your word" (Luke 1:38), but Eve, disobedient, for she disobeyed while still a virgin. For just as Eve had Adam for a husband but was still a virgin – "for they were both naked" in Paradise "and had no shame" (Gen.2:25), since, recently created, they had no understanding of procreation: they had to grow up first and then multiply (1:28) – and by disobeying became the cause of death for herself and the whole human race, so also Mary, with a husband predestined for her but yet a virgin, was obedient and became the cause of salvation for herself and the whole human race. For this reason the Law calls the one betrothed to a man the wife of the one betrothing her, even though she is still a virgin, signifying the recycling that Mary effected for Eve. For what has been tied cannot be loosed unless one reverses the ties of the knot so that the first ties are undone by the second, and the second free the first: thus it happens that the first tie is unknotted by the second and the second has the place of a tie for the first. This is why the Lord said that the first would be the last and the last first (Matt.19:30; 20:16); and the prophet indicates the same thing by saying, "In place of the fathers that they were, they became your sons" (Ps.45:16).

For the Lord, becoming the First-born from the dead (Col.1:18) and receiving the ancient fathers into his bosom, regenerated them into the life of God, himself becoming the first of the living because Adam had become the first of the dead. This is why Luke (3:23–38) began his genealogy with the Lord to trace it back from him to Adam, thus indicating that the fathers did not give life to the Lord but he regenerated them in the Gospel of life. So too the knot of Eve's disobedience was loosed by Mary's obedience, for what the virgin Eve had bound by her unfaith, the virgin Mary loosed by her faith.[11]

23.3 Therefore at the beginning of Adam's transgression, as the scripture tells, God did not curse Adam himself but the earth that he worked. As one of the ancients says, "God transferred the curse to the earth so that it would not continue in man." In condemnation for his transgression man received weariness and earthly labor and eating bread by the sweat of his brow and returning to the earth from which he was taken (Gen.3:1–19); and likewise the woman received weariness and labor and groaning and the pangs of birth and servitude, that is, to her husband (3:16), so that they might not be accursed by God and utterly perish or remain unpunished and despise God. The whole curse, however, fell upon the serpent who led them astray. "And God said to the serpent, 'Because you did this, you are accursed among all the domestic animals and all the wild beasts of the earth'" (3:14). The Lord in the Gospel pronounced the same curse to those found on his left: "Depart, you accursed, into the eternal fire which my Father has prepared for the devil and his angels" (Matt.25:41), signifying that the eternal fire has not been prepared primarily for man, but for the one who led him astray and made him sin and inaugurated apostasy, and for the angels who became apostates with him. This is the fire which they who like the angels persevere in wicked works, without penitence and return, will justly experience.

23.5 This is why God interrogates them, so that the accusation may fall upon the woman; then he interrogates her, so that she may turn the accusation against the serpent. She tells what had happened: "The serpent seduced me and I ate" (3:13). God did not interrogate the serpent, for he knew that he was the instigator of the transgression. But he made his curse fall first on him, so that he might turn to man with a second condemnation. For God hated the one who seduced man, while he gradually felt pity for the one seduced.

Tatian denies Adam's salvation

23.8 Becoming the synthesis of all heresies, as we have shown, he [Tatian] personally invented this doctrine. By thus adding something novel he was trying with words devoid of meaning to gain hearers devoid of faith. In his attempt to pass himself off as a teacher, he tried to use expressions often found in Paul, <such as> "In Adam we all die" (1 Cor.15:22); but he was ignorant that "Where sin abounded, grace superabounded" (Rom.5:20).

24.1 Where the church is, there is the Spirit of God, and where the Spirit of God is, there is the church and all grace; and the Spirit is truth (1 John 5:6).

Plato's view of God was better than Marcion's

25.3 Therefore Marcion, who divides God in two and says that one is good and the other judgmental, makes God perish in both ways. For the judgmental one, if he is not good, is not God, for a God without goodness is not God; and again, one who is good and not also judgmental will suffer the same lot as the other, and will be deprived of being God.

Furthermore, how can they call the Father of all things wise if they do not assign the judgmental to him? For if he is wise he is also an examiner; but the judgmental belongs to the examiner, and justice accompanies the judgmental for judging justly; justice calls forth judgment, and in turn judgment when made with justice, proceeds to wisdom. In wisdom, then, the Father surpasses all human and angelic wisdom because he is Lord and just Judge and Ruler over all.

But he is merciful, good, and patient, and he saves those he should and judges those who deserve judgment; and his justice is not cruel, since his goodness goes before it.

25.4 Thus God, who in goodness makes his sun rise on all and rains on the just and the unjust (Matt.5:45), will judge those who having benefited equally from his kindness will not have similarly lived worthily of his gift but have lived in pleasures and carnal passions, opposing his benevolence and blaspheming the one who gave them such great benefits.

25.5 Plato appears to be more religious than they are, for he acknowledged the one God who is both just and good, has power over all, and himself performs judgment.

And God, according to an ancient tradition, holds the beginning and the end and the middle of everything that exists, and rightly completes it on a path in accordance with his nature. Justice always accompanies him and takes vengeance on those who break the divine law' (*Laws* 4.715E).[12]

And again, he shows that the Maker and Creator of this universe is good. "In him who is good, envy never arises over anything" (*Timaeus* 29E).[13] Thus he sets as the beginning and the cause of the making of the world the goodness of God, not an Ignorance or a fallen Aeon or a "fruit of deficiency" or a weeping and lamenting Mother or another God and Father.

25.7 We pray that they may not continue in the ditch they have dug [Eccl.10:8] but may separate from such a Mother . . .

This is our prayer for them; we love them more expediently than they think they love themselves. For since our love is true it saves them, if they accept it. It is like a harsh medicine that eats away the foreign and superfluous flesh formed on a wound; it takes away their pride and exaltation. This is why we shall try, with all our strength and without weariness, to offer our hand to them.

BOOK IV

BOOK IV ON THE LORD'S WORDS WILL CONVERT HERETICS

Pr.1   In sending you as I promised, beloved, this fourth book of my work *On the Detection and Refutation of False Knowledge*, we are going to confirm what we already said by the Lord's words, so that you may receive what you asked for, the means of refuting all the heretics in every way, so that you will not permit them to be weakened and fall deeper into the Abyss of error and drown in the ocean of ignorance but by turning them to the port of truth they may attain salvation from it.

Pr.2   Anyone who wants to convert them must know their systems exactly. It is impossible for anyone to cure the sick if he does not know the disease of those who are not well.[1] For this reason those who were before us and indeed far superior to us were not able to refute the disciples of Valentinus adequately, for they did not know the system of theirs which we delivered to you with all diligence in the first book, in which we also showed that their doctrine is the summation of all heresy. For the same reason, in our second book we took them for the target of our whole refutation, for those who adequately oppose such people oppose all holders of false opinions, and those who refute them refute every heresy.

Their blasphemy against the Creator

3.1   These evil persons say, "If the heaven is a throne and earth a footstool (Is.66:1), and if it is said that heaven and earth will pass away (Luke 21:33), then when they pass away this God seated on them must pass away, and therefore he is not the God above all." But first they do not know how heaven is a throne and earth a footstool, nor do they know what God is, but they suppose that he sits in human fashion and is contained but does not contain. They also are ignorant of the passing away of heaven and earth; but Paul was not ignorant when he said, "The fashion of this world is passing away" (1 Cor.7:31).

4.1 Furthermore, concerning Jerusalem and the house [of God] they venture to say, "If it had been the city of the great King it would not have been abandoned." This is like saying that if chaff were the creation of God, it would not have been abandoned by the wheat, or if the twigs of the vine had been made by God they would never have been pruned when they were deprived of grapes. But these things have been done essentially not for themselves but for the fruit that grows on them, Once this fruit ripens and is picked, they are abandoned and disappear because they are no longer useful for the bearing of fruit. So it was with Jerusalem.

4.2 Since the law began with Moses, it consequently ended with John, for its completion, Christ, had come and therefore with them "the law and the prophets were until John" (Luke 16:16). Jerusalem too, beginning with David and completing the time of legislation, had to have an end when the new covenant appeared. For God makes everything with measure and order, and nothing with him lacks measure, for nothing lacks number (Wisd.11:20). And he spoke well who said: "The immeasurable Father is measured in the Son"; for the Son is the measure of the Father, since he comprehends him (Luke 10:22).

The one God and his Son

6.2 Justin well said in his book *Against Marcion*, "I should not have believed the Lord himself had he proclaimed a God other than the Creator." But since from the one God, who made this world and formed us and contains and administers everything, the only Son came to us, recapitulating in himself what he had formed, my faith is firm in him and my love unshakeable toward the Father, since the Lord provides us with both faith and love.[2]

God's guidance

11.2 In this God differs from man: God makes, man is made. He who makes is always the same, while he who is made has a beginning, a middle, and an end, and ought to receive growth. God gives benefits, while man receives them. God is perfect in every respect, equal to himself and uniform; he is all Light, all Mind, all substance, the source of all good things, while man receives progress and growth toward God. For as God is always the same, so man, being in God, will always advance toward God. God will never cease to benefit and enrich man, nor will man cease receiving benefit and wealth from God. For the man who is grateful to him who made him will be the recipient of his goodness and the instrument of his glorification, but again the man who is ungrateful and spurns the one who fashioned him and is not subject to his Word will receive just judgment. For he himself has promised to give much to those who do not stop bearing fruit and multiplying the Lord's money: "Well done," he says, "good and faithful servant; since you were faithful with a little, I will set you over much; enter into the joy of your Lord" (Matt.25:21; Luke 19:17). It is the Lord himself who promises much.

Natural precepts and the law

13.1 The natural precepts of the law, through which man is justified and which those men observed who were justified by faith and pleased God, even before the gift of the law, he did not abolish but extended and made full (Matt.5:17), as is shown from his words: "It was said to the ancients, 'You shall not commit adultery.' But I say to you, whoever sees a woman to lust for her has already committed adultery with her in his heart" (5:27–28). And again: "It was said, 'You shall not kill.' But I say to you, whoever is angry with his brother without cause will be liable to judgment" (5:21–22). And: "It was said, 'You shall not commit perjury.' But I say to you not to take oaths at all. Let your word be Yes, yes and No, no" (5:33–34,37). And so on. All these do not contain the contradiction and abolition of previous things, as the Marcionites assert, but the fullness and extension, as he himself says, "Unless your justice exceeds that of the scribes and Pharisees you will not enter into the kingdom of heaven" (5:20).

The service of God

14.1 At the beginning it was not as if God needed man that he formed Adam, but to have someone to whom to present his benefits. For not only before Adam but before the whole creation the Word was glorifying his Father, while remaining in him, and he was being glorified by the Father, as he himself says: "Father, glorify me with the glory that I had with you before the world came to be" (John 17:5). He did not order us to follow him because he needed our service but because he was offering us salvation. To follow the Savior is to share in salvation, just as to follow the light is to perceive the light. Those who are in the light do not illuminate the light but are illuminated and made splendid by it. They supply nothing to it but receiving benefit are illuminated by the light. Such is the service of God. Nothing is added to God nor does God need human service, but to those who follow and serve him he provides life and imperishability and eternal glory, benefits to those who serve him because they serve him, and to those who follow him because they follow him. He does not receive benefit from them, for he is perfect and without need. God uses the service of men so that being good and merciful he may benefit those who continue in his service. For while God needs nothing, man needs communion with God. This is the glory of man, to continue and remain in the service of God. Therefore the Lord said to the disciples, "You did not choose me but I chose you" (John 15:16), indicating that they were not glorifying him by following him but that because they followed the Son of God they were glorified by him. And again, "I want them also to be where I am so that they may see my glory" (17:24), not boasting of it but willing to share his glory with his disciples, of whom the prophet Isaiah (43:5–7) said:

> From the east I will bring your seed and from the west I will gather you. I will say to the north, Gather them, and to the south, Do not hold them back. Gather my sons from afar and my daughters from the ends of the earth, all those I have called in my name, for I prepared him and formed and made him for my glory (Is.43:5–7).

And because "where the corpse is, there the eagles will gather" (Matt.24:28), they will share in the glory of the Lord, who formed and prepared them so that with him they may share in his glory.

The Mosaic law figurative

14.3 Thus the Word ordained laws for the people on the construction of the tabernacle, the building of the temple, and the choice of the Levites, as well as the sacrifices and offerings and purifications and all the rest of the observances. He himself needed none of these things, for he is always full of all good things and every sweet-smelling odor and all the smoke of perfumes, before Moses ever existed. But he was educating a people always inclined to return to idols, instructing them through many callings[3] to persevere in the service of God, calling them through secondary to primary matters, that is through the figurative to the true, through the temporal to the eternal, through the carnal to the spiritual, through the earthly to the celestial. Thus it was said to Moses, "You shall do everything after the model of the things you have seen on the mountain" (Exod.25:40). For during forty days he learned to retain the words of God, the celestial characters, the spiritual images and prefigurations of things to come, as Paul also said, "They drank from the rock that followed them, and the rock was Christ" (1 Cor.10:4). Then after relating the events in the law (10:7), he added, "All these things happened to them as prefigurations, and they were written down for the instruction of us on whom the end of the ages has come" (10:11). By the prefigurations, then, they learned to fear God and persevere in his service.

Natural precepts and concessions

15.1 Therefore for them the law was at once a demand upon them and a prophecy of things to come. For God at first admonished them through the natural precepts which from the beginning he had given to men and implanted in them, that is, through the Decalogue – whoever does not obey it does not have salvation – and he required nothing more of them, as Moses says in Deuteronomy (5:22): "These are all the words which the Lord spoke to the whole assembly of the sons of Israel on the mountain, and he added nothing, and he wrote them on two tablets of stone and gave them to me." And this is why the Lord ordered those who wanted to follow him to keep the commandments (Matt.19:17).

But when they turned to make a calf and turned back to Egypt in their minds, desiring to be slaves rather than free men, then they received a slavery conformed to their desire, not separating them from God but taming them under a yoke of slavery, as Ezekiel the prophet explains the causes of such legislation: "Their eyes followed the desire of their heart, and I gave them precepts that were not good, and prescriptions by which they would not live" (20:24–25). And indeed Luke writes that Stephen, the first to be killed for his witness to Christ, thus spoke of Moses (Acts 7:38–43):

He received the commandments of the living God, to give you, but your fathers refused to obey him; they repulsed him and turned in their heart to Egypt, saying to Aaron, "Make for us gods to go ahead of us, for we do not know what has happened to Moses, who led us out of the land of Egypt." And they made a calf in those days and offered sacrifices to the idol and rejoiced in the work of their hands. And God turned and delivered them to the service of the armies of heaven, as it is written in the book of the prophets [Amos 5:25–26]: "Have you offered me sacrifices and oblations during forty years in the desert, house of Israel? You have accepted the tabernacle of Moloch and the star of the god Rempham, these images that you made to worship them."

By that he clearly indicates that it was not another god but God himself who gave such a law, suited to their slavery. Therefore in Exodus (33:2–3) he says to Moses, "I will send my angel to you; for I will not go up with you, for you are a people with a stiff neck."

Why various precepts of the law?

15.2 And the Lord showed not only this but also that certain precepts were given them by Moses because of their hardness and because they would not obey. As they said to him, "Why did Moses forbid giving a bill of divorcement and repudiating one's wife," he said to them, "He allowed this for you because of the hardness of your heart, but from the beginning it was not so" (Matt.19:7–8). Thus he excused Moses as a faithful servant; he also recognized as one the God who from the beginning made male and female; and he accused them of being hard and disobedient. This is why they had received from Moses the precept of divorce suited to their hardness.

Concessions in the New Testament

But why speak of the Old Testament, when in the New the apostles are found doing the same for the reason already mentioned? Thus Paul says, "I say these things, not the Lord" (1 Cor.7:12), and again, "I say this as a concession not as a precept" (7:6), and again, "As for virgins, I do not have a precept of the Lord, but I give advice, having obtained mercy from the Lord to be faithful" (7:25). But in another place he says, "Lest Satan tempt you because of your incontinence" (7:5). If therefore in the New Testament the apostles are found agreeing on certain precepts by way of concession because of the incontinence of some and for fear that these, hardened and despairing of their salvation, might become apostate from God, we must not marvel if also in the Old Testament the same God wanted to do something similar for the benefit of the people. He drew them on through the practices already mentioned so that having swallowed the saving hook of the Decalogue and remaining held by it they would not return to idolatry or become apostate from God, but would learn to love him with their whole heart. If anyone, because the Israelites disobeyed and were lost, says this legislation is "weak," he should find in our own calling that "many are called but few are chosen" (Matt.22:14), and inside are wolves but outside clad in sheepskins (7:15); and that God has always preserved both human free will and his own exhortation, so that those who disobey may be justly judged for having disobeyed, and those who obey and believe will be crowned with imperishability.

God, his word and his wisdom

20.1   So then it is not possible to know God in his greatness, for it is not possible to measure the Father, but in his love – for this is what leads us to God through his Word – those who obey him always learn that he is so great a God and that it is he who by himself created and adorned and contains everything. This "everything" includes us and our world. We too, with everything the world contains, were made by him. Of him scripture says, "And God formed man, taking dust of the earth, and he breathed in his face a breath of life" (Gen.2:7). Angels did not make or form us, for angels could not have made an image of God, nor any other but the true God, nor any power far distant from the Father of all things. God needed none of these to make whatever he had foreordained to make, as if he did not have hands of his own. For always with him are his Word and Wisdom, the Son and the Spirit, through whom and in whom he made everything freely and independently, to whom he also speaks when he says, "Let us make man after our image and likeness" (1:26), taking the substance of the creatures from himself as well as the pattern of the things he adorned.

20.2   The writing well says, "First of all, believe that there is one God, who created and completed all things and made everything exist out of the non-existent, he who contains all and alone is contained by none."[4] Among the prophets, Malachi also well says: "Is it not one God who made us? Is there not one Father for us all?"

(Mal.2:10). In agreement, the Apostle also says, "There is one God the Father, who is above all and in us all" (Eph.4:6). And likewise also the Lord: "All things have been delivered to me by my Father" (Matt.11:27), obviously by him who made all; for it was not another's property but his own that he gave. Nothing was left out from this total. Therefore he is "judge of living and dead" (Acts 10:42). "He has the key of David: he will open and no one will close; he will close and no one will open" (Rev. 3:7). For "no one" else "in heaven or on earth or under the earth could open the book" of the Father "or look at him" (5:3) but "the Lamb that was slain" (5:12) and "redeemed us by his blood" (5:9), after receiving power over everything, when "the Word became flesh" (John 1:14) from the God who made all things by his Word and adorned them by his Wisdom. So also, as in heaven he had the first place as Word of God, so he held it on earth as being a just man "who committed no sin, neither was guile found in his mouth" (1 Pet.2:22). He also had the first place over those under the earth, becoming "firstborn of the dead" (Rev.1:5), so that all things saw their king, as we have said, and that the paternal light shone forth in the flesh of our Lord and then, radiant from his flesh, came among us and thus mankind reached imperishability, enveloped by the paternal light.

Wisdom as Spirit

20.3 We have provided many proofs to show that the Word, that is, the Son, was always with the Father. But that Wisdom, which is the Spirit, was with him before all creation, it says through Solomon: "God by Wisdom founded the earth, he prepared the heaven by understanding; by his knowledge the abysses burst forth, and the clouds dropped down the dew" (Prov.3:19–20). And further: "The Lord created me as the beginning of his ways for his works; before the ages he established me; in the beginning, before he made the earth and established the abysses, before the fountains came forth, before the mountains were made firm, and all the hills, he generated me" (8:22–25). And again: "When he prepared the heaven I was with him; when he made firm the fountains of the abyss and the foundations of the earth I was with him to adjust. I was the one with whom he found joy, and daily I rejoiced before his face all the time, while he rejoiced to have finished the world and took pleasure among the sons of men" (8:27–31).[5]

20.4 Therefore there is one God who by Word and Wisdom made and harmonized everything. He is the Creator, who assigned this world to the human race. In his greatness he is unknown to all who were made by him, for no one has investigated his height among the ancients or the moderns.

Primacy of the Word

In his love, however, he is always known through the one through whom he created everything. This is his Word, our Lord Jesus Christ, who in the last times was made man so that he might join the end to the beginning, that is, man to God. And therefore the prophets, after receiving the prophetic gift from the same Word, predicted his coming in the flesh, by which the mingling and communion of God and man was achieved according to the good pleasure of the Father. From the beginning the Word foretold that God would be seen by men, that he would live and speak with them on earth (Bar.3:38), and that he would be present to the work he fashioned, to save it and be perceptible to it, to "free us from the hands of all who hate us" (Luke 1:71), that is, from every spirit of transgression, making us able "to serve him in holiness and justice all our days" (1:74–75) so that, embracing the Spirit of God, man might come into the glory of the Father.

The work of the Spirit

20.6 Therefore men will see God in order to live, becoming immortal by the vision and attaining to God. That is what, as I have said, was figuratively shown through the prophets, that God will be seen by the men who bear his Spirit and always await his coming, as Moses said in Deuteronomy (5:24), "In that day we shall see, because God will speak to a man and he will live." Some of them saw the prophetic Spirit and its work in all kinds of gifts poured forth; others saw the coming of the Lord and his ministry from the beginning, by which he achieved the will of the Father as in heaven, so on earth (Matt.6:10); still others saw the Father's glories adapted in various times to men who saw and then heard, and to those who would hear subsequently. Thus, then, God was manifested; for through all these things God the Father is shown forth, as the Spirit works and the Son administers and the Father approves, and man is made perfect for his salvation. As he said through the prophet Hosea (12:11), "I have multiplied visions and have been represented by the hands of the prophets." The Apostle sets forth the same thing when he says, "There are varieties of gifts but the same Spirit; and there are varieties of ministries but the same Lord; there are varieties of workings, but the same God, who works all in all. To each is given the manifestation of the Spirit for his benefit" (1 Cor.12:4–7).

The work of the Word

But he who works all in all is invisible and inexpressible, as to his power and his greatness, for all beings made by him, though he is by no means unknown, for all learn through his Word that there is one God the Father, who contains all and gives existence to all, as it is written in the Gospel: "No one has ever seen God; the only-begotten God, who is in the Father's bosom, has revealed him" (John 1:18).

20.7 Thus from the beginning the Son is the Revealer of the Father, since from the beginning he was with the Father: prophetic visions, diversities of gifts, his ministries, the glorification of the Father, he has shown forth all that to men for their benefit at the right time, like a well-composed and harmonious melody. Where there is composition there is melody; where there is melody it is at the right time; where there is the right time, there is benefit. And because the Word became the dispenser of the Father's grace for the benefit of the men for whom he made such great "economies", he showed God to man and man to God, preserving the invisibility of the Father so that man would not become a despiser of God but would always have a goal toward which to advance, and at the same time making God visible to men through his many "economies" so that man might not be totally deprived of God and perish. For the glory of God is the living man, and the life of man is the vision of God. If the revelation of God by the creation already gives life to all the beings living on earth, how much more does the manifestation of the Father by the Word give life to those who see God!⁶

The Incarnation of the Word prefigured

22.1 In the last times, "when the fullness of the time" of liberty "came" (Gal.4:4), the Word in person "washed away the filth of the daughters of Zion" (Is.4:4), with his own hands washing the feet of the disciples (John 13:5), that is, of the human race inheriting God at the end, so that just as at the beginning through the first human beings we were all enslaved by the death we owed, so at the end, through the last human beings, all who from the beginning were disciples, cleansed and washed from death, might come into the life of God. For he who washed the disciples' feet sanctified the whole body and brought it to cleansing (John 13:10).

This is why he served them a meal while they reclined, to indicate those who were reclining in the earth, to whom he came to bring life. As Jeremiah says: "The Lord, the Holy One of Israel, remembered his dead asleep in the land of the tomb, and he went down to them to proclaim the good news of his salvation, to save them."[7]

This is why the eyes of the disciples were heavy when Christ came to his passion (Matt.26:43). Finding them asleep, the Lord first left them, to indicate the patience of God over the sleep of men; but when he came a second time he awoke them and made them arise, to indicate that his passion would be the awakening of his sleeping disciples. For them he "descended into the lower parts of the earth" (Eph.4:9), to see with his eyes the unfinished part of the creation, of which he said to the disciples, "Many prophets and just men desired to see and hear what you see and hear" (Matt.13:17).

22.2 For Christ did not come just for those who believed him from the times of Tiberius Caesar, nor did the Father exercise his providence just for the men who live now, but for all the men who from the beginning feared and loved God as they were able and lived in justice and piety toward their neighbors and desired to see Christ and hear his voice. Therefore at his second coming he will awaken all these and raise them up before the others, that is, before those who will be judged, and he will establish them in his kingdom.

"For there is one God" who led the patriarchs in his "economies," and "who justified the circumcised by faith and the uncircumcised through faith" (Rom.3:30). Just as we were prefigured and foretold in the first men, they again are shaped in us, that is, in the church, and receive the wage of their labors.

23.1 This is why the Lord said to the disciples, "Behold, I tell you, lift up your eyes and see the fields, that they are white for the harvest. For the reaper receives his wage and gathers fruit for eternal life, that he who sows and he who reaps may rejoice together. In this the saying is true: one sows, another reaps. I have sent you to reap what you did not work for; others worked, and you have entered into their labors" (John 4:35–38). Who are they, then, who have worked and served the "economies" of God? Obviously, the patriarchs and the prophets, who prefigured our faith and sowed on earth the coming of the Son of God, announcing who and what he would be, so that the men who would come later might have the fear of God and readily accept the coming of Christ, being instructed by the scriptures.

This is why, when Joseph recognized that Mary was pregnant and thought of sending her away secretly, an angel said to him in dreams, "Do not fear to take Mary your wife, for what she has in her womb comes from the Holy Spirit; she will bear a son and you will call him Jesus, for he will save his people from their sins" (Matt.1:20–21). And to convince him he added, "All this took place that what was spoken by the Lord through the prophet might be fulfilled: 'Behold, the Virgin will conceive and bear a son, and his name will be called Emmanuel'" (1:22–23; Is.7:14), persuading him and excusing Mary by the words of the prophet, showing that she was this Virgin, who was to generate Emmanuel, foretold by Isaiah. Therefore Joseph agreed without hesitation and took Mary, and during the whole time he cared for Christ he gladly served him, even going out to Egypt and coming back and migrating to Nazareth. Indeed, those who do not know the scriptures and the promise of God[8] and the "economy" of Christ considered him the father of the boy.

This is why the Lord himself read the prophecies of Isaiah at Capernaum. "The Spirit of the Lord is upon me, and therefore he anointed me, he sent me to preach to the poor, to cure the broken-hearted, to announce to the captives their deliverance and to the blind their sight" (Luke 4:18; Is.61:1). And to show that he was the one who had been foretold by the prophets, he said to them: "Today this scripture is fulfilled in your ears" (Luke 4:21).

23.2 This is why the apostle Philip, after finding the eunuch of the queen of Ethiopia reading the words of Isaiah: "Like a sheep he was led to the slaughter and like a lamb, mute before his shearer, did not open his mouth; in humility his judgment was taken away" (Acts 8:32–33; Is.53:7), and the other details the prophet went through about his passion and coming in the flesh and how he was dishonored by those who did not believe him), easily persuaded him to believe that Jesus Christ, who was crucified under Pontius Pilate and suffered all that the prophet predicted, was the Son of God who gives eternal life to men (Acts 8:37). As he baptized him he left him at once, for nothing was lacking to one precatechized by the prophets; he did not fail to know either God the Father or the rules of moral life, but only the coming of the Son of God. And when he had quickly come to know him, "he went his way rejoicing" (8:39), to be the herald of Christ's coming in Ethiopia. Philip did not have to labor overmuch with him, for he had been preformed by the prophets in the fear of God.

This is why the apostles, gathering "the lost sheep of the house of

Israel" (Matt.10:6), showed them by speaking to them from the scriptures that this crucified Jesus was the Christ, the Son of the living God. They thus persuaded a great multitude who had the fear of God, and in one day three, four, and five thousand men were baptized (Acts 2:41; 4:4).

Paul's preaching to the gentiles

24.1 This is why Paul, the apostle to the gentiles, says, "I labored more than them all" (1 Cor.15:10). For them, in fact, the teaching was easy, since they had proofs from the scriptures; those who heard Moses and the prophets (Luke 16:31) easily accepted the "firstborn from the dead" (Col.1:18) and the "prince of the life" (Acts 3:15) of God, the one who by extending his hands destroyed Amalech (Exod.17:10–13) and through the faith that was in him made the man live after the snake's bite (Num.21:6–9).

But to the gentiles the Apostle first taught, as we have shown in the previous book, how to give up superstition about idols and worship one God, the Maker of heaven and earth and Creator of the whole universe, and that the Son of this God is his Word, through whom he produced everything, and that he became man among men in the last times in order to struggle for humanity, defeat the enemy of man, and give his work the victory over its adversary. Even when those of the circumcision did not practice the words of God because they despised them, they still were instructed in advance not to commit adultery or fornication, not to steal or defraud (Mark 10:19), and that whatever harmed their neighbor is evil and hated by God; therefore they easily agreed to abstain from these, since they had already learned these things.

24.2 But the gentiles had to learn this very thing, that actions of this kind were evil, harmful, and useless, and damaged those who committed them. Therefore he who received the apostolate to the gentiles labored more than those who proclaimed the Son of God among the circumcised. The scriptures aided the latter because the Lord confirmed and fulfilled them when he came just as he had been predicted. For the former, however, it was an alien learning and a novel teaching: the gods of the gentiles not only were not gods, but they were idols of demons; there is only one God, who is "above every principality and power and dominion and every name that is named" (Eph.1:21), and his Word, by nature invisible, became tangible and visible among men, and went "down to death, even death on a cross" (Phil.2:8). Those who believe in him will become imperishable and impassible and will attain to the kingdom of the heavens. All that was preached orally to the gentiles, without any scriptures; this is why those who preached to the gentiles "labored more."

Predictions and prefigurations

25.3 It was necessary for some things to be predicted in a patriarchal mode by the patriarchs, and for others to be prefigured by the prophets in the mode of the law, and for yet others to receive from those who received adoption a formation corresponding with their formation according to Christ, but all things are shown forth in one God.

26.1 When the law is read by the Jews in our time it is like a fable, for they do not have what is the explanation of all, that is, the human coming of the Son of God. But when read by Christians it is a treasure hidden in a field, revealed and explained by the cross of Christ, enriching the mind of men, showing forth the wisdom of God and manifesting his "economies" for man, prefiguring the kingdom of Christ and foretelling the heritage of the holy Jerusalem. It predicts that the man who loves God will advance to see God and hear his word and will be so glorified by the hearing of this word that other men will not be able to look upon his glorious face, as was said by Daniel: "Those who understand will shine like the splendor of the firmament and, among the multitude of the just, like stars, eternally and forever" (Dan.12:3). If then anyone reads the scriptures in the way we have just shown – as the Lord explained them to the disciples after his resurrection from the dead, proving from the scriptures themselves that "it was necessary that the Christ should suffer and enter into his glory" (Luke 24:26,46) and that "in his name the remission of sins should be preached" (24:47) in the whole world – he will be a perfect disciple, "like the master of the house who brings forth from his treasure things new and old" (Matt.13:52).

The authority of the presbyters

26.2 This is why one must hear the presbyters who are in the church, those who have the succession from the apostles, as we have shown, and with the succession in the episcopate have received the sure spiritual gift of truth according to the good pleasure of the Father. As for all the others who are separate from the original succession, in whatever place they gather, they are suspect. They are heretics with false doctrine or schismatics full of pride and audacity and self-willed or, again, hypocrites looking only for gain and vainglory.

26.4 So one must turn away from all men of this kind, and adhere to those who, as we have said, guard the teaching of the apostles and with the rank of presbyter provide a healthy word and way of life (Tit.2:8) for the example and correction of others.

The teaching of a presbyter

27.1 As I have heard from a certain presbyter, who had heard it from those who had seen the apostles, and from their disciples,[9] the deeds committed by the ancients without the counsel of the Spirit received sufficient condemnation from the scriptures, for God, who does not respect persons, imposed a suitable correction on deeds not in accordance with his good pleasure.

27.2 And this is why the Lord went down under the earth (Eph.4:9) to proclaim to them his coming, the remission of sins for those who believe in him. They all believed in him, those who set their hope in him (1:12), that is, proclaimed his coming in advance and served his 'economies' – the just and the prophets and patriarchs.[10] And he remitted their sins like ours, so that we can no longer blame them for them without despising the grace of God. For as they do not reproach us for the incontinent acts we performed before Christ was manifest among us, so it is not right for us to accuse those who sinned before us. For "all fall short of the glory of God" (Rom.3:23) but those who have eyes turned toward the light are justified, not by themselves but by the Lord's coming. Their acts were written down for our instruction (1 Cor.10:11), first so that we might know that our God and theirs is one, to whom sins are not pleasing even if committed by illustrious men, and second so that we should abstain from evil.

The Exodus story defended

29.2 God hardened the heart of Pharaoh so that, while he saw that the finger of God led the people out, he did not believe it but precipitated himself into the sea of unbelief, imagining that their exodus took place through magic and that the Red Sea offered passage to the people not by God's power but naturally.

30.1 As for those who criticize and accuse the people at the Exodus for taking, by God's order, the vessels of every sort as well as clothing from the Egyptians, out of which the tabernacle in the desert was made, they prove themselves ignorant of the judgments of God and his "economies," as the presbyter used to say. For if God had not consented to this, in the prefigurative Exodus, today in our Exodus, that is, in the faith in which we are set, through which we have come out of the number of the gentiles, no one could be saved. For all of us are accompanied by possessions either modest or great, which we acquired from "the mammon of iniquity" (Luke 16:9). Whence come the houses in which we live, and the clothing we wear, and the vessels we use, and everything that serves our daily life, but from what we acquired by avarice when we were pagans or received from pagan parents, relatives, or friends, who acquired it by injustice, not to mention what we are still acquiring even in the faith? For who sells and does not want to gain from the buyer? Who buys and does not want to take advantage of the seller? Who does business unless to gain his living? Do not even the believers who are in the imperial palace receive what is necessary from Caesar's goods, and does not each of them give as he can to those in need? The Egyptian people owed not only their property but life itself to the earlier goodness of the patriarch Joseph, but what do the pagans owe us, when we receive profits and benefits from them? Whatever they produce by their labor we in the faith use without labor.

30.2   The people underwent the worst slavery to the Egyptians, as scripture says. "And the Egyptians oppressed the children of Israel and made their life hateful by hard labors, with mud and brick-making and all the work they did in the fields, through all the works with which they forcibly oppressed them" (Exod.1:13–14). And they built fortified cities for them (1:11), laboring much and increasing their fortune for many years and through every form of slavery, since they not only were ungrateful to them but wanted to destroy them all. What then was done unjustly if out of much they took a little, and those who could have possessed much wealth and gone away rich, had they not been slaves, left with the slightest pay for their long slavery?

Just as if some free man is forcibly abducted by someone and is his slave for many years and increases his wealth, but then obtains some help and could seem to possess certain modest sums that belong to his master, he really would depart with little recompense for his great labors and the great wealth acquired. Anyone who accused him of having acted unjustly would seem to be an unjust judge in regard to the man who had been forcibly enslaved. Such are people of this kind, who accuse the people of taking a few things from their many labors but do not accuse themselves for the favors received from their pagan parents and, without having been in slavery, have received the maximum benefit from them. They accuse them of having received for their labors uncoined gold and silver in a few vessels, as we said, but – we will tell the truth, even should it seem ridiculous to some – they themselves, out of the labors of others, carry in their girdles coins of gold and silver and bronze with the superscription and image of Caesar (cf. Matt.22:20–21) and say they are acting justly.

30.3 But if we compare ourselves with them, who will appear to have received more justly? The people, from the Egyptians who owed them all sorts of debts? Or us, from the Romans and the other nations which owe us nothing of this kind? The world enjoys peace through them, so that we may walk without fear on the roads and sail wherever we wish.

The truly spiritual disciple judges all . . .

33.1 A disciple who is truly "spiritual," because he has received the Spirit of God which was with men from the beginning in all the "economies" of God and predicted the future, showed forth the present, and told about the past, "judges all and himself is judged by none" (1 Cor.2:15).

For he judges the gentiles, who "serve the creature rather than the Creator" and with "depraved mind" (Rom.1:25,28) waste all their activity. He also judges the Jews, who do not receive the Word of liberty nor wish to be freed, though they have the Liberator in their midst, but out of season and apart from the law they pretend to serve the God who needs nothing, and do not recognize the coming of Christ for the salvation of men nor desire to understand that all the prophets announced his two advents.

33.7 He will also judge those who produce schisms, those who lack the love of God and look out for their own advantage rather than the unity of the church, and for insignificant and trivial causes rend and divide the great and glorious body of Christ, and insofar as they can, kill it – speaking peace and making war, they truly "filter a fly and swallow a camel" (Matt.23:24). No reform can come from them as great as the damage their schism causes.

... and is judged by none

"But he himself is judged by no one" (1 Cor.2:15), for with him everything is unshakably firm, He has a full faith in one God Almighty, "from whom is everything" (1 Cor.8:6), and a firm assent to the Son of God, Jesus Christ our Lord, "through whom is everything" (8:6), and to the "economies" through which the Son of God was made man, and in the Spirit of God, who gives knowledge of the truth (1 Tim.2:4), who makes known to men the "economies" of the Father and the Son in each generation, as the Father wills.

The one true Gnosis

33.8 This is true Gnosis: the teaching of the apostles, and the ancient institution of the church, spread throughout the entire world, and the distinctive mark of the body of Christ in accordance with the successions of bishops, to whom the apostles entrusted each local church, and the unfeigned preservation, coming down to us, of the scriptures, with a complete collection allowing for neither addition nor subtraction; a reading without falsification and, in conformity with the scriptures, an interpretation that is legitimate, careful, without danger or blasphemy.

Gnosis with love and martyrdom

Above all there is the special gift of love, more precious than knowledge, more glorious than prophecy, pre-eminent among all the gifts of grace.
33.9 Therefore the church in every place, because of its love for God, sends forth in every time a throng of martyrs to the Father. All the others are unable to make this showing, but even deny that such martyrdom is necessary. In their view their doctrine is the true testimony. Therefore in the whole time since the Lord appeared on earth hardly one or two of them, as if obtaining mercy, has borne the disgrace of the Name with our martyrs and has been punished with them as a kind of supplement being given them.

Varieties of Gnostic exegesis

35.4 They say that above these matters [spoken by the Mother] there are things said by the Principality, but they are refuted by what is reported in the scriptures concerning the coming of Christ. As for what they are, they are not in agreement but make different responses about the same texts. For if someone wants to test them and asks individually the most distinguished among them about some text, he will find that one of them sees in it an allusion to the Propator, the Abyss; another to the Beginning of all, the Only-Begotten; another to the Father of all, the Word; another to one of the Aeons in the Pleroma; another to Christ, and another to the Savior. The most learned of them, after remaining silent for a long time, says it was spoken of Limit, but another says the Sophia within the Pleroma is indicated; another, that the Mother outside the Pleroma is announced; another will speak of the God who made the world. So many are the differences among them on one point, and so many the varied opinions they profess on the same scriptures! When one and the same text has been read, all furrow their brows and shake their heads, saying, "This is a very profound word, and not all understand the greatness of the meaning it contains; therefore silence is the greatest thing for the wise." The Silence above must be expressed in the silence present among them. So they all go away, however many they are, giving birth to so many great thoughts from a single text and secretly taking their subtleties with them. If they ever agree on what was predicted in the scriptures, we ourselves will then refute them. Meanwhile, holding erroneous opinions they refute themselves, disagreeing over the same words. But we, following the Lord as the one and only true teacher and taking his words as the rule of truth, all always say the same things of the same texts, since we know one God, maker of this universe, who sent the prophets, brought the people out of the land of Egypt, and in the last times manifested his Son in order to confound unbelievers and reclaim the fruit of justice.

BOOK V

BOOK V SUPPLEMENTS BOOKS I–IV

Pr. In the four books we have already edited and sent you, beloved, with the doctrines revealed and the inventors of irreligious opinions overthrown, sometimes starting from the doctrine of each one as left in their writings, sometimes out of reasoning proceeding from various demonstrations, we have thus made known the truth and proclaimed the message of the church, which the prophets had already announced (as we have shown), which Christ perfected, which the apostles transmitted, from whom the church received it and, alone keeping it safe throughout the world, delivers to its children. We have resolved all the questions proposed to us by the heretics, explained the doctrine of the apostles, and revealed most of what the Lord said or did through parables.

In this fifth book of the whole work *On the Detection and Refutation of the Knowledge Falsely So Called* we shall try to provide proofs based on the rest of our Lord's teaching and on the apostolic letters, as you requested us to do. We are obeying your command, since we were appointed also for the ministry of the word (Acts 6:4), and are applying ourselves in every way, according to our power, to provide you with all possible resources against the contradictions of the heretics, to bring back wanderers and convert them to the church of God, and also to strengthen the mind of neophytes so that they may preserve unshaken the faith which they received, well-guarded, from the church, and in no way be corrupted by those who try to teach them wrongly and turn them from the truth.

You and all future readers of this writing must read very carefully what we have said so that you may know the very theses for which we are providing refutations. For only thus will you oppose them suitably and yourself will be able to take on the task of refuting all the heretics, rejecting their doctrines as ordure with the help of the celestial faith and following the only sure and true Teacher, the Word of God, Jesus Christ our Lord, who because of his immeasurable love became what we are in order to make us what he is.

Incarnation and revelation

1.1 For we could not learn the mysteries of God had not our teacher, the Logos, been made man; nor could anyone have revealed the secrets of the Father (John 1:18) except his own Word. "Who has known the mind of the Lord? Or what" other one "has been his counselor?" (Rom.11:34). Nor, again, could we have known them except by seeing our teacher and perceiving the sound of his voice with our own ears; for by imitating his works and doing his words (Matt.7:24) we have communion with him, and thus we who are newly created receive growth from him who was perfect before the whole creation, who alone is excellent and good.

Corporeal resurrection and the Eucharist

2.2 Those who reject the whole "economy" of God, deny the salvation of the flesh and reject its regeneration, saying that it is not capable of receiving imperishability, are absolutely vain. If this flesh is not saved, the Lord did not redeem us by his blood (Col.1:14) and the cup of the Eucharist is not communion with his blood and the bread we break is not communion with his body (1 Cor.10:16). For blood comes only from veins and flesh and the rest of the human substance, which the Word of God became when he redeemed us by his blood. As his Apostle says, "In him we have redemption by his blood, the remission of sins" (Col.1:14). And because we are his members (1 Cor.6:15) and are nourished by means of the creation (which he himself provides, making his sun rise and raining as he will [Matt.5:45]), he declared that the cup from the creation is his blood, out of which he makes our blood increase, and the bread from the creation is his body, out of which he makes our body grow.

2.3 If then the cup of mixed wine and the bread that is made receives the word of God and becomes the Eucharist of the blood and the body of Christ, and from these it grows and consists of the substance of our flesh, how can they deny that the flesh is receptive of the gift of God, which is eternal life, when it has been nourished by the body and blood of the Lord and is a member of him? When the blessed Apostle said in the letter to the Ephesians, "that we are members of the body, of his flesh and his bones" (Eph.5:30), he was saying these things not of some spiritual and invisible man ("For a spirit does not have bones or flesh" [Luke 24:39]) but of the real man's constitution, consisting of flesh and sinews and bones, which is nourished from the cup, which is his blood, and grows from the bread, which is his body.

5.1 Bodies endured for a long time as long as this pleased God. If heretics read the scriptures they will find that our ancestors lived beyond 700, 800, and 900 years ...

5.2 It seems incredible and impossible to modern people, ignorant of God's "economies," that a man can live so many years, but our ancestors lived that long, as do those who have been translated to prefigure the future "length of days" (Ps.23:6; 91:16). It seems incredible that men came out safely from the belly of the sea-monster and the fiery furnace, but they were led out as by the Hand of God to show his power.

Breath of life and Spirit

12.1 The former life was driven out because it had been given not through the Spirit but through a "breath."

12.2 The breath of life (Gen.2:7), which makes the man psychic, is one thing and the life-giving Spirit (1 Cor.15:45) is another. And therefore Isaiah said, "Thus says the Lord, who made heaven and made it fast, who made firm the earth and what is in it, and gave breath to the people who are on it and the Spirit to those who walk on it" (Is.42:5): by that he says that breath was given in common to all the people on earth, while Spirit is properly for those who tread upon earthly lusts. Therefore Isaiah says, making the distinction again, "For the Spirit will come forth from me and it is I who made every breath" (57:16), properly setting the Spirit in God, who in the last days has spread it forth on the human race by adoption, but setting breath generally in the creation and referring to it as something made. What has been made is different from him who made it. So breath is something temporary, while Spirit is eternal. And breath grows for a moment and stays for a time and then goes away, leaving breathless what it was in before; but Spirit possessing a man inside and outside, always remains and will never leave him.

But, says the Apostle, addressing us men, "It is not the spiritual which is first, but first is the psychic, then what is spiritual" (1 Cor.15:46). This is reasonable, for man had to be formed first and when formed receive a soul and then receive the communion of the Spirit. Therefore "the first Adam was made a living soul but the last Adam was made a life-giving Spirit" (15:45). Just as the one who had been made a living soul, when he inclined toward evil, lost his life, so this same one, returning to the better and receiving the life-giving Spirit, will find life.

Flesh dies, Spirit lives

12.3 For it is not one thing that dies and another that is made alive, just as it is not one thing that is lost and another that is found, but the Lord came to look for that very sheep that was lost (Matt.18:11). What was dead? Evidently the substance of flesh, which had lost the breath of life and became without breath and dead. This is what the Lord came to make alive so that as we all die in Adam because psychic, so we all live in Christ because spiritual, after having put off not the work shaped by God but the desires of the flesh, and put on the Holy Spirit.

Paul's language about death and resurrection

As the Apostle says in his letter to the Colossians, "Put to death your members on earth." What are these members? He explains: "Fornication, impurity, passion, evil desire and the avarice which is idolatry" (Col.3:5). The Apostle preaches the rejection of these and says that those who commit such deeds, as being merely "flesh and blood," cannot "inherit the kingdom of heaven" (Gal.5:21; 1 Cor. 15:50), for their soul, having inclined to the worse and descended into worldly lusts, shares the same name as themselves. He orders us to put these off and says again in the same letter, "Having put off the old man with his deeds" (Col.3:9). By saying this he did not repudiate the old formation, for otherwise we should kill ourselves and separate from the life here below.

12.4 But the Apostle himself wrote to us as one formed in the womb and born out of it (Gal.1:15) and he acknowledges in the letter to the Philippians that "life in the flesh is a fruitful labor" (1:22). Now the fruit of the labor of the Spirit is the salvation of the flesh; for what could the visible fruit of the invisible Spirit be if not to make the flesh mature and receptive of imperishability? If then "to live in the flesh is the fruit of a work for me", the Apostle surely does not despise the substance of the flesh when he says "Putting off your old man with his works" (Col.3:9) but indicates the putting off of our old way of life which grows old and perishes (Eph.4:22), and therefore he continues, "And putting on the new man, who renews himself in knowledge according to the image of him who created him" (Col.3:10). When he says, "Who renews himself in knowledge," he shows that that man who previously found himself in ignorance, that is, who did not know God, renews himself by the knowledge of him; for the knowledge of God renews man. And in saying, "According to the image of him who created him," he indicates the recapitulation of this man who at the beginning was made after the image of God (Gen.1:26).

12.5 That the Apostle was the same being who was born from the womb, that is, of the ancient substance of flesh, he himself said in the letter to the Galatians: "When he who set me apart from my mother's womb and called me through his grace was pleased to reveal his Son in me so that I should proclaim him among the gentiles" (1:15–16). For there was not one born from the womb and another who proclaimed the Son of God, as we said, but the same one formerly ignorant who persecuted the church (1:13), when revelation was made to him from heaven and the Lord spoke with him, as we showed in the third book, preached the Gospel of the Son of God Christ Jesus, who was crucified under Pontius Pilate, with his past ignorance abolished by his later knowledge.

Gnostics cannot appeal to 1 Corinthians 15:50

13.2 Vain and truly unfortunate are those who do not want to look at things so evident and clear but flee from the light of truth, blinding themselves like the Oedipus of tragedy. It happens that novice wrestlers, struggling with others, forcibly grab a part of their adversary's body and are thrown to the ground by the part they hold; as they fall they suppose they are winning because they vigorously hold that member they first seized, but in fact they are held in derision because they have fallen. Thus when the heretics take two expressions from Paul, "Flesh and blood cannot inherit the kingdom of God" (1 Cor.15:50), they have not understood the mind of the Apostle or studied the meaning of his expressions. Simply holding to the mere words, they die in relation to them, overturning the whole "economy" of God as far as they can.

13.4 What proves that the Apostle does not speak of some other body, but of the body of flesh, is that he says to the Corinthians plainly, indubitably, and without any ambiguity:

Always bearing about the death of Jesus in our body, that the life of Jesus Christ may also be manifest in our body. For if we the living are delivered to death because of Jesus, that the life of Jesus may also be manifest in our mortal flesh . . . (2 Cor. 4:10–11).

And that the Spirit is bound with the flesh, when he says in the same letter, "You are a letter of Christ, ministered by us, written not with ink but with the Spirit of the living God, not on tablets of stone but on tablets of flesh in your hearts" (3:3). If, then, our hearts of flesh are capable of receiving the Spirit, what wonder if at the resurrection they receive the life given by the Spirit? Of this resurrection the Apostle says in his letter to the Philippians: "Conformed to his death, if I may attain to the resurrection from the dead" (Phil. 3:10–11). Therefore, in what other mortal flesh can life be understood as manifest except in this substance which is also made dead because of the confession of God?

Incarnation means flesh and blood

14.1   What proves that it is not the substance of flesh and blood that the Apostle attacks when he says it does not possess the kingdom of God (1 Cor.15:50) is the fact that he constantly uses the terms flesh and blood of our Lord Jesus Christ, sometimes to show that he was a man (for the Lord himself called himself Son of man) and sometimes to confirm the salvation of our flesh. For if the flesh were not to be saved the Word of God would not have become flesh (John 1:14) and if the blood of the just were not to be requited the Lord would not have had blood.

But since from the beginning the blood of the just spoke, as God said to Cain when he had killed his brother, "The voice of your brother's blood cries out to men" (Gen.4:10). And that their blood would be requited, he said to those about Noah, "I will require your blood of your souls from the hand of every beast" (9:5), and again: "Whoever sheds the blood of a man, his own blood will be shed in return" (9:6). Likewise the Lord said to those who were going to shed his blood, "The blood of every just man shed on the earth will be requited, from the blood of the just Abel to the blood of Zechariah son of Barachiah, whom you killed between the temple and the altar; truly, I tell you, all that will come upon this generation" (Matt.23:35–36). He was pointing to the future recapitulation in himself of the shedding of the blood of all the just and the prophets from the beginning and the requital of their blood through himself. He would not have demanded requital unless it was to be saved, and the Lord would not have recapitulated these things in himself if he too had not been made flesh and blood in accordance with the first-formed work, thus saving in himself at the end what had perished at the beginning in Adam.

14.2 If, however, the Lord became incarnate by means of another "economy" and took flesh from a different substance, then he did not recapitulate man in himself, and one cannot even call him flesh, since flesh really is what succeeded to the work first modeled from earth. But if he had to take matter from a different substance, from the beginning the Father would have taken a different substance for his clod of earth. But now the saving Word was made what the man who perished was, through himself effecting communion with him and obtaining his salvation. What was lost (cf. Luke 19:10) had blood and flesh; for taking earth from the ground God fashioned man, and for him was the whole "economy" of the Lord's coming. Therefore he too had flesh and blood, recapitulating in himself the original work of the Father, not something different, and seeking what was lost (19:10). And therefore the Apostle says in the letter to the Colossians, "And you were formerly aliens and enemies of his purpose in evil works but are now reconciled in the body of his flesh through his death, to present yourselves holy and pure and without blame before him" (Col.1:21–22). "You have been reconciled in the body of his flesh," because the just flesh has reconciled the flesh that was captive to sin and brought it into friendship with God.

14.3 So if anyone says that the flesh of the Lord was different from ours in that it did not sin "nor was guile found in his mouth" (1 Pet. 2:22), while we are sinners, he speaks correctly. But if he imagines that the flesh of the Lord was different in substance from ours, the word of the Apostle on reconciliation will have no weight for him, for what is reconciled was formerly in enmity. If the Lord took flesh of another substance, what became hostile by transgression is not reconciled to God. But now by our communion with him the Lord reconciled man with the Father, reconciling us by the body of his flesh (Col.1:22) and redeeming us by his blood, as the Apostle says to the Ephesians: "In whom we have redemption through his blood, the remission of sins" (1:7). And again to the same: "You who were formerly far off have been made near by the blood of Christ" (2:13). And again: "In his flesh he destroyed enmity, the Law of precepts in decrees" (2:14–15). And in the whole letter the Apostle clearly testifies that we have been saved by the flesh of our Lord and his blood.

14.4 If then flesh and blood are what make life for us, it was not

literally said of flesh and blood that they cannot inherit the kingdom
of God (1 Cor.15:50), but of the carnal actions we have mentioned,
which turn man toward sin and deprive him of life. And therefore in
the letter to the Romans he says, "Let not sin reign in your mortal
body so that you obey it. Do not deliver your members to sin as
weapons of injustice, but deliver yourselves to God as living from
the dead and your members as weapons of justice for God"
(Rom.6:12–13). Thus by the same members with which we served sin
and bore fruit to death, he desires us to serve justice in order to bear
fruit to life (6:6;7:5;6:19).

Remember therefore, beloved, that you have been redeemed by the
flesh of our Lord and bought by his blood, and "holding to the head
from which the whole body" of the church "is knit together and
grows" (Col.2:19), that is, at the carnal coming of the Son of God;
confess him as God and hold firmly to him as man, using the proofs
drawn from the scriptures. Thus you will easily avoid, as we have
shown, all the opinions later invented by the heretics.

Recapitulation and the Word of God

18.3 The Maker of the world is truly the Word of God: he is our
Lord, who in the last times was made man, existing in this world
(John 1:10), and invisibly contains everything that was made
(Wisd.1:7) and was imprinted in the shape of a Chi in everything,[1] as
Word of God governing and disposing everything. Therefore he
came in visible form into his own region (John 1:11) and was made
flesh (1:14) and was hanged from the wood, in order to recapitulate
everything in himself. And his own did not receive him (1:11), as
Moses announced by saying to the people, "And your life will be
hanging before your eyes and you will not believe your life"
(Deut.28:66). Therefore those who did not receive him did not
receive life. "As many as received him he gave them power to become
children of God" (John 1:12). For he is the one who has power over
all from the Father, as Word of God and true man.

19.1 Therefore when the Lord obviously came into his own
domain, with his own creation bearing him up as it was borne by him,
and by his obedience on the tree recapitulating the disobedience in
the tree, and with the seduction of that betrothed virgin Eve dissi-
pated by the truth announced by the angel to Mary, also a betrothed
virgin – as the first one was seduced by the word of an angel to escape
God and lie about his word, so the second was given the good news

by the word of an angel to bear God and obey his word; and as the first was seduced into disobeying God, so the second was persuaded to obey God so that the virgin Mary might become the advocate of the virgin Eve; and just as the human race was subjected to death by a virgin, it was freed by a virgin, with the virginal disobedience balanced by virginal obedience; thus the sin of the first man was corrected by the rectitude of the Firstborn, and the prudence of the serpent was overcome by the simplicity of the dove (Matt.10:16), and by that the bonds were dissolved by which we had been tied to death.

Review on heretics

19.2 Then all the heretics are stupid and do not know the "economies" of God and do not know his "economy" for man – blind as they are concerning the truth – when they contradict their own salvation, some introducing a Father other than the Demiurge, others saying that the world and its substance were made by angels, others saying that this matter, far removed from their so-called Father, flourished spontaneously and innately, and others deriving its substance from deficiency and ignorance in what the Father contains. Yet others despise the visible coming of the Lord and reject his incarnation. Still others, again, ignorant of the "economy" of the Virgin, say he was generated by Joseph. Some say that neither soul nor body can receive eternal life, but only the "inner man," which they identify with their mind, judging it alone to rise to perfection. Others say the soul is saved, but the body cannot share in salvation from God, as we said in the first book, where we set forth the doctrines of all of them, and we showed their inconsistency in the second.

Review on the church

20.1 All these are much later than the bishops to whom the apostles entrusted the churches, and we have set this forth with all due diligence in the third book. All the aforementioned heretics, since they are blind to the truth, have to go to one side or the other off the road and therefore the traces of their doctrine are scattered without agreement or logic. The way of church members surrounds the whole world, contains the firm tradition from the apostles, and lets us view one and the same faith with all, for all believe in one and the same God and in the "economy" of the incarnation of the Son of God and know the same gift of the Spirit and care for the same commandments and preserve the same organization in the church and await the same coming of the Lord; they hope for the same salvation of the whole man, that is, of soul and body. Therefore the proclamation of the church is true and solid, since in it one and the same way of salvation is shown forth in the whole world. To it has been entrusted the light of God, and this is why the "wisdom" of God, by which he saves men, "is celebrated on the roads, acts confidently in public places, is proclaimed at the top of walls, and speaks with assurance at the city gates" (Prov.1:21). Everywhere the church proclaims the truth: and this is the seven-branched lamp which bears the light of Christ.

20.2 Those who abandon the message of the church criticize the simplicity of the holy presbyters, not observing how much better a simple religious man is than a blasphemous and impudent sophist. Such are the heretics: imagining they have found something superior to the truth and following the doctrines just described, they proceed along various, manifold, and uncertain ways, not always maintaining the same doctrines. They are like blind men led by the blind and naturally fall into the open ditch of ignorance (Matt.15:14), always seeking and never finding the truth (2 Tim.3:7). We must flee from their doctrines and carefully avoid being harmed by them, but take refuge with the church and be nursed by its breast and the scriptures of the Lord. For the church has been planted in the world like paradise. "You will eat the fruit of every tree in paradise" (Gen.2:16), says the Spirit of God; that is, eat from every scripture of the Lord, but do not eat with a spirit of pride and have no contact with the dissent of heretics. They profess to possess the knowledge of good and evil, and stretch their impious minds beyond the God who made them. They think beyond the measure of thought. Therefore the Apostle says, "Do not think more highly than you ought to think, but think with sober judgment" (Rom.12:3), so that we may not taste their "knowledge," which is more than one ought to think, and be expelled from the paradise of life. Into this the Lord brings those who obey his preaching, "recapitulating in himself everything heaven and on earth" (Eph.1:10).

Recapitulation as framework

The things in the heavens are spiritual, while those on earth are the dispensation related to man. Therefore he recapitulated these in himself by uniting man to the Spirit and placing the Spirit in man, himself the head of the Spirit and giving the Spirit to be the head of man: for it is by this Spirit that we see and hear and speak.

21.1 So in recapitulating everything he recapitulated our war against the enemy. He called forth and defeated the one who at the beginning in Adam had led us captive, and he trod on his head, as in Genesis God said to the serpent: "And I will set enmity between you and the woman, between your seed and her seed; she will watch your head and you will watch her heel" (Gen.3:15). From that point he who was to be born of a virgin after the likeness of Adam was announced as "watching the head" of the serpent. This is the "seed" of which the Apostle speaks in the letter to the Galatians: "The law of works was established until the seed should come to which the promise was made" (Gal.3:19). He explains it more clearly in the same letter when he says: "When the fullness of time came, God sent his Son, born of a woman" (4:4). For the enemy would not justly have been overcome had not the one who defeated him been "born of a woman." He controlled man through a woman, having set himself from the beginning as the foe of man. Therefore the Lord acknowledged himself as Son of man, recapitulating in himself that primal man from whom the formation of the woman was made, so that as through the defeated man our race went down to death, so again through man the victor we might ascend into life, and as death won the prize over us by a man, so again by a man we might win the prize over death.[2]

Recapitulation by the devil

24.1 Just as the devil lied at the beginning, he also lied at the end when he said, "All this has been delivered to me and I give it to whom I will" (Luke 4:6). He did not delimit the kingdoms of this age, but God did, for "the king's heart is in the hand of God" (Prov.21:1). And the Word says by the mouth of Solomon, "Through me kings reign and the powerful keep justice; through me princes are exalted and tyrants rule the earth" (8:15–16). And the apostle Paul says on this, "Be subject to all the higher powers, for there is no power except from God. Those that exist have been established by God" (Rom.13:1). And again he says of them, "Not without reason does it [the power] bear the sword, for it is the minister of God to execute his wrath upon the wrongdoer" (13:4). And because he says this not of angelic powers or invisible principalities, as some dare to interpret him, he adds, "For this reason you pay tribute, for they [the magistrates] are the ministers of God, attending to this" (13:6). The Lord confirmed this by not doing what the devil urged and by ordering the tribute paid to the collectors for himself and for Peter (Matt.17:27), for "they are the ministers of God, attending to this very thing."

Government not diabolical; Romans 13 irrelevant

24.2 Since man, separating from God, became so savage that he considered his kinsman by blood as an enemy, and without fear entered upon all disorder and murder and avarice, God imposed the fear of man on them, for they did not know the fear of God, so that in submission to the authority of men and educated by their laws they might attain to some measure of justice and act with moderation toward one another, fearing the sword plainly set before them, as the Apostle says: "Not without reason does it bear the sword, for it is the minister of God to execute his wrath on the wrongdoer." And for this reason the magistrates themselves, who have the laws as a cloak of justice, will not be interrogated or punished for what they do justly and legitimately, but will perish for everything they do to harm the just, iniquitously and illegally and in tyrannical fashion; for the just judgment of God comes to all equally and is unfailing. Authority on earth has been established for the benefit of the "gentiles" by God (not by the devil, who is never at rest and does not want the "gentiles" to live in peace) so that, fearing this authority, men may not devour one another like fish but by the imposition of laws may check the great injustice of the "gentiles." Thus the magistrates are the ministers of God. <If then they are ministers of God> who exact tribute from us, serving this very purpose,
24.3 <and> if the powers that exist have been established by God (Rom.13:1), it is clear that the devil lied when he said, "It has been delivered to me and I give it to whom I will" (Luke 4:6). For he by whose order men are born is also the one by whose order kings are appointed, suited to those reigned by them at the time. Among them some are given for the amendment and benefit of their subjects, and for the preservation of justice; others for fear and punishment and reprimand; still others, for mockery, insolence, and pride, as the subjects deserve, by God's just judgment, as we said; which reaches all equally. As for the devil, who is merely an apostate angel, he can only do what he did in the beginning, that is, seduce and lead astray the mind of man to transgress the commandments of God and gradually blind the hearts of those who hear him and forget the true God, worshiping this one as God.

Predictions of regal power

26.1 John the Lord's disciple spoke yet more clearly about the last time and the ten kings who live in it, among whom the empire now in power will be divided. He explained what the ten horns seen by Daniel were, saying that thus it was said to him:

> And the ten horns you saw are ten kings who have not yet received power, but they will receive it as kings for an hour, together with the beast. These agreed to give their power and authority to the beast. They will fight against the Lamb and the Lamb will defeat them, since he is Lord of lords and King of kings (Rev.17:12–14).

It is clear that the one to come will kill three of these, the rest will be subject to him, and he will be the eighth of them. They will devastate Babylon and burn it with fire and give their kingdom to the beast and persecute the church. Afterwards they will be destroyed by the coming of our Lord.

The Lord said that the kingdom must be divided and thus perish: "Every kingdom divided against itself will be made desolate and every city or house divided against itself will not stand" (Matt.12:25). And therefore the kingdom and city and house must be divided into ten parts, and therefore he already prefigured their partition and division. Also Daniel carefully identifies the end of the fourth kingdom by the toes of the statue seen by Nebuchadnezzar, upon which comes the stone cut without hands, as he says: "The feet of the statue were part iron and part clay; a stone was cut without hands and it struck the image on its iron and clay feet and completely smashed them" (Dan.2:33–34). After that he says in the explanation:

> Since you saw the feet and toes part clay, part iron, the kingdom will be divided and the firmness of iron will be in it, as you saw iron mixed with clay. And the toes are part iron, part clay (2:41–42).

Therefore the ten toes are ten kings among whom the kingdom will be divided; some of them are strong and active, while others are weak and idle and they will not agree, as Daniel says:

> A part of the kingdom will be strong and another will be broken. Since you saw the iron mixed with clay, they will be mingled by the seed of men, and they will not hold together, as iron does not hold with clay (2:42–43).

And he says what the end will be:

> And in the days of those kings God will set up a kingdom that will never be destroyed, and his kingdom will not be left to another people. He will break and destroy all the kingdoms (2:44).

The end of the world and salvation

28.3 The world will come to an end in as many millennia as the days in which it was made. And therefore the scripture of Genesis says, "And heaven and earth and all their adornment were finished. God finished on the sixth day all his works that he made, and he rested on the seventh day from all his works that he made" (2:1–2). This is an account of past events as they took place and a prophecy of the future. For if "a day of the Lord is like a thousand years" (2 Pet.3:8), and if the creation was finished in six days, it is clear that the end of things will be the 6,000th year.

28.4 This is why during this whole period of time the man formed at the beginning by the Hands of God, that is, the Son and the Spirit, comes to be in the image and likeness of God (Gen.2:7; 1:26). The chaff, that is, apostasy, is taken away, while the wheat is taken into the barn (Matt.3:12; Luke 3:17). This is why tribulation is necessary for those who are saved, so that in a certain way winnowed and mingled with the Word of God by patience and finally set on fire, they may be suited for the festival of the King. As one of us, condemned to the beasts for his witness to God, said: "I am the wheat of Christ, ground by the teeth of the beasts, in order to become the pure bread of God."[3]

29.1 At the end when the church is suddenly lifted up "there will be tribulation such as has not existed since the beginning or will exist" (Matt.24:21). For this will be the last contest of the just, in which the winners will be crowned with imperishability.

The number of the beast in Revelation

30.1 If . . . this number is placed in all the genuine and ancient copies, and those who saw John face to face provide attestation, and reason teaches us that the number of the name of the beast according to the Greek was of counting by the letters in it is 666, that is, with tens equal to hundreds and hundreds equal to units (for the number six preserved the same through all indicates the recapitulation of all the apostasy at the beginning and in the middle and at the end) – I do not know how certain people went wrong following a special opinion and giving up the middle number of the name, deducting fifty and wanting only one ten in place of six. I am sure this was a scribal error, common enough when numbers are written by letters, for the letter Xi (60) is easily spread out as Iota (10) in Greek. Some then accepted the new number without investigation; others used it simply and unskillfully and some stupidly ventured to look for names for the erroneous number. We think that pardon is given by God to those who did this simply and without malice; but all those who for vainglory determine names containing the false number, and define the name they find as that of him who is to come, will not go out without penalty for having led astray both themselves and those who believe them. First, there is the penalty of abandoning the truth and supposing that the nonexistent exists; then, if he who adds or subtracts anything from scripture will have a significant punishment (Rev.22:18–19), such a person will necessarily fall into this. And another danger, no slight one, will ensue for those who have falsely imagined they know the name of the Antichrist: if they posit one name and he comes with another, they will be easily seduced by him, as if the one they should fear were not yet present.

30.3   It is more certain and less dangerous to wait for the fulfillment of this prophecy than to undertake researches and make conjectures about random names, for one can find many names containing the number mentioned, but the same problem will remain: if one finds many names with this number, which one will the man to come bear? We speak in this way not because we lack names with the number of the Antichrist but because of fear of God and zeal for truth. For the word EUANTHAS has the required number but we cannot say anything about it.[4] Also LATEINOS has the number 666, and it is very likely because the last kingdom has this name: the Latins are ruling in this time, but we make no boast about this. Also TEITAN, with the two vowels Epsilon and Iota in the first syllable,[5] is of all those found among us, the most worthy of credit. It contains the number mentioned and consists of six letters, each syllable with three letters. It is an ancient and exceptional name, for none of our kings is called Titan, and none of the idols worshipped in public among Greeks and barbarians has this name. It is considered divine by many, so that the sun is called Titan by our present rulers.[6] The name also evokes vengeance and an avenger, because Antichrist will pretend to avenge the victims of oppression. Moreover it is royal and even tyrannical.[7] Thus the name Titan has enough persuasiveness and probability for us to conclude out of many names that it could well be that of the man who is to come. However, we will not risk a pronouncement on this or assert positively that he will have this name, for we know that if his name had to be proclaimed openly at present, it would have been spoken by the one who saw the Apocalypse. It was seen not long ago but nearly in our generation, toward the end of the reign of Domitian.[8]

Resurrection and the kingdom on earth

31.2 If then the Lord observed the law of the dead, to become the Firstborn from the dead (Col.1:18) and stayed until the third day in the lower regions of the earth (Eph.4:9), and then rose in flesh so that he might even show the prints of the nails to the disciples (John 20:25,27), and thus ascended to the Father, how are those persons not confused who call this world hell and say that the "inner man" leaving the body here ascends into the supercelestial place? For since the Lord "went into the middle of the shadow of death" (Ps.22:4) where the souls of the dead were, and then rose bodily and only after the resurrection was taken up into heaven, it is obvious that thus the souls of his disciples, on whose account the Lord effected these things, will go into the invisible place assigned to them by God and will stay there until the resurrection while waiting for it. Then they will take back their bodies and rise perfect, that is, bodily, as also the Lord rose, and thus will come to the vision of God. "For no disciple is above his master, but every perfect disciple will be like his master" (Luke 6:40). Our Master did not fly away at once but first he waited for the time of resurrection fixed by the Father and indicated through Jonah; then after three days he rose and was taken up. Thus we too must await the time of our resurrection fixed by God and predicted by the prophets, and rising thus, those of us whom the Lord deems worthy will be ţaken up.

Miraculous fertility and peace

33.3 When the just rise from the dead and reign; when also the creation renovated and freed will abundantly produce a multitude of all foods out of the rain from the heaven and the fertility of the earth: as the presbyters who had seen John the Lord's disciple remembered hearing from him how the Lord used to teach about times and say,

The days will come when vines come up each with ten thousand branches and on each branch ten thousand twigs and on each twig ten thousand shoots and on each shoot ten thousand grapes, and each grape when pressed will give twenty-five measures of wine. And when one of the saints picks a cluster, another will shout, "I am a better cluster; pick me, bless the Lord through me." Similarly a grain of wheat will produce ten thousand ears, and each ear will have ten thousand grains, and each grain ten pounds of pure flour; and the other fruits and seeds and herb in like proportions; and all the animals, using those foods which are taken from the ground, will become peaceful and harmonious, subject to men with all subjection.

33.4 This is what Papias, hearer of John and colleague of Polycarp, a man of ancient times, attests in writing in the fourth of his books, of which there are five in all. And he adds:

These things are credible to believers. And when the betrayer Judas did not believe and asked, "How, then, will such production be achieved by the Lord?" the Lord said, "Those who come in that time will see."

Predicting these times, Isaiah says:

And the wolf shall feed with the lamb, and the leopard shall rest with the kid; the calf, the bull, and the lion shall feed together, and a little boy shall lead them. The ox and the bear shall feed together, and their young shall live together; the lion and the ox shall eat straw. An infant boy shall thrust his hand into the asp's den and into the nest of young asps, and they shall do no harm nor hurt to anyone upon my holy mountain (11:6–9).

Again, recapitulating, he says, "Then wolves and lambs shall feed together; the lion like the ox shall eat straw; the serpent shall eat earth as bread; and they shall do no harm or hurt upon my holy mountain, says the Lord" (65:25). I am aware that some try to refer these texts metaphorically to savage men who out of various nations and various occupations come to believe, and when they have believed live in harmony with the just. But though this now takes place for men who come from various nations into the one doctrine of the faith, nevertheless it will take place for these animals at the resurrection of the just, as we have said; for God is rich in all things, and when the world is re-established in its primeval state all the animals must obey and be subject to man and return to the first food given by God, as before the disobedience they were subject to Adam (Gen.1:28–30) and ate the fruit of the earth. This is not the time to show that the lion will eat straw, but this indicates the size and opulence of the fruits. For if an animal like the lion eats straw, what will be the quality of the wheat whose straw is food fit for lions?

Eschatology combined with growth

34.2 Isaiah also says that according to God's will every creature must grow and reach maturity, to produce such fruits and make them mature:

> On every high mountain and every hill there will be flowing water in that day when many perish and towers fall. The light of the moon will be like the light of the sun, <and the light of the sun will be> sevenfold, the day when <the Lord> will bring a remedy for the ruin of his people and will cure the grief of your blow (Is.30:25–26).

The grief of the blow is the blow with which man was originally struck when he disobeyed in Adam, that is, death, which God will cure by raising us from the dead and restoring us to the heritage of the fathers, as <the benediction of Japheth says: "May God give room to Japheth, and may he dwell in the abodes of Shem" (Gen.9:27), and> again Isaiah says, "You will put faith in the Lord, and he will make you walk over every land, and he will feed you from the heritage of Jacob your father" (Is.58:14). This is also what the Lord said:

> Blessed are those servants whom the Lord will find watching when he comes. Verily I say to you that he will gird himself and will make them recline and will serve them, and if it is the second or the third watch when he comes, blessed are they (Luke 12:37–38).

John says the same in the Apocalypse. "Blessed and holy is he who has his part in the first resurrection" (Rev.20:6). Similarly Isaiah announced the time in which these things will take place.

> And I said, "Till when, Lord?" Until the cities are desolate and there are no inhabitants for them or the houses, and the earth is left deserted. After that the Lord will take men far away and those who remain will multiply on the earth (Is.6:11–12).

Daniel says the same:

> The kingdom, the power, and the greatness of the kings who are under the heaven has been given to the saints of the Most High God. His kingdom is an everlasting kingdom, and all powers will serve and obey him (Dan.7:27).

And so that the promise might not be referred to the present time, it was said to the prophet, "As for you, come, and stand in your heritage at the end of days" (Dan.12:13).

34.3 That the promises were announced not only to prophets and patriarchs but also to the churches gathered from the nations, which the Spirit calls "islands" because they are placed in the midst of tumult, undergo the tempest of blasphemies, and are a port of safety for those in danger and a refuge for those who love the truth and try to escape the Abyss or depth of error, Jeremiah speaks thus:

> Nations, hear the word of the Lord and proclaim it to the islands far away; say, "He who scattered Israel will gather it together and will keep it as a shepherd keeps his flock of sheep, for the Lord has redeemed Jacob and delivered him from the hand of a stronger one." They will come and rejoice on Mount Zion, they will come to the goods of the Lord, to a land of wheat, wine, fruits, cattle and sheep. Their soul will be like a fruitful tree, and they will never hunger again. Then the young women will rejoice in the company of the young men, and the elders will rejoice, and I shall change their grief into joy and make them rejoice. And I shall magnify the soul of the priests, sons of Levi, and make it drunk, and my people will be filled with my good things (Jer.31[38]:10–14).

The Levites and the priests, as we showed in the preceding book, are all the Lord's disciples, who also "profane the Sabbath in the temple and are not guilty" (Matt.12:5). Such promises clearly refer to the feast in the kingdom of the just, to be provided out of the creation, which God promised to serve.

34.4 Further, Isaiah says of Jerusalem and the one who will reign there, "Thus says the Lord: 'Blessed is he who has a posterity in Zion and descendants in Jerusalem. Behold, a just king will reign, and princes will govern with judgment'" (Is.31:9–32:1). And of the preparation for rebuilding he says,

> Behold, I shall prepare for you a stone of carbuncle and your foundations of sapphire; I shall set your parapets of jasper and

your gates of crystal stone and wall you about with precious stones; and all your sons will be taught by the Lord and your sons will be in great peace and you will be built up in justice (Is.54:11–14).

And again he says,

Behold, I make Jerusalem for gladness and my people <for joy>. And now the sound of weeping will no longer be heard in her, nor the sound of clamor; there will no longer be a man struck down by a premature death nor an elder who does not fill out his time. The young man will be a hundred, and the sinner will be a hundred at death and will be accursed. They will build houses and dwell in them; they will plant vines and eat their fruits. They will not build houses for others to live in. They will not plant for others to eat. For the days of my people will be like the days of the tree of life. They will use the works of their hands (Is.65:18–22).

These predictions are not allegoies

35.1 If any try to understand such prophecies as allegories, they will not even be able to agree completely with themselves, and will be convicted of error by the texts themselves, which say: "Until the cities are desolate and there are no inhabitants for them or the houses, and the earth is left deserted" (Is.6:11). "For behold," Isaiah says, "the day of the Lord comes, without healing, full of fury and anger, to reduce the earth to desert and exterminate sinners" (13:9). He says further, "Let the impious man be done away, that he may not see the glory of the Lord" (26:10). And after this is done, "God will go far from men and those who are left will multiply on the earth" (6:12). "They will build houses and live in them themselves; they will plant vines and eat from them" (65:21).

All such statements indubitably refer to the resurrection of the just, to take place after the coming of Antichrist and the destruction of all the nations under him, in which the just will reign on earth, growing because of the vision of the Lord. Thanks to him, they will grow accustomed to contain the glory of God the Father and will receive life with the holy angels and communion and unity with spiritual realities in the kingdom. And those whom the Lord finds in their flesh awaiting him from the heavens after enduring the tribulation and escaping the hands of the lawless one, they are the ones of whom the prophet says: "And those who are left will multiply on the earth" (6:12). These are also those among the gentiles whom God will prepare, after being left, for multiplying on earth to be under the reign of the saints and to serve in Jerusalem.

The new Jerusalem on earth

<More plainly yet, on Jerusalem> and the kingdom in it Jeremiah the prophet declared:

> Look to the east, O Jerusalem, and see the joy which comes to you from God himself. Behold, your sons whom you sent out will come, gathered from the east to the west at the word of the Holy One, rejoicing in the glory of God ... (Bar.4:36–37).

35.2 Such events cannot be understood as occurring in the supercelestial regions – "for God," he says, "will show forth your splendor to all the earth under heaven" (Bar.5:3) – but they will take place in the times of the kingdom, when the earth has been renewed by Christ and Jerusalem has been rebuilt after the model of the Jerusalem above.

This was the city which John in the Apocalypse saw coming down upon the new earth. For after the times of the kingdom, he says, "I saw a great white throne and him who sat on it, from whose face earth and heaven fled, and no place was found for them" (Rev.20:11). Then he set forth the details of the general resurrection and judgment, saying that he saw "the dead, great and small, for the sea," he says, "gave up the dead found in it; death and hell gave up the dead who were in them, and the books were opened. The book of life," he says, "was also opened, and the dead were judged, after what was written in these books, according to their works. The death and hell were thrown into the fiery lake, the second death" (Rev.20:12–14). This is what is called Gehenna, which the Lord called eternal fire (Matt.25:41). "And whoever was not found written in the book of life was thrown into the fiery lake" (Rev.20:15). He goes on to say,

> I saw a new heaven and a new earth; for the first heaven and earth passed away, and there was no more sea. And I saw the holy city, the new Jerusalem, coming down from heaven, prepared like a bride adorned for her husband. And I heard a great voice coming forth from the throne, which said, "Behold, the tabernacle of God is with men; he will dwell with them and

they will be his peoples, and God himself will be with them as their God. And he will wipe away every tear from their eyes, and death will be no more, and there will be no grief or cry or suffering, for the first things have passed away" (21:1–4).

Isaiah says the same: "There will be a new heaven and a new earth, and they will not remember the prior things nor will they come to their heart, but they will find gladness and exultation in it" (Is.65:17–18). This is what was said by the Apostle: "The fashion of this world is passing away" (1 Cor.7:31). Similarly the Lord said, "Earth and heaven will pass away" (Matt.26:35). When all these things take place, John the Lord's disciple says that the Jerusalem above will descend upon the new earth, like a bride adorned for her husband, and this will be the tabernacle of God, in which God will dwell with men. The Jerusalem of the former earth will be the image of this Jerusalem, in which the just will experience imperishability and will prepare themselves for salvation, and the model of this tabernacle Moses received on the mountain.

And none of this can be taken allegorically, but everything is solid and true and substantial, made by God for the enjoyment of just men. For as God is really the one who raises man, so man will really rise from the dead, and not allegorically, as we have shown by so many examples. And as he truly will rise, so also he will truly exercise imperishability and grow and be strong in the times of the kingdom, so that he may be receptive of the glory of the Father. Then when everything is renewed, he will really live in the city of God. "For the one," he said, "who sits on the throne said, 'Behold, I make all things new.' And the Lord said, 'Write everything, for these words are faithful and true.' And he said to me, 'It is done'" (Rev. 21:5–6), and rightly.

36.1 Since men are real, their transformation must also be real, since they will not go into non-being but on the contrary will progress in being. For neither the substance nor the matter of the creation will be annihilated – true and solid is the one who established it – but "the fashion of this world passes away" (1 Cor.7:31), that is, in which the transgression took place, since man grew old in them. Therefore this "fashion" was temporal, since God knew everything in advance, as we have shown in the previous book, where we explained as well as possible the reason for the creation of a temporal world. But when this "fashion" passes away, man will be renewed for imperishability so that he can no longer grow old, and "that will be the new heaven and the new earth" (Is.65:17), in which the new man will dwell, conversing with God in a manner always new. That this will last forever and without end, Isaiah states thus: "For as the new heaven and the new earth which I make will last in my sight, says the Lord, so your posterity and your name will last" (66:22).

And as the presbyters say, then those who are judged worthy of life in the heavens will arrive there, that is, in the heavens, others will enjoy the delights of paradise, and still others will possess the splendor of the city, but God will be seen everywhere, insofar as those who see him are worthy.

36.2 Such will be the difference in dwelling for those who have produced a hundred for one, sixty for one, and thirty for one (Matt.13:8). The first will be raised into heaven, the second will live in paradise, the third will dwell in the city: this is why the Lord said there are many "abodes" with the Father (John 14:2). For everything belongs to God, who provides for each the abode which befits him: as his Word said, the Father shares with all as each is worthy. There is the banquet hall in which those invited to the marriage will recline and feast (Matt.22:1–14). Such, say the presbyters, the disciples of the apostles, are the order and the rhythm of those who are saved, as well as the degrees through which they progress: by the Spirit they will ascend to the Son, through the Son to the Father, when the Son concedes his work to the Father, as was said by the Apostle: "He must reign until he puts all enemies under his feet. The last enemy to be destroyed is death" (1 Cor.15:25–26). For in the times of the kingdom the just man, living on the earth, will forget dying. He also says,

> When it says that everything has been subjected to him, obviously this is apart from the one who subjected everything. And when everything has been subjected to him, then the Son himself will be subjected to him who has subjected everything, that God may be all in all (15:27–28).

36.3 Thus John exactly foresaw the first resurrection of the just and the inheritance of the earth in the kingdom; in agreement with him the prophets predicted this resurrection. This too the Lord taught, when he promised to drink the new mixed cup with his disciples in the kingdom (Matt.26:29) and further when he said,

> The days will come when the dead in their tombs will hear the voice of the Son of Man and will rise, those who have done good to a resurrection of life but those who have done evil to a resurrection of judgment (John 5:25,28–29).

By that he said that those who have done good will rise first, to go to rest, and that next those who must be judged will rise, as the scripture of Genesis says that the end of this age is on the sixth day (Gen.1:31–2:1), that is, the 6,000th year; then will come the seventh day of rest, of which David says, "This is my rest, the just will enter it" (Ps.131:14; 117:20); this seventh day is the seventh millennium of the kingdom of the just, in which they will exercise imperishability, after the creation has been renewed for those who have been preserved for this, as Paul the Apostle acknowledged that the creation will be liberated from the slavery of perishability to take part in the glorious liberty of the sons of God (Rom.8:19–21).

CONCLUSION

In and through all this the same God the Father will be shown forth. It is he who formed man and promised the fathers the heritage of the earth. It is he who will give it at the resurrection of the just and will fulfill the promises in the kingdom of his Son. It is he who as Father will provide "what eye has not seen nor ear heard and has not entered the heart of man" (1 Cor.2:9). For there is one Son who achieved the will of the Father, and one human race, in which are achieved the mysteries of God, mysteries that "angels desired to see" (1 Pet.1:12), but they could not investigate the Wisdom of God, through which his work was shaped and made concorporate with the Son. For God wanted his firstborn Word to descend into his creation and be held by it, and in turn for the creation to hold the Word and ascend to him, thus surpassing the angels and coming to be in the image and likeness of God (Gen.1:26).

NOTES

1 THE LIFE OF IRENAEUS

1 Eusebius *Church History* 5.20.4–8.
2 Perhaps Irenaeus did not hear the story from John (whoever he was). Epiphanius (*Heresies* 30.24) says the encounter was with Ebion in Asia – one of his typical errors?
3 In his letter to the Philippians (7.1) Polycarp had thus denounced "anyone who says there is neither resurrection nor judgment." Did he meet Marcion at Rome?
4 *Heresies* 3.3.4.
5 Eusebius *Church History* 5.24.16–17, part of a longer account cited below.
6 W. H. C. Frend, "A note on the influence of Greek immigrants on the spread of Christianity in the West," in *Mullus: Festschrift T. Klauser*, 125–29; cf. A. Jülicher, "Eirenaios (8)," *RE* 5 (1905), 2125; R. Turcan, "Les religions 'orientales' à Lugdunum en 177," in *Les martyrs de Lyon 177* (Paris: CNRS, 1978), 195–210. On second-century economic conditions, A. Grenier, "La Gaule romaine," in T. Frank (ed.), *An Economic Survey of Ancient Rome*, 3 (Paterson, NJ: Pageant, 1959), 379–644, esp. 509–62. "'Lyons was not only the great clearing-house for the commerce in corn, wine, oil, and lumber; she was also one of the largest centres in the Empire for the manufacture and the distribution of most of the articles consumed by Gaul, Germany, and Britain" (M. Rostovtzeff, *The Social and Economic History of the Roman Empire*, 2nd edn (Oxford: Clarendon Press, 1957), 166).
7 Corpus Inscriptionum Latinorum XII 2007, XIII 2004, 2005.
8 Ibid. XIII 1950, 1969, 2004.
9 The possibly contemporary epitaph of Euteknios, from Lyons, contrasts persuasion with speaking among Celts, and imitates a line of Homer; cf. C. P. Jones, "L'inscription grecque de Saint-Just," in *Les Martyrs de Lyon* (1978), 120–22.
10 *Heresies* 1 praef.3.
11 Ibid. 4.30.3.
12 Ibid. 1.10.2.

13 Polycarp would have done the same (Eusebius *Church History* 5.20.7).

14 *Heresies* 3.4.2. This recalls Tacitus' primitivistic rhapsody on the Germans; and Irenaeus himself notes identical Christian traditions in Germanies and Iberias (Roman provinces) as well as among the Celts (1.10.2).

15 Gregory of Tours *History of the Franks* 1.29 (*Monumenta Germaniae Historica, Scriptores rerum Merovingicarum* 1.47).

16 Eusebius *Church History* 5.1.57–58.

17 Ibid. 5.4.2.

18 Ibid. 5.3.2; 5.1.3.

19 One of the first anti-Montanists was Claudius Apollinaris, bishop of Hierapolis, who in an apology referred to the rain-miracle depicted on the Column of Marcus Aurelius in Rome. The event in question can be dated 173/174.

20 Eusebius *Church History* 5.7, from *Heresies* 2.31.2; 32.4; 5.6.1.

21 Eusebius *Church History* 5.16–19.

22 See SC 152, 195. Irenaeus' contemporary Theophilus of Antioch produced two interrelated books *To Autolycus*, then a separate third one.

23 *Oxyrhynchus Papyri* 3.405; cf. 4, 264–65 (*Heresies* 3.9.2–3). A larger papyrus fragment from the fourth century includes *Heresies* 5.3.12–13.3.

24 The Valentinian Ptolemaeus in Epiphanius *Heresies* 33.7.9.

25 Botte argued ("Saint Irénée et l'Épître de Clément," *Revue des Études Augustiniennes* 2 (1956), 67–70) that Irenaeus treats 2 Clement as an appendix to 1 Clement, but the fire mentioned in 2 Clement is not for "the devil and his angels." Irenaeus is making 1 Clement his own.

26 *Heresies* 3.3.3.

27 Ibid. 3.3.4.

28 Eusebius *Church History* 5.24.8; 5.23.3–4.

29 Ibid. 5.25; 5.23.2.

30 Harvey, *Irenaeus*, Fragmenta Syriaca, 27; from British Museum Codex 12158, folio 41.

31 *Church History* 5.24.12–17.

32 Ibid. 5.20.2.

33 Ibid. 4.23.12.

34 Ibid. 5.26.

35 *Epideixis* 3 and 61.

2 GNOSTIC ORIGINS

1 Justin *Apology* 1.26.6.

2 Justin *Dialogue* 35.6.

3 *Heresies* 1.25.6; 1.26.2; 1.27.4; 1.28–31.

4 Justin *Apology* 1.26.1–5.

5 Justin was aware of these debates (*Dialogue* 2.2); cf. Aristocles in Eusebius *Gospel Preparation* 11.3.4–5; Numenius, ibid. 14.4.16–59 (= frag. 24 Des Places).

6 *Oxyrhynchus Papyri* 29.2506.

7 *Phaedrus* 243A.

8 Hippolytus *Refutation* 7.20–27. In defense of the originality of Irenaeus'

account see R. M. Grant, "Place de Basilide dans la théologie chrétienne ancienne," *Revue des Études Augustiniennes* 25 (1979), 201–16.

9 Equal to 1+2+100+1+200+1+60.

10 See also *Second Treatise of the Great Seth* VII 2, trans. in J. M. Robinson (ed.), *The Nag Hammad: Library in English*, rev. edn (San Francisco: Harper & Row, 1988), 365 (hereafter Robinson).

11 The same situation obtains in Matt.27:32–35, but Mark is traditionally associated with Alexandria. John 19:17 says that Jesus bore his own cross.

12 Cf. Kaulakau, Saulasau, and Zeesar in Hippolytus *Refutation* 5.8.4.

13 *Gospel of Thomas* 23; p. 129 Robinson.

14 Gaius of Rome confuses the picture by denouncing Cerinthus as author of the book of Revelation; this is confirmed by Dionysius of Alexandria (Eusebius *Church History* 3.28.2,5; 7.25.1–3). Misunderstanding both Gaius and Dionysius, Eusebius wrongly treats Cerinthus as a Jewish Christian; cf. Grant, *Eusebius as Church Historian* (Oxford: Clarendon Press, 1980), 133–34.

15 The virtuous, not sinners, are baptized, as in Josephus' account of John's baptism (*Antiquities* 18.117).

16 Irenaeus claims to be refuting Marcion from his writings, *ex eius scriptis*. Perhaps, then, the exegesis comes from a lost early *Letter* to which Tertullian referred (cf. A. von Harnack, *Marcion* (Leipzig: Hinrichs, 1924), 27, 74, 21*–23*). Tertullian says that Marcion later rescinded the orthodox beliefs he once held, "as you yourself confess in a certain letter which your followers do not reject" (*On the Flesh of Christ* 2.4). Again, he writes that "his disciples will not deny that he shared his former faith with us, as his own letter attests" (*Against Marcion* 1.1.6).

17 Harnack *Marcion*, 218* (Tertullian *Against Marcion* 4.30.5; Epiphanius *Heresies* 42.11.6.40 [2.112,13–17 Holl]).

18 Justin *Dialogue* 72.4; cf. O. Skarsaune, *The Proof from Prophecy* (1987), 41, 283–85, 452: six quotations of Pseudo–Jeremiah in *Heresies* 3.20.4; 4.22.1; 4.33.1,12; 5.31.1 and *Demonstration* 78.

19 *Heresies* 4.27.2. Similarly Tertullian suggested in his relatively late treatise *On the Soul* that Christ descended "to the souls of the patriarchs" or to the "patriarchs and prophets" (7.3; 55.2).

20 Epiphanius *Heresies* 42.1.7, 2.2.

21 Irenaeus *Heresies* 1.28.1; Tatian *Oration* 35.3, p.66, 15 Marcovich.

22 Irenaeus *Heresies* 3.23.8.

23 Clement *Miscellanies* 3.81.1–2.

24 W. C. Till, *Die Gnostischen Schriften des Koptischen Papyrus Berolinensis 8502, TU* 60 (Berlin: Akademie, 1955).

25 M. Krause and P. Labib, *Die drei Versionen des Apokryphon des Johannes im Koptischen Museum zu Alt-Kairo* (Wiesbaden: Harrassowitz, 1962), 153–60, 189–90, 195–98. English translations in pp 104–23 Robinson.

26 F. Wisse, "The Epistle of Jude in the History of Heresiology," in M. Kranse (ed.), *Essays on the Nag Hammadi Texts in Honour of Alexander Böhlig*, NHS 3 (Leiden: Brill, 1972), 133–43, speaks of Jude's "catholic authority," lack of specific references, and emphasis on primitive unchanging faith as against heresy introduced later.

27 Contrast 1 John 4:18: "perfect love casts out fear."

3 AGAINST THE VALENTINIANS

1 *Heresies* 1.23.1, 27.1–2; 3.4.3; 1.25.6.
2 Ibid. 3.4.3.
3 Ibid. 1.13.5,7.
4 Ibid. 1 praef.2.
5 Ibid. 4.35.4.
6 Cf. Ignatius *Romans* 7.2: "My Eros has been crucified."
7 *Heresies* 1.1.3; 1.3.1–6; 1.8.1–4.
8 Does his evidence come from Tatian, who accepted the Valentinian aeons with the teaching of Marcion and Saturninus that marriage was corruption and fornication (1.28.1) – and in his *Oration* (22–23) tells of witnessing festivals and gladiatorial shows?
9 *Heresies* 1.13.1–2.
10 Pliny *Natural History* 35.175; cf. E. Schwartz, "Anaxilaides," in *RE* 1 (1894), 2083.
11 *Heresies* 1.13.3; *Galen On Prognosis to Epigenes* 6 (14.632–35 Kühn).
12 *Heresies* 1.16.3; 2.26.3.
13 Ibid. 1.4.3. F.-M. Sagnard, *La gnose valentinienne et le témoignage de saint-Irénée* (Paris: Vrin, 1947), 266–89, studies Irenaeus' use of irony chiefly in theological contexts.
14 *Heresies*. 3.11.9; for this Gospel see pp. 40–51 Robinson.
15 Galen *Commentary on Hippocrates Epidemics Book III*, p. 78, 7–9 Wenkebach.
16 *Heresies* 1.11.1. The predecessors of Valentinus are specifically the "Gnostics" of 1.29–30; cf. SC 263, 296–300. Tertullian disagrees, ascribing individuated Aeons to Ptolemaeus, not Valentinus (*Against Valentinians* 4.2).
17 *Heresies* 1.11.2.
18 Ibid. 1.11.3.
19 Ibid. 1.11.4. In this parody he was able to use the long Homeric compound verb *proprokylindomenos*, "keep rolling before" or "wandering," as if it meant "pre-prerotund." Since his parody involved melons, he could also revise an attack on the Achaeans in *Iliad* 2.235. There Thersites rebukes them as "melons [i.e. "soft ones"], Achaean women, no longer Achaean men." Irenaeus may not have noticed that Thersites was accustomed to say "whatever he thought would raise a laugh among the Argives" (2.215), but he turned the words against the Gnostics as "melons, only vile sophists and not men." These passages show the emphasis on literature in Irenaeus' education, as well as his application to study.

4 CHRISTIAN BOOKS AND TRADITIONS

1 *Heresies* 2.27.3; 1.9.2; 1.3.6; 2.10.1; 1.4.3.
2 *Demonstration* 43.
3 Cf. Graffin in SC 263, 270–71.
4 *Heresies* 3.8.1; cf. 4.30.1,3.
5 Hippolytus *Refutation* 6.42.1.
6 *Heresies* 3.21.2; 2 Esdr. 14:20–22.

7 The memory of Ptolemy as a great book collector was still alive in Irenaeus' day, as Galen makes clear (*Commentary on Hippocrates Epidemics III*, pp. 78–80 Wenkebach; cf. W. D. Smith, *The Hippocratic Tradition* (Ithaca, NY: Cornell University Press, 1979), 199–201).

8 *Epistle of Aristeas*; embellishments in Philo *Life of Moses* 2.29–39; Josephus *Antiquities* 12.85–114; the first Christian witness, Justin *Apology* 1.31.

9 Jerome *Preface on the Pentateuch* (PL 28.181–82); cf. *Preface in Paralipomena* (PL 28, 1393A) and *Apology against Rufinus* 2.25 (PL 23, 470A–B)

10 Augustine *City of God* 18.42–43.

11 Theophilus used similar materials: Bar.2:4 (3.11) and probably 2 Macc.7:28 on creation (1.4). I now think he did not use 2 Esdr.1:8 but Josephus *Antiquities* 11.93 (3.25), not 1 Esdr.2:25 but Josephus *Against Apion* 1.154 (3.29).

12 *Heresies* 3.21.1–2.

13 Ibid. 4.16.2, summarized from 1 Enoch 12–16.

14 Bar.3:37 (*Heresies* 4.20.4); 4:36–5:9; 5:2 (5.35.1–2).

15 Dan.13–14 = Susanna (3.25.6; 4.5.2; 4.26.3).

16 Eusebius *Church History* 3.39.15–16.

17 Hippocrates *The Number Seven* (*De septenario*) 5 (8.636 Littré); Philo *Creation* 105.

18 *Heresies* 3.21.3 (birth); *Demonstration* 74 (death).

19 Ibid. 3.11.7–8.

20 Similarly Theophilus began his volumes *To Autolycus* with a clear allusion to 2 Tim.3:8; later (3.14) he ascribes (Tit.3:1 +) 1 Tim.2:(1–)2 to "the divine Word" along with Rom.13:(1–3 +)7–8. There are many allusions to the Pastorals in the letter of Polycarp.

21 Ibid. 3.3.3.

22 Ibid. 1.16.3; 3.3.4.

23 Ibid. 1.6.3 (cf. 1 Cor.6:9; in any event, some Pauline epistle).

24 Stephanus Gobarus in Photius (PG 103, 1104D).

25 1 Peter (*Heresies* 4.9.2; 4.16.5; 5.7.2); 2 Peter (5.28.3).

26 *Heresies* 3.16.5,8: John in his epistle, 1 John 2:18–19,21–22, in his epistle already cited, 2 John 7–8; again in the epistle, 1 John 4:1–3.

27 *Heresies* 5.30.1,3; presumably including Polycarp. The fifth-century Codex Ephraemi rescriptus reads "616."

28 Cf. F. Wisse, "The Epistle of Jude in the History of Heresiology," NHS 3 (1972), 133–43.

29 See "The Bible of Theophilus of Antioch," *Journal of Biblical Literature* 66 (1947), 173–96.

30 *Heresies* 3.3.2–4.

31 Ibid. 1.20.1; cf. *Infancy Gospel of Thomas* A 6.3; B 7.1; Latin 6.6 (pp. 145,160,172 Tischendorf). For Gnostic use of apocryphal gospels cf. SC 263, p. 263.

32 Heresies 1.21.5 = *First Apocalypse of James* (A. Böhlig and P. Labib, *Koptisch-gnostische Apokalypsen aus Codex V von Nag Hammadi*, (Halle-Wittenberg: Martin-Luther-Universität, 1963), 43–45, pp. 265–66 Robinson.

33 *Heresies* 1.24.6 = *Gospel of Thomas* 23, p. 129 Robinson.
34 He clearly rejects the Valentinians' *Gospel of Truth* (*Heresies* 3.11.9).
35 Thomas and Matthew are associated in Matt.3:3, Mark 3:18, and Luke 6:15; James and John frequently in the synoptic gospels but not in John.
36 Eusebius *Church History* 3.39.3–4 and 15.
37 Ibid. 3.39.11.
38 This would make 500,000,000 choinixes of flour.
39 Eusebius *Church History* 3.39.1,13.
40 Cf. *Apocalypse of Paul* 22, p. 51 Tischendorf (more fully in the Coptic version).
41 Polycarp *Philippians* 3.2; 11.2–3. Ignatius, Polycarp's junior contemporary, similarly calls the Ephesians "fellow-initiates with Paul" (*Ephesians* 12.2) but not with John.
42 H. von Campenhausen, "Polykarp von Smyrna und die Pastoralbriefe," *Sitzungsberichte der Heidelberger Akademie der Wissenschaften*, Philosophisch-historische Klasse (1951) 2.
43 *Philippians* 7.1. Neither Papias nor Polycarp reflects the Apocalypse of John.
44 For the emended text cf. SC 100*, 263 (note on SC 100**, 729). If we do not emend the text, Irenaeus spoke of two sets of witnesses: the elder saw the apostles, as did his contemporaries (cf. Papias).
45 The presbyters thus would have accepted an anti-Marcionite reading of 1 Peter.
46 Clement of Alexandria, who knew Irenaeus' work, clearly referred to 1 Clement and Hermas as "scripture," but this proves nothing for Irenaeus himself.
47 Hermas *Visions* 2.4.3. He uses the word *episkopos* only in the plural (*Similitudes* 9.27.2).
48 Cf. W. R. Schoedel, "Enclosing, not enclosed," in W. R. Schoedel and R. L. Wilken (eds), *Early Christian Literature and the Classical Intellectual Tradition* (Paris: Beauchesne, 1979), 75–86.
49 Justin *Apology* 1.26.2–4; *Dialogue* 120.6 (Samaria); *Apology* 1.26.5 (Rome).
50 Eusebius *Church History* 4.18.9.
51 Justin *Dialogue* 81.4; for Papias' witness to its "trustworthiness," Andrew of Caesarea *On the Apocalypse* (PG 106, 220).
52 Ignatius *Polycarp* 8.1; *Romans* 4.1–2; 5.2.
53 For Irenaeus' doctrine cf. J. A. Robinson, *St. Irenaeus: The Apostolic Preaching* (London: SPCK, 1920), 51–59.
54 D. T. Runia, *Philo in Early Christian Literature* (Assen: Van Gorcum; Minneapolis: Fortress, 1993), 110–18.

5 GREEK EDUCATION AGAINST GNOSTICISM

1 Justin expresses regret for his ignorance of music, astronomy, and geometry (*Dialogue* 2.4).
2 Jerome *Epistle* 53.6.
3 Sextus Empiricus *Against Professors* 1.85; cf. 299–312.
4 The manuscripts refer to Antifanus or Antiphanus, but Irenaeus has the

Birds (693–702) of Aristophanes in mind; cf. SC 293, 254–55.

5 Cf. A. Körte's editions in 1938 and 1953; add *Oxyrhynchus Papyri* 33 (1968) 2656, 2657 (fourth and third centuries); also 59 (1992), 3967 (38 verses).

6 Diogenes Laertius 7.13; Epictetus 4.1.19–23, with two lines from the *Misumenos* (partly cited on the ill effect of lust by Clement *Miscellanies* 2.64.2).

7 *Heresies* 1.4.3; 1.15.4; 1.11.4 (Plato too criticized tragedy, *Republic* 595B).

8 Ibid. 2.12.3; 4.39.3; 5.13.2 (cf. Sophocles *Oedipus Rex* 1268–79). In a later discussion of vision, without reference to tragedy, he simply refers to those who "have blinded themselves or have been blinded by others" (5.27.2).

9 W. C. van Unnik, "Theological speculation and its limits," in W. R. Schoedel and R. L. Wilken (eds), *Early Christian Literature and the Classical Intellectual Tradition* (Paris: Beauchesne, 1979), 33–43.

10 *Heresies* 2.28.2; Seneca *Benefits* 7.1.5.

11 *Heresies* 2.26.2, 28.9, based on Matt.10:29–30.

12 Diels–Kranz 21 B 24: Sextus Empiricus *Adv. math.* 9.144 (from Theophrastus' doxography, according to Diels), trans. J. H. Lesher, *Xenophanes of Colophon: Fragments* (*Phoenix* suppl. vol. 30; University of Toronto Press, 1992), 103; cf. Pseudo-Aristotle *Xenophanes* 977a37: "power to see and hear and all the senses wholly (*pantéi*)" (cf. Diels 1879, 565, 26; 580, 16).

13 Diogenes Laertius 9.19.

14 *Natural History* 2.14.

15 *Heresies* 2.13.3. Source of good: Philo *Creation* 21, *Decalogue* 81, *Virtuous Man* 84; Numenius, frag. 52 des Places (Calcidius 296); Dionysius of Alexandria in Athanasius *Views of Dionysius* 23.2; Eusebius *Church Theology* 2.7, p. 106, 23 Klostermann.

16 *Miscellanies* 7.5.5; 7.37.6.

17 The Greeks are Cyril *Catechism* 6.7 (PG 33, 549A) and Theodoret on Psalm 129:2 (PG 80, 1900BC). The Latins are Novatian *Trinity* 6 (PL 3, 923C); the three from Gaul, Hilary of Poitiers on Psalm 129, 3 (PL 9, 719C); Victricius of late fourth-century Rouen *Praise of Saints* 8 (PL 20, 450B); Claudianus Mamertus (fifth-century) precisely from Vienne, *Soul* 1.21.

18 Irenaeus quotes Plato's *Laws* and *Timaeus* to prove the point.

19 *Heresies* 1.12.2.

20 Ibid. 2.13.8.

21 Ibid. 2.28.4.

22 Hilary of Poitiers, using this text, supplies references to Jer.23:23 and Acts 17:28 (*On the Psalms* 129, 3; PL 9, 720A). Irenaeus mentions both texts elsewhere (*Heresies* 4.19.2, 3.12.9), but has in mind John 1:1 (Word), John 4:24 (Spirit), and 1 John 1.5 (Light).

23 *Heresies* 4.11.2.

24 Lesher, *Xenophanes of Colophon*, 115–18.

6 RHETORIC IN THEOLOGY

1 Eusebius *Church History* 5.1.26; 5.3.2–3; *Heresies* 3.12.14.

2 H. J. Lawlor and J. E. L. Oulton, *Eusebius* (London: SPCK, 1928), 2.156.

3 Frances Young, "The rhetorical schools and their influence on patristic exegesis," in R. Williams (ed.), *The Making of Orthodoxy: Essays in Honour of Henry Chadwick* (Cambridge University Press, 1989), 182–99.

4 *Heresies* 1 praef.2–3.

5 W. R. Schoedel, "Philosophy and Rhetoric in the Adversus Haereses of Irenaeus," *VC* 12 (1959), 22–32 (27): Defense of Socrates in Plato *Apology* 17b; Lysias *Oration* 19.1.2; Isaeus 10.1; Hermogenes *Peri Ideon* 2.6, 2.370, 23 Spengel = p.346, 18 Rabe.

6 The rhetorician Hermogenes treats "detection" as "refutation" (*Progymnasmata* 5, p. 11, 2–3 Rabe), but Hippolytus (*Refutation of All Heresies* 9.31.2) insists that one must go beyond "detection." He notes that Valentinians denied Irenaeus' accurate reporting (6.42.1).

7 Eusebius *Church History* 5.13.3 (Irenaeus' book in 5.7.1).

8 A. Mai and P. Buttmann, *Scholia Antiqua in Homeri Odysseam* (Berlin, 1821), 39 (on 1.328); 356 (on 11.38); summaries at the beginning of each book. At *Odyssey* 1.328 the minstrel Phemius does not sing about Odysseus' impending return, for had he done so Telemachus would not have left home and Penelope's suitors would have left her; and "the whole *oikonomia* (arrangement) of the *hypothesis* (plot) would have fallen apart." At *Odyssey* 11.38 many critics regarded the list of the souls of the dead as an interpolation because it mixed up brides, unmarried youths, old men, and virgins, or because the souls had not yet come on the scene. The "vulgate" scholion explains the list as an *anakephalaiôsis* (summary) of what is said next.

9 *Heresies* 1.9.4, contrasting the verses with the arrangement or structure.

10 Polybius 1.2.1; Theon *Progymnasmata* 1 (2.61.21 Spengel); Sextus Empiricus *Against Professors* 3.3; second- and third-century hypotheses for Sophocles and Euripides, *Oxyrhynchus Papyri* 52 (1984), 3650–53; Theophilus 2.13.

11 *Heresies* 1.9.4.

12 On Gnostic hypotheses cf. B. Reynders, "La polémique de saint Irénée: méthode et principes," *Recherches de théologie ancienne et médiévale* 7 (1935) 5–27 (17–18).

13 *Heresies* 3.4.2; 4.20.2 (Hermas *Mandates* 1.1); cf. W. R. Schoedel (1979), 'Enclosing not enclosed.'

14 *Heresies* 3.3.3.

15 It is true, as Rousseau and Doutreleau note (SC 210, 237) that these items are found in Genesis, Exodus, the major prophets, and Matt.25:41; but not as such in 1 Clement. The Matthaean text is absent.

16 Diodorus 5.1.1–2; Dionysius *Composition* 25 (*Critical Essays* 2, LCL 1985, 224, 17); *To Pompeius* 4 (ibid. 386, 19–12); Lucian *On Writing History* 50.

17 *Heresies* 1.10.2; 3.19.2; 4.33.1.

18 Ibid. 3.14.1.

19 An old scholion on Hesiod's *Theogony* differentiates his poem from his encomium of the Muses and his *anakephalaiôsis* (L. Di Gregorio, *Scholia vetera in Hesiodi Opera et Dies* [Milan: "Vita e pensiero," 1975], 22); cf. Dionysius *On Lysias* 9, also 19 (*anakephalaiôtikon*); *Roman Antiquities* 1.90.2; Hermogenes *Method* 12, p. 427, 15, 17 Rabe; Theophilus 3.1; Clement *Tutor* 2.75.1–2.

20 *Heresies* 4.6.2 (Eusebius *Church History* 4.18.9). Justin never uses the word in his writings.

21 *Heresies* 1.9.2.

22 Ibid. 2.22.4–6.

23 They could have cited Luke 2:47: "All were astonished at his answers" (at the age of 12); Irenaeus knows the passage (*Heresies* 1.20.2) but has forgotten it.

24 *Heresies* 3.21.3 (starting from 44 BC).

25 Cf. J. T. Nielsen, *Adam and Christ in the Theology of Irenaeus of Lyons* (Assen: Van Gorcum, 1968), 76–82; unlike other critics, he finds Irenaeus twisting Paul.

26 *Heresies* 1.3.4.

27 Justin *Dialogue* 100.5; cf. 124.3–4 (84.7); *Heresies* 3.21.10–23.7.

28 F. R. M. Hitchcock, *Irenaeus of Lyons* (Cambridge University Press, 1914), 147.

29 *Heresies* 5.33.3–4.

30 *Church History* 3.39.13.

31 *Dialogue* 80.5.

32 K. Holl, *Fragmente vornicänischer Kirchenväter aus den Sacra Parallela* (*TU* 20.2, 1899), 82; SC 152, 28–29.

BOOK I AGAINST HERESIES

1 "Knowledge falsely so called" echoes 1 Tim.6:20; so also Theophilus begins *To Autolycus* with an echo of 2 Tim.3:8.

2 Ptolemaeus claimed that his secret teaching was "the apostolic tradition, which we too received from a succession." He means that he received it from Valentinus, who in turn received from Theudas, a disciple of Paul – whose own tradition, according to 1 Corinthians 11:23, came from the Lord.

3 The possibly contemporary epitaph of Euteknios contrasts persuasion with speaking among Celts, and imitates *Iliad* 1.249 (cf. C. P. Jones, "L'inscription grecque de Saint-Just," in *Les martyrs de Lyon* (1978), 120–22).

4 That is, the *toga praetexta* of the equestrian or even senatorial class. Like these Gnostics, contemporary Cynics were accused of avarice (Lucian *Fugitives* 17, 30–31; cf. Tatian *Oration* 19.2, p. 39, 7 Marcovich).

5 So contemporary Cynics were said to seduce the wives of their hosts (Lucian *Fugitives* 18, cf. 30, and his account of a false prophet in *Alexander* 42).

6 SC 263, 264–65 emends the text and cites Logion 38 of the Nag Hammadi *Gospel of Thomas*: "Often you desired to hear these words that I spoke to you, and you had no other from whom to hear them."

7 For Graffin's emendations and translations see SC 263, 270–71.

8 Irenaeus "translates" thus: "I invoke what is above every power of the Father and is called Light and Spirit and Life; for you have reigned in a body."

9 Irenaeus "translates" thus: "I do not divide the Spirit, the heart, and the supercelestial merciful power of Christ; may I enjoy your Name, Savior of Truth."

10 This is essentially the same as the second "Hebrew" formulary above.

11 The Delphic formula "Know thyself."

12 These formulas are exactly the same as those in the Nag Hammadi *First Apocalypse of James* (A. Böhlig and P. Labib, *Koptisch-gnostische Apokalypsen aus Codex V von Nag Hammadi* (Halle-Wittenberg, Martin-Luther-Universität, 1963), 43–45, pp. 265–66 Robinson; cf. SC 263, 272–76).

13 Irenaeus has already quoted Acts 8:9–23 on Simon.

14 Ps.2:2: "The kings of the earth rose up and the archons gathered together against the Lord and against his Christ."

15 Mark 15:21–24 (cf. Matt.27:32–35) names Simon and continues, "and they crucified him." Cf. *Second Treatise of the Great Seth* (VII 2, p. 365 Robinson).

16 1 Cor. 2:8: the Wisdom of God "which none of the archons of this aeon knew; for if they had known they would not have crucified the Lord of Glory."

17 Ps.2:4: "He who dwells in heavens will ridicule them and the Lord will mock them."

18 John 20:17: "I ascend to my Father and your Father, my God and your God;" 7:33; 16:5: "I go to him who sent me."

19 This number equals 1+2+100+1+200+1+60.

20 Matt.5:25–26; Luke 12:58–59.

21 Mark 4:11: "To you is given the mystery"; 4:34: "he explained everything privately to his own disciples."

22 Gal.5:6: "Faith made effective through love"; Ignatius *Ephesians* 14:1: "the beginning is faith and the end is love."

23 Jewish synagogues were oriented toward the temple. For early Christians cf. Tertullian *Apology* 16.10 and Origen *On the Prayer* 32; also Clement *Miscellanies* 7.43.6; and especially Origen *Homilies* on *Numbers* 5.1, p. 26, 17 Baehrens.

24 For these "Gnostics" see *Heresies* 1.11.1.

25 So the Coptic *Apocryphon of John*. The names of the second and third lights come from the Old Testament: Raguel is an angel in the book of Tobit and David is the king and author of the mysterious psalms, but the first and the last cannot be identified.

26 For the Coptic versions see Robinson, pp. 104–23.

27 "Son of Man" is a Gospel name of Jesus; for "Second Man" cf. 1 Cor.15:47.

28 Compare Ignatius *Ephesians* 19.2–3.

29 We follow the emendation of SC 264, 370; cf. 263, 306–7.

BOOK II AGAINST HERESIES

1 An especially unfortunate Gnostic term, repeatedly noted by Irenaeus (SC 293, 201–2).
2 The manuscripts refer to Antifanus or Antiphanus, but Irenaeus has the *Birds* (693–702) of Aristophanes in mind; cf. SC 293, 254–55.
3 *Theogony* 561–62; *Works and Days* 60–61.
4 On this difficult passage cf. SC 293, 260–62.
5 *Works and Days* 78–82.
6 Pindar *Olympian Ode* 1.49–51 (Pindar himself says the myth is false).
7 The expression echoes 1 Clement 20.8.
8 Cf. Theophilus 1.7 (Jer.38:22).
9 These materials are headings in the compendium of Pseudo-Plutarch, printed by H. Diels (*Doxographi Graeci*, 1879).
10 Cf. the argument of John 3:12.
11 Cf. Quadratus in Eusebius *Church History* 4.3.2

BOOK III AGAINST HERESIES

1 Not based on 1 Clement; see Introduction.
2 Polycarp would have done the same; see Introduction.
3 This recalls Tacitus' primitivistic rhapsody on the Germans; and Irenaeus himself notes identical Christian traditions in the Germanies and the Iberias as well as among the Celts (1.10.2).
4 The four animals come from Rev.4:7.
5 For the interpretation cf. SC 210, 289.
6 Marcion and almost all New Testament manuscripts read "We did not yield." Cf. W. Sanday and C. H. Turner, *Novum Testamentum Sancti Irenaei Episcopi Lugdunensis* (Oxford: Clarendon Press, 1923), 154.
7 Cf. Ignatius *Ephesians* 20:2: "the drug of immortality, the antidote not to die but live forever in Jesus Christ."
8 An echo of the Delphic maxim.
9 Here *gloria* mistranslates *doxa* (SC 210, 351).
10 The reading of Justin (*Dial.* 103.8) and several early manuscripts.
11 On loosing and binding cf. Matt.16:19 (18:18); W. C. van Unnik, "Les cheveux défaits des femmes baptisées," *VC* 1 (1947), 77–100, esp. 98–100; Hermas *Similitudes* 9.13.8–14.2 (women with loosed hair contrasted with virgins).
12 Also cited in Clement of Alexandria *Exhortation* 69.4; *Miscellanies* 2.132.2.
13 Also cited in Clement *Miscellanies* 5.24.2.

BOOK IV AGAINST HERESIES

1 Marcosians apparently criticized Irenaeus' report (Hippolytus *Refutation* 6.42.1).
2 The rest of this text is sometimes ascribed to Justin, but he does not use the word *anakephalaiôsis*.

3 Reading *vocationes* with Codex Corbeiensis.
4 Hermas *Mandate* 1.1.
5 Theophilus (1.7; 2.10) also refers these texts to Word and Wisdom.
6 For the form of the sentence cf. Rom.5:10,15,17.
7 The text comes from Pseudo-Jeremiah; see Introduction.
8 Perhaps a modification of "You do not know the scriptures or the power of God" (Matt.26:29; Mark 12:24).
9 In this passage there is the same kind of ambiguity as in Papias' remarks about eyewitnesses (Eusebius *Church History* 3.39.4). The paraphrase includes *Heresies* 4.27.1–32.1.
10 This reverses Marcion's doctrine (1.27.3).

BOOK V AGAINST HERESIES

1 For the translation cf. SC 152, 296–302; from Plato *Timaeus* 36BC via Justin *Apology* 1.60.1,5.
2 The model for this passage is Rom.5:15–17 (cf. 1 Cor.15:21).
3 Ignatius of Antioch Romans 4.1.
4 It is equal to 5+400+1+50+9+1+200 = 666, but EUANTHAS is not a Greek word.
5 The name was spelled TITAN but Iota sometimes became Epsilon-Iota (cf. *Heresies* 1.15.1).
6 The Titans fought the gods in mythology; for the sun cf. Cicero *Nature of the Gods* 2.112; Virgil *Aeneid* 4.119; 6.725.
7 For the text cf. SC 152, 334 (n. 1 on 2.383: following the Armenian version).
8 Domitian, Roman emperor 81–96. Irenaeus believed the apostle John lived into the reign of Trajan (98–117).

BIBLIOGRAPHY

(A) IRENAEUS

(1) Texts, Indexes, Translations

Harvey, W. W. (1857) *Sancti Irenaei Episcopi Lugdunensis*. Cambridge: Typis Academicis.

Lampe, G. W. H. (1968) *A Patristic Greek Lexicon*. Oxford: Clarendon Press.

Reynders, B. (1954) *Lexique comparé du texte grec et des versions latine, arménienne et syriaque de l'"Adversus Haereses" de Saint Irénée*. Louvain: Durbecq, 1954 (pages/lines of Harvey printed in the SC margins)

——(1958) *Vocabulaire de la "Démonstration" et des fragments de Saint Irénée*. Louvain: Durbecq.

Roberts, A. and Donaldson, J. (trans.) (1880) *Irenaeus*. Ante-Nicene Christian Library, vols. 5, 9. Edinburgh: T. & T. Clark; also later reprints.

Robinson, J. A. (trans.) (1920) *St Irenaeus: The Demonstration of the Apostolic Preaching*. London: SPCK.

Rousseau, A. *et al.* (1965–82) *Irénée de Lyon Contre les hérésies Livres I–V*, 10 vols. Paris: Cerf (pages/lines of Harvey printed in the SC margins). Book I = SC 263–64; Book II = SC 293–94; Book III = SC 210–11; Book IV = SC 100*–**; Book V = SC 152–53.

Sanday, W. and Turner, C.H. (1923) *Novum Testamentum Sancti Irenaei Episcopi Lugdunensis*. Oxford: Clarendon Press.

Smith, J. P. (trans.) (1952) *Proof of the Apostolic Preaching*. Ancient Christian Writers, 16, Westminster, MD: Newman.

Unger, D. J. and Dillon, J. J. (trans.) *St. Irenaeus of Lyons Against the Heresies*, vol. 1. Ancient Christian Writers 55, New York: Paulist Press.

(2) Studies

Audet, T. A. (1943) "Orientations théologiques chez saint Irénée," *Traditio* 1: 15–54.

Beckwith, R. (1985) *The Old Testament Canon of the New Testament Church*. London: SPCK.

Benoît, A. (1960) *Saint Irénée: Introduction à l'étude de son théologie*. Paris: Presses Universitaires.

Botte, B. (1956) "Saint Irénée et l'Épître de Clément," *Revue des Études augustiniennes* 2: 67–70

Brox, N. (1966) *Offenbarung, Gnosis und gnostischer Mythos bei Irenäus von Lyon*. Salzburg: Pustet.

Campenhausen, H. von (1951) "Polykarp von Smyrna und die Pastoralbriefe," *Sitzungsberichte der Heidelberger Akademie der Wissenschaften*, Philosophisch-historische Klasse, 2.

Di Berardino, A. (ed.) (1992) *Encyclopedia of the Early Church*. New York: Oxford University Press.

Fantino, J. (1994) *La théologie d'Irénée. Lecture des Écritures en réponse à l'exégèse gnostique. Une approche trinitaire*. Paris: Cerf.

Frend, W. H. C. (1964) "A note on the influence of Greek immigrants on the spread of Christianity in the West," in *Mullus: Festschrift T. Klauser* (*Jahrbuch für Antike und Christentum*, suppl. vol. 1), 125–29.

Grant, R. M. (1949) "Irenaeus and Hellenistic Culture," HTR 42: 41–51.

——(1966) *The Early Christian Doctrine of God* (Richard Lectures). Charlottesvilla, VA: University of Virginia Press.

——(1980) *Eusebius as Church Historian*. Oxford: Clarendon Press.

——(1986) "Carpocratians and Curriculum," *HTR* 79: 127–36.

Grenier, A. (1959) "La Gaule romaine," in T. Frank (ed.), *An Economic Survey of Ancient Rome*, 3. Paterson, NJ: Pageant, 379–644.

Hefner, P. (1964) "Theological Methodology and St. Irenaeus," *Journal of Religion* 44: 294–309.

Hitchcock, F. R. M. (1914) *Irenaeus of Lugdunum*. Cambridge University Press.

Holl, K. (1899) *Fragmente vornicänischer Kirchenväter aus den Sacra Parallela. TU* 20.2, Leipzig: Hinrichs.

Houssiau, A. (1955) *La christologie de saint Irénée*. Louvain: Publications Universitaires.

Jaschke, H.-J. (1987) "Irenäus von Lyon," *Theologische Realenzyklopädie* 16: 258–68.

Jones, C. P. (1978) "L'inscription grecque de Saint-Just," in *Les Martyrs de Lyon*, 119–27.

Jülicher, A. (1905) "Eirenaios (8)," *RE* 5: 2125.

Lawlor, H. J. and Oulton, J. E. L., (1928) *Eusebius*. London: SPCK.

Lawson, J. [1948] *The Biblical Theology of St. Irenaeus*. London: Epworth.

Le Boulluec, A. (1985) *La notion d'hérésie dans la littérature grecque IIe-IIIe siècles*. 2 vols. Paris: Études Augustiniennes, 1985

Lesher, J. H. (1992) *Xenophanes of Colophon: Fragments*. Phoenix suppl. vol 30, University of Toronto Press.

Les Martyrs de Lyon 177. (1978) Colloques Internationaux du Centre National de la Recherche Scientifique, 575. Paris: Éditions du Centre National de la Recherche Scientifique.

Minns, D. (1994) *Irenaeus*. Outstanding Christian Thinkers Series. London: Geoffrey Chapman.

Nautin, P. (1961) *Lettres et écrivains chrétiens des IIe et IIIe siècles*. Paris: Cerf.

Nielsen, J. T. (1968) *Adam and Christ in the Theology of Irenaeus of Lyons*. Assen: Van Gorcum.

Norris, R. A. (1979) "The transcendence and freedom of God: Irenaeus, the Greek tradition and Gnosticism," in Schoedel and Wilken (1979), 87–100.

——(1994) "Theology and language in Irenaeus of Lyon," *Anglican Theological Review* 76: 285–95.

Orbe, A. (1992) "Irenaeus," in Di Berardino (1992), 413–16.

Osborn, E. (1990) "The logic of Recapitulation," in *Pléroma* (1990), 321–35.

Pietri, C. (1978) "Les origines de la mission lyonnais: remarques critiques," in *Les martyrs de Lyon* (1978), 211–31.

Pléroma: Salus carnis. Homenaje a Antonio Orbe, S.J. (1990), ed. E. Romero-Pose. Santiago de Compostela.

Reynders, B. (1935) "La polémique de saint Irénée: Méthode et principes," *Recherches de théologie ancienne et médiévale* 7: 5–27.

Rotovtzeff, M. (1957) *The Social and Economic History of the Roman Empire*. 2nd edn, Oxford: Clarendon Press.

Runia, D. T. (1993) *Philo in Early Christian Literature*. Assen: Van Gorcum; Minneapolis: Fortress.

Schoedel, W. R. (1959) "Philosophy and rhetoric in the Adversus Haereses of Irenaeus," *VC* 12: 22–32.

——(1979) "Enclosing not enclosed: the Early Christian Doctrine of God," in Schoedel and Wilken (1979), 75–86.

——(1984) "Theological method in Irenaeus (*Adv. Haer.* 2.25–28)," *JTS* 35: 31–49.

Schoedel, W. R. and Wilken, R. L. (eds) (1979) *Early Christian Literature and the Classical Intellectual Tradition*. Théologie Historique, 54, Paris: Beauchesne.

Skarsaune, O. (1987) *The Proof from Prophecy*. Supplements to *Novum Testamentum*, 56.

Smith, W. D. (1979) *The Hippocratic Tradition*. Ithaca, NY: Cornell University Press.

Turcan, R. (1978) "Les religions 'orientales' à Lugdunum en 177," in *Les martyrs de Lyon* (1978), 195–210.

Unnik, W. C. van. (1977) "The authority of the presbyters in Irenaeus' works," in *God's Christ and His People: Studies in Honour of N. A. Dahl*. Oslo: Universitets-forlaget, 248–60.

——(1977) "An interesting document of second century theological discussion (Irenaeus, Adv. haer. 1.10.3)," *VC* 31: 196–228.

——(1979) "Theological speculation and its limits," in Schoedel and Wilken (1979), 33–43.

Widmann, M. (1957) "Irenäus und seine theologische Väter," *Zeitschrift für Theologie und Kirche* 54: 156–73.

Wilken, R. L. (1967) "The Homeric Cento in Irenaeus, 'Adversus Haereses' I,9,4," *VC* 21: 25–33.

Young, Frances (1989) "The rhetorical schools and their influence on patristic exegesis," in R. Willliams (ed.), *The Making of Orthodoxy: Essays in honour of Henry Chadwick*. Cambridge University Press, 182–99.

(B) GNOSTICS

(1) Texts, Translations

Böhlig, A. and Labib, P., (1963) *Koptisch-gnostische Apokalypsen aus Codex V von Nag Hammadi*, Halle-Wittenberg: Martin-Luther-Universität.

Chadwick, H. (1953) *Origen Contra Celsum*. Cambridge University Press.

Krause, M. and Labib, P. (1962) *Die drei Versionen des Apokryphon des Johannes im Koptischen Museum zu Alt-Kairo*. Wiesbaden: Harrassowitz.

Robinson, J. M. (ed.) (1988) *The Nag Hammadi Library in English*, rev. edn. San Francisco: Harper & Row.

Till, W. C. (1955) *Die Gnostischen Schriften des Koptischen Papyrus Berolinensis 8502, TU* 60, Berlin: Akademie.

(2) Studies

Frickel, J. "Unbekannte gnostische Schriften in Hippolyts *Refutatio*," in M. Krause (ed.), *Gnosis and Gnosticism: Papers Read at the Seventh International Conference on Patristic Studies*. NHS 12, Leiden: Brill, 119–37.

Grant, R. M. (1977) "Gnostics and the inspiration of the Old Testament," in A. L. Merrill and Overholt, T. W. (eds), *Scripture in History and Theology: Essays in Honor of J. Coert Rylaarsdam*, Pittsburgh: Pickwick, 269–77.

——(1979) "Place de Basilide dans la théologie chrétienne ancienne," *Revue des Études Augustiniennes* 25: 201–16 (French version by Marcel Simon).

——(1986) "Carpocratians and curriculum," *HTR* 79: 127–36 (for K. Stendahl).

——(1994) "Old Testament saints and sinners," in C. Elsas (ed.), *Tradition und Translation: Festschrift für Carsten Colpe*, Berlin/New York: De Gruyter, 356–61.

Harl, M. (1980) "Les mythes valentiniennes de la création et de l'eschatologie dans le langage d'Origène: le mot HYPOTHESIS," in B. Layton (ed.), *The Rediscovery of Gnosticism*. Supplements to Numen 41 (1): 417–25.

Harnack, A. von (1924) *Marcion: Das Evangelium vom fremden Gott*, 2nd edn. Leipzig: Hinrichs.

Koschorke, K. (1978) *Die Polemik der Gnostiker gegen das kirchliche Christentum*. NHS 12, Leiden: Brill.

Norris, R. A. (1979) "The transcendence and freedom of God: Irenaeus, the Greek tradition and Gnosticism," in Schoedel and Wilken (1979), 87–100.

Rudolph, K. (1983) *Gnosis*, trans. R. McL. Wilson *et al.* Edinburgh: T. & T. Clark.

Sagnard, F.-M. (1972) *La gnose valentinienne et le témoignage de saint-Irénée*. Paris: Vrin.

Schoedel, W. R. (1972) "Topological theology and some Monistic Trends in Gnosticism," in M. Krause (ed.), *Essays on the Nag Hammadi Texts in Honor of Alexander Böhlig*. NHS 3, Leiden: Brill, 88–108.

——(1980) "Gnostic Monism and the Gospel of Truth," in B. Layton, (ed.), *The Rediscovery of Gnosticism*. Supplements to Numen 41(1): 379–90.

Scopello, M. (1977) "Les citations d'Homère dans le traité de l'exégèse de l'âme," in M. Krause (ed.), *Gnosis and Gnosticism: Papers Read at the Seventh International Conference on Patristic Studies*. NHS 8, Leiden: Brill, 3–12.

Unnik, W. C. van (1961) "Die Gotteslehre bei Aristides und in gnostischen Schriften," *Theologische Zeitschrift* 17: 166–74.

Wisse, F. (1972) "The Epistle of Jude in the History of Heresiology," in M. Krause (ed.), *Essays on the Nag Hammadi Texts in Honor of Alexander Böhlig*. NHS 3, Leiden: Brill, 133–43.

INDEX

Abrasax, in Basilides 15, 92

Abyss: and Ophites 99; in
Ptolemaeus 59, 61, 68; in
Valentinianism 27, 42, 43, 73–4,
77, 85, 88, 107, 110–11, 162

Achamoth (Desire): and Ophites
103; in Valentinianism 22–3, 26,
62–4, 65–7, 72, 85, 87, 115

Acts of Peter 19

Adam: Christ as recapitulation 52,
139–40, 141, 166, 169, 173; and
Ophites 101–2; salvation 18, 97,
142; and service of God 146

Adonai, and Ophites 19, 100, 103,
122

Adoptionism, syllogisms 18

Aeons: and Barbelo-Gnostics 97–8;
in Basilides 111–12; Christian use
62; in Mark the magician 79–81;
and Ophites 99, 103; in
Ptolemaeus 22, 23, 44–5, 59–63,
66–9, 72; in Tatian 18, 97; in
Valentinianism 27–8, 42, 73, 85,
110, 111–16, 135, 162

Alexander, and apostolic succession
8, 125

Alexandria: and apocrypha 46; and
Christian Platonism 53; and
Gnosticism 1; and Paschal dispute
8–9; and Septuagint 32

allegory: and eschatological
predictions 182–3, 184; Gnostic
use 24, 62

alphabet, in Marcosian system 79,

80, 81, 82, 106

Anacletus, and apostolic succession
7, 125

anakephalaiosis 50–1, 53, 197 n.2c;
see also recapitulation

Anaxagoras 43, 44

Anaxilaos 25, 75

Anaximander 43

Andrew of Caesarea 192 n.51

angels: in Basilides 15, 16, 91–2; in
Irenaeus 150; in Menander 90; and
Ophites 29, 101; in Saturninus 14,
90; in Simon Magus 12–13, 89; in
Valentinianism 31, 63, 65, 87, 105,
171

Anicetus: and apostolic succession
8, 9, 125; and early Gnosticism 11,
18, 94, 127–8; and Polycarp 3–4,
9, 126

Antichrist: and earthly kingdom 182;
and number of the Beast 176–8

Antioch, and rhetorical schools 46

Antithesis-Gospel-Apostle 18

Apelles, *Syllogisms* 18, 47

Apocalypse of Baruch 36

Apocalypse of John *see* Johannine
literature

apocrypha and pseudepigrapha 1,
11, 16, 34–5, 46, 84

Apocryphon of John 11, 19

Apostolic Fathers, Irenaeus'
knowledge of 1

Aquila 32

archons: in Basilides 15–16, 91–2;

204

Breinigsville, PA USA
09 September 2009
223786BV00001B/24/A

9 780415 118385